Governance of Distressed Firms

CORPORATIONS, GLOBALISATION AND THE LAW

Series Editor: Janet Dine, *Director, Centre for Commercial Law Studies, Queen Mary College, University of London, UK*

This uniquely positioned monograph series aims to draw together high-quality research work from established and younger scholars on what is an intriguing and under-researched area of the law. The books will offer insights into a variety of legal issues that concern corporations operating on the global stage, including interaction with the World Trade Organization (WTO), international financial institutions and nation states, in both developing and developed countries. While the underlying foundation of the series will be that of company law, broadly defined, authors are encouraged to take an approach that draws on the work of other social sciences, such as politics, economics and development studies and to offer an international or comparative perspective where appropriate. Specific topics to be considered will include corporate governance, corporate responsibility, taxation and criminal liability, amongst others. The series will undoubtedly offer an important contribution to legal thinking and to the wider globalisation debate.

Titles in the series include:

Corporate Governance in the 21st Century
Japan's Gradual Transformation
Edited by Luke Nottage, Leon Wolff and Kent Anderson

National Corporate Law in a Globalised Market
The UK Experience in Perspective
David Milman

Transnational Corporations and International Law
Accountability in the Global Business Environment
Alice de Jonge

The Corporate Objective
Andrew Keay

Secured Credit and the Harmonisation of Law
The UNCITRAL Experience
Gerard McCormack

A Legal Framework for Emerging Business Models
Dynamic Networks as Collaborative Contracts
Emily M. Weitzenboeck

Directors' Duties and Shareholder Litigation in the Wake of the Financial Crisis
Edited by Joan Loughrey

Governance of Distressed Firms
David Milman

Governance of Distressed Firms

David Milman

Professor of Law, Lancaster University, Professorial Associate at Exchange Chambers and formerly Visiting Fellow at the Institute of Advanced Legal Studies, UK

CORPORATIONS, GLOBALISATION AND THE LAW

Edward Elgar
Cheltenham, UK • Northampton, MA, USA

Published by
Edward Elgar Publishing Limited
The Lypiatts
15 Lansdown Road
Cheltenham
Glos GL50 2JA
UK

Edward Elgar Publishing, Inc.
William Pratt House
9 Dewey Court
Northampton
Massachusetts 01060
USA

A catalogue record for this book
is available from the British Library

Library of Congress Control Number: 2013932951

This book is available electronically in the ElgarOnline.com Law Subject Collection,
E-ISBN 978 1 78100 019 9

MIX
Paper from
responsible sources
FSC® C013056
FSC
www.fsc.org

ISBN 978 1 78100 018 2

Typeset by Cambrian Typesetters, Camberley, Surrey
Printed and bound in Great Britain by T.J. International Ltd, Padstow

For those who departed in 2006

Contents

Preface

It is now 30 years since the Cork Committee, *Insolvency Law and Practice: Report of the Review Committee* (Cmnd 8558, 1982) reported and set in train a series of reforms that changed the landscape of the regulation of insolvency practice in the UK. Now is an opportune time to reflect upon this watershed moment. We shall look at specific aspects of the reforms inspired by the Cork Committee as we proceed through our study, but a few words by way of overview may prove helpful. The Cork Committee reforms in the context of our subject area may be broken down into two elements. First, there was the 'stick and carrot' strategy deployed against directors of distressed companies. This amounted to offering incentives on corporate rescue and increased sanctions for those directors who adopted the ostrich approach of trading on regardless. Second, there were major reforms to the role of insolvency practitioners by imposing mandatory qualifications and conferring modern powers. Taken together, the aim was to promote higher standards of stewardship. Our goal is to evaluate the degree of success achieved by this strategy.

The Institute of Advanced Legal Studies has supported this research by granting me a six-month visiting fellowship in 2012. I am grateful to all of the staff at the Institute, but particular thanks on my part should be recorded to Eliza Boudier, Belinda Crothers and the library staff.

I have had the opportunity to hold discussions with a number of practitioners over the past two years. I have received strong support from the Insolvency Team at Exchange Chambers, particularly Mark Cawson QC, Lisa Linklater, Giles-Maynard Connor, David Mohyuddin and Carly Sandbach. Their support is appreciated and the opportunity to participate in their Yorkshire Insolvency Forum has been invaluable.

Attendance and participation at academic conferences/seminars held at the University of Sheffield (4 July 2012), the University of Leeds (21 September 2012) and the Institute of Advanced Legal Studies (29 November 2012) has provided me with a range of valuable insights to reflect upon. I am grateful for the invitations received from the respective organizers of these seminars, namely John de Lacy, Michael Galanis and Belinda Crothers (once again). A particular word of thanks should be reserved for John Tribe, who chaired my talk at the IALS.

More generally, Professor Len Sealy, as always, has offered me invaluable support through the sharing of his incisive insights, as has Peter Bailey in our almost daily interactions/discussions on company law and insolvency law. My former doctoral research student, Paul Moorhead, who now has his own insolvency practice, has been an invaluable source of reference on many practical issues.

At Lancaster, I remain heavily indebted to my colleague Philip Lawton for sharing his expertise on corporate governance over many an informal discussion. Angus MacCulloch and David Sugarman have also provided valuable assistance in specific areas of complexity. Eileen Jones has provided first-class logistical support. Lorna Pimperton has been most supportive in terms of facilitating access to library resources. Alan Katz has made available his years of practical experience to enable me to clarify my thoughts on a number of issues. I acknowledge the support given to me by Lancaster University through its research leave scheme.

I have been fortunate for many years to have worked with many overseas postgraduates from a range of jurisdictions. My interactions with them have broadened my horizons and enhanced my understanding of a range of systems of corporate law.

At Edward Elgar, particular thanks are due to Luke Adams, John-Paul MacDonald and Laura Seward.

Finally, I thank Dr Catherine Deering for her support on this project, and on all of the other legal writing ventures that have gone before.

Responsibility for the views expressed in this monograph (and any errors therein) rests solely at my door. The law is stated as at 15 December 2012, though a few later developments have been noted at proof stage. This area of law never stands still and any such revisions are necessarily brief.

Abbreviations used for law reports and periodicals

AC	Appeal Cases
Acc Ref	Accounting Reform
ACLR	Australian Corporate Law Reports
ACSR	Australian Corporate and Securities Reports
Act Jur	Acta Juridica
All ER	All England Law Reports
All ER (D)	All England Law Reports (Digest)
ALR	Australian Law Reports
Amic Cur	Amicus Curiae
Am Jo of Compar Law	American Journal of Comparative Law
Am Jo of Int Law	American Journal of International Law
App Cas	Appeal Cases
Ariz Law Rev	Arizona Law Review
Aust Insolv Jo	Australian Insolvency Journal
Aust Jo of Corp Law	Australian Journal of Corporate Law
Aust Jo of Man	Australian Journal of Management
BCC	British Company Cases
BCLC	Butterworths Company Law Cases
BJIBFL	Butterworths Journal of International Banking and Financial Law
Bond Law Rev	Bond Law Review
BPIR	Bankruptcy and Personal Insolvency Reports
Can Bus L Jo	Canadian Business Law Journal
CFILR	Company Financial and Insolvency Law Review
Ch	Chancery
Ch App	Chancery Appeals
CJQ	Civil Justice Quarterly
CLJ	Cambridge Law Journal
CLP	Current Legal Problems
CLR	Commonwealth Law Reports
CLWR	Common Law World Review
CMLR	Common Market Law Reports

Co Law	The Company Lawyer
Conv	Conveyancer and Property Lawyer
Corp Gov	Corporate Governance International
CRI	Corporate Rescue and Insolvency
CSIH	Court of Session Inner House (neutral citation)
C&SLJ	Corporate and Securities Law Journal
CSOH	Court of Session Outer House (neutral citation)
DLR	Dominion Law Reports
EBLR	European Business Law Review
EBOL Rev	European Business Organisations Law Review
ECFLR	European Company and Financial Law Review
ECHR	European Court of Human Rights (neutral citation)
Econ of Trans	Economics of Transition
ECR	European Cases Reports
Edin L Rev	Edinburgh Law Review
EHRR	European Human Rights Reports
ELR	European Law Review
Ent Theory and Pract	Entrepreneurship Theory and Practice
ER	English Reports
EWCA Civ	England and Wales Court of Appeal Civil Division (neutral citation)
EWCA Crim	England and Wales Court of Appeal Criminal Division (neutral citation)
EWHC	England and Wales High Court (neutral citation)
Exch	Exchequer Cases
FCA	Federal Court of Australia
Ford Int Law Jo	Fordham International Law Journal
Griff L Rev	Griffith Law Review
Harv L Rev	Harvard Law Review
HCA	High Court of Australia (neutral citation)
HL Cas	House of Lords cases
ICCLR	International Company and Commercial Law Review
ICLQ	International and Comparative Law Quarterly
ICR	International Corporate Rescue
IEHC	Irish High Court (neutral citation)
IESC	Irish Supreme Court (neutral citation)
IIR	International Insolvency Review
IJLMA	International Journal of Law and Management
IL & P	Insolvency Law and Practice
ILRM	Irish Law Reports Monthly
Ins Intell	Insolvency Intelligence

Ins Law	Insolvency Lawyer
Insolv Pract	Insolvency Practitioner
Int Jo of Disc and Gov	International Journal of Disclosure and Governance
Int Jo of Ent Behav and Res	International Journal of Entrepreneurial Behaviour and Research
Int Rev of Law and Econ	International Review of Law and Economics
IR	Irish Reports
Ir Jur	Irish Jurist
IRLR	Industrial Relations Law Reports
JAL	Journal of African Law
JBL	Journal of Business Law
JCLS	Journal of Corporate Law Studies
JLS	Journal of Law and Society
Jo of Econ Hist	Journal of Economic History
Jo of Fin	Journal of Finance
Jo of Fin Crime	Journal of Financial Crime
Jo of Fin Reg and Comp	Journal of Financial Regulation and Compliance
Jo of L Hist	Journal of Legal History
Jo of Law and Soc	Journal of Law and Society
Jo of Law Soc Scot	Journal of the Law Society of Scotland
Jo of Pol Econ	Journal of Political Economy
KB	King's Bench
Law and Cont Prob	Law and Contemporary Problems
Law and Fin Mark Rev	Law and Financial Markets Review
Law Teach	Law Teacher
Leg Hist	Legal History
Leg Stud	Legal Studies
Lloyds Rep	Lloyds Law Reports
LMCLQ	Lloyds Maritime and Commercial Law Quarterly
LQR	Law Quarterly Review
Maas Jo of Euro and Compar Law	Maastricht Journal of European and Comparative Law
Manag Law	Managerial Law
McGill LJ	McGill Law Journal
Melb Univ L Rev	Melbourne University Law Review
MLR	Modern Law Review
NI	Northern Irish Reports
NICh	Northern Ireland Chancery Division (neutral citation)
NILQ	Northern Ireland Legal Quarterly

NI Master	Northern Ireland Master's Decisions (neutral citation)
Nottm Law Jo	Nottingham Law Journal
NSWCA	New South Wales Court of Appeal
NSWLR	New South Wales Law Reports
NUJS Law Rev	National University of Juridical Science Law Review
NZBLQ	New Zealand Business Law Quarterly
NZLR	New Zealand Law Reports
Ox Univ Comm LJ	Oxford University Commonwealth Law Journal
PCC	Palmers Company Cases
P & CR	Property and Compensation Reports
QB	Queen's Bench
RALQ	Receivers, Administrators and Liquidators Quarterly
Recov	Recovery
SALJ	South African Law Journal
SA Merc L Jo	South African Mercantile Law Journal
SC	Session Cases
SCC	Supreme Court of Canada
Sing AcLJ	Singapore Academy of Law Journal
SJ	Solicitors' Journal
SLT	Scots Law Times
SMCLN	Sweet and Maxwell's Company Law Newsletter
Stan L Rev	Stanford Law Review
Stat L Rev	Statute Law Review
STC	Simon's Tax Cases
STI	Simon's Tax Intelligence
Syd L Rev	Sydney Law Review
TLR	Times Law Reports
UKFTT	UK First Tier Tax Tribunal (neutral citation)
UKHL	House of Lords (neutral citation)
UKPC	United Kingdom Privy Council (neutral citation)
UKSC	United Kingdom Supreme Court (neutral citation)
Univ Chic L Rev	University of Chicago Law Review
US	US Supreme Court Reports
Utah L Rev	Utah Law Review
Vand L Rev	Vanderbilt Law Review
WASCA	Western Australia Supreme Court of Appeal
Wash U LQ	Washington University Law Quarterly
WLR	Weekly Law Reports
WN	Weekly Notes

Table of cases

UNITED KINGDOM

EUROPEAN COURT OF JUSTICE

EUROPEAN COURT OF HUMAN RIGHTS

AUSTRALIA

CANADA

IRELAND

NEW ZEALAND

USA

Table of legislation

UK STATUTES

UK STATUTORY INSTRUMENT

EU MEASURES

EUROPEAN CONVENTION ON HUMAN RIGHTS AND FUNDAMENTAL FREEDOMS

AUSTRALIAN LEGISLATION

CANADIAN LEGISLATION

GERMAN LEGISLATION

INDIAN LEGISLATION

IRISH LEGISLATION

MALAYSIAN LEGISLATION

NEW ZEALAND LEGISLATION

SINGAPOREAN LEGISLATION

SOUTH AFRICAN LEGISLATION

US LEGISLATION

Federal Legislation

State Law

1. Introduction to concepts and dramatis personae

1.1 SETTING THE SCENE

The aim of the study is to focus on how the well-established corporate governance debate can be applied to firms (and in particular small firms) experiencing financial distress. This aspect of the broader governance discourse is less well documented than the usual scenario applicable in the case of listed solvent concerns. Tens of thousands of firms of all sizes in the UK endure this debilitating economic condition each year[1] and it is important that we understand the regulatory context in which they, their managers, their 'gatekeepers'[2] and ultimately their undertakers[3] have to subsist. The macro-economic climate prevailing in 2011 and 2012 has been especially testing and has consequently thrown up this issue into sharp relief. But we should not be over-alarmist because if we refer to Companies House Annual Companies Statistics for 2011–12, we find in Table A1 some 2 663 100 companies registered in England and Wales. Table A4 from the same source tells us that the average life span of a limited company is 8.8 years.

The research methodology to be adopted in this study is primarily doctrinal in nature (but including usage of some comparative material). Nevertheless, it has been supported by insights collected from fellow academics and practitioners via many a discussion in recent years. I am grateful to those practitioners and experts who have spared the time to share their thoughts with me,

---

1 Figures for 2011 show 21 843 companies entering formal insolvency proceedings in England and Wales. In the EU some 220 000 companies were liquidated in 2010 – see *Consultation on Future of European Insolvency Law* (21 June 2012). But that is only the tip of the iceberg; many thousands of businesses teeter on the brink of insolvency each year but manage to survive on a hand-to-mouth basis. Such companies are increasingly referred to as 'zombie' companies – see L. Manning [2012] (Winter) Recov 5. It is sometimes suggested that banks are too concerned at the present about the amount of bad debt on their balance sheets to precipitate the formal insolvency of such firms.

2 See John Coffee, *Gatekeepers: The Professions and Corporate Governance* (2006) – this term is wide enough to cover auditors and professional advisers.

3 That is, insolvency office-holders.

though I stress that the views expressed in this text are my personal insights, for which I take sole responsibility. The author was fortunate enough to be awarded a six-month visiting fellowship at the Institute of Advanced Legal Studies in London in the first half of 2012 to facilitate research into the stewardship aspects of this project.

The study is 'dynamic' in the sense that it will observe and analyse the changing goals of governance as the financial well-being of the company declines. It will become apparent that the stewardship emphasis switches from a primary (but no longer exclusive) focus on the protection of shareholders to the safeguarding of other stakeholder groups (especially creditors and employees). The pivotal role of banks in their capacity as secured creditors in this changing financial environment will attract particular attention.

A historical perspective will be included, and the question will be asked whether the dominant theories and rules operating in this field are appropriate to the challenging social and economic conditions encountered by company stewards in the early decades of the twenty-first century in the wake of the global economic crisis that first hit us badly in the latter part of 2008.[4] Should we adopt a more sympathetic approach towards those who struggle to keep companies afloat against a combination of adverse trading conditions? Alternatively, should we move away from the current vogue for attempting business rescue and instead embrace the potential opportunities generated by the forces of destructive economics?[5] More radically, is it now an opportune time to reconsider our liberal approach towards the general availability of limited liability to all entrepreneurs?[6] When set against the very high mortality rate for new SMEs, this is surely not an outlandish question to ask, though for those wedded to established ideas, this is tantamount to a heresy.

The author will consider whether the current UK regime for the governance of distressed firms is adequate and will examine the implications of making

---

[4] For an excellent account of this global event see C.A.E. Goodhart, *The Regulatory Response to the Financial Crisis* (2010) (Edward Elgar) and L.E. Mitchell and A.E. Wilmarth, Jr, *The Panic of 2008* (2010) (Edward Elgar).

[5] See the work of Joseph Schumpeter, in particular *The Theory of Economic Development: an Inquiry into Profits, Capital, Credit, Interest and the Business Cycle* (1934). This work was first produced in German in 1912, but did not receive global attention until translated into English in 1934. The idea of creative destruction was more to the fore in Schumpeter's later text *Capitalism, Socialism and Democracy* (1942). See also P. Ormerod, *Why Most Things Fail: Evolution, Extinction and Economics* (2005). Schumpeter's wide-ranging work can be applied to the corporate governance debate in a number of ways – see for example A. Belcher [1996] 47 NILQ 322.

[6] See A. Hicks [1997] JBL 306 and [2001] JBL 433. Further discussion of this vital issue is provided by S. Griffin (2004) 25 Co Law 99 and B. Pettet [1995] CLP 124.

changes in this area (for example by enhancing recoveries for creditors and promoting measure for the rescuing of firms). Those changes *may* well be informed by the experience of other jurisdictions in dealing with common problems (see Chapter 5). But caution must be exercised here, as we shall discover.

This is an important area for study because, with the reality of globalization, it is vital that the UK is seen to have effective rules operating in this area, as those many foreign companies who are now taking advantage of our insolvency procedures may have migrated here solely for the exploitation of that limited tactical purpose.[7] Allowing regulatory inefficiencies to develop in the way we tackle insolvent companies could stultify this development, which provides valuable employment and income for the professional services sector, and could thereby damage the UK economy as a whole. The World Bank has commented favourably upon the relative efficiency of using insolvency processes in the UK.[8] Under the 2012 survey the UK ranks sixth in the world. That said, we should not prostitute fundamentals (such as basic tenets of distributional justice and essential ethical standards of stewardship) simply to attract the business associated with foreign bankruptcies; in other words, we should resist the temptation to become the 'bankruptcy brothel of Europe', as some critics have alleged.

1.2 'CORPORATE GOVERNANCE' DEFINED

We need to explain what we mean by the term 'corporate governance' for the purposes of this project. Corporate governance theory will be analysed in Chapter 2. In the context of a corporate entity, various definitions of corporate governance are available.[9] There is no agreement here on the precise wording of a definition but there exists a broad consensus on what we are talking about.

---

[7] We thus have the 'bankruptcy tourism' syndrome – see for example *Hellas Telecommunications (Luxembourg) II SCA* [2009] EWHC 3199 (Ch), [2010] BCC 295 (foreign company relocated to this jurisdiction to use controversial prepack procedure under the umbrella of an administration). For later proceedings involving a dispute as the most appropriate exit route from administration see [2011] EWHC 3176 (Ch), where the actions taken in the administration were upheld. Compare *Hans Brochier Holdings v Exner* [2006] EWHC 2594 (Ch), [2007] BCC 127, where the English courts eventually declined to claim jurisdiction because the evidence suggested that the centre of main interests (COMI) of the company was located in Germany.

[8] See World Bank, *Doing Business* (2012). Note also A. Reisberg [2010] CLP 315.

[9] See A. Keay, *Directors' Duties* (2009) at paras 3.02–3.10.

The Cadbury Committee[10] viewed corporate governance in terms of a system which operates to control and direct companies. Giles Proctor and Lilian Miles also lay emphasis on the element of systems.[11] John Parkinson in a posthumous essay[12] helpfully described the notion as having both internal and external aspects, in the sense that it encompasses both domestic governance elements and external regulation of companies. More recently, Alan Dignam and Michael Galanis explain corporate governance in terms of an institution that weighs up competing stakeholder interests.[13] The perspective favoured by the OECD is also one that focuses upon the relationship that exists between the board and the various stakeholder constituencies. Generally, North American perspectives focus on the relationship between boards and their shareholders, whereas European analyses tend to take in the wider stakeholder interest.

Taking all of these useful perspectives into account, at the end of the day the working definition we have adopted for this survey is:

> *That system of legal rules and other social norms that seeks to regulate how firms are managed in the interests of the appropriate stakeholders.*

This definition is wide enough to encompass material that exists beyond the law (such as codes of practice, conventions and social norms); it also invites us to consider who are the appropriate stakeholders at any one point in time. The definition is not restricted to the governance of companies, but would be capable of applying to other entities, such as LLPs, whose members enjoy the characteristic attribute of limited liability.

If we are to focus on systems of regulation, we should now identify the essential components of this governance system. This is not always entirely clear. As far as English law is concerned, we will be looking at legislation (in its various forms), European measures (both EU and ECHR[14] related) and jurisprudence developed by the courts. There is also a significant self-regulatory component, for example the UK Corporate Governance Code (introduced in 2010 and updated in September 2012). The courts in developing the law will clearly have recourse to principle but will also keep a keen eye on custom and practice to inform their decisions, particularly when reviewing the actions

---

10 (1992) at para 2.5.

11 See G. Proctor and L. Miles, *Corporate Governance* (2003) at 3.

12 See 'Corporate Governance and the Regulation of Business Behaviour' in S. Macleod (ed.) *Global Governance and the Quest for Justice: Vol 2 – Corporate Governance* (2006).

13 See their Preface to *The Globalisation of Corporate Governance* (2009).

14 Now forming part of English law through the medium of the Human Rights Act 1998.

of insolvency practitioners.[15] Lord Mansfield, the father of UK commercial law, would surely commend such an approach. Generally, we would expect the courts to be promoting the highest standards of stewardship, though they do enjoy discretion to 'whitewash' procedural lapses that do not negatively impact upon reasonable stewardship expectations. Witness their role on applications under s. 1157 of the Companies Act 2006 and in dealing with formal lapses in insolvency procedures.[16] There is one negative feature of judicial input into the governance matrix that is worth flagging up at this early stage of the exercise. Judicial decisions are in effect a form of retrospective guidance in that they constitute a legal pronouncement upon conduct that has gone before. In a climate where legal uncertainty is not uncommon, this declaratory aspect of judicial decision-making can have serious consequences for insolvency practitioners and it is doubly important that the views within the profession as to the acceptability of a practice are taken account of (but not necessarily slavishly followed). Misconceptions on acceptable practices have a nasty habit of being converted into a form of orthodoxy with the result that disappointing judicial rulings receive unfair criticism. On the positive side, the prompt reporting of decisions through the neutral citation system and the agency of BAILII (British and Irish Legal Information Institute) have helped to mitigate some of the problems here. We return to this thorny issue in Chapter 6.

Moving on, the use of the concept of governance presupposes that someone is going to be governed. For the purposes of our study that subject group will be those who manage firms, whether such firms be with or without a formal insolvency regime.

1.3 'FIRMS'

A secondary definitional issue requires clarification. This study as suggested above will encompass governance regimes both in relation to limited companies and limited liability partnerships (LLPs). Both are corporate entities[17]

---

[15] For recognition of this see G. Lightman (2001) 14 Ins Intell 57 at 70. Also note the comments of Neuberger J in *MTI Trading Systems v Winter* [1998] BCC 591 at 595.

[16] They have statutory authority to do this via Insolvency Rule 7.55. Note also the precedent of *Re G Tech Construction Ltd* [2007] BPIR 1275. On this see the discussion in Chapter 4.

[17] See Limited Liability Partnerships Act 2000 s. 1(2). The similarity between companies and LLPs and the distinctions with the partnership form are borne out by Sales J in *F & C Alternative Investments v Barthelemy* [2011] EWHC 1731 (Ch),

with sophisticated layers of legal regulation. So under the LLP Act 2000 basic rules of company law are introduced via s. 15 and basic rules of corporate insolvency law via s. 14. The details of LLP regulation are found in secondary legislation, such as the LLP Regulations 2001 (SI 2001/1090) and the LLP (Application of the Companies Act 2006) Regulations 2009 (SI 2009/1804). The Practice Direction on Insolvency Proceedings[18] treats LLPs as equivalent to a company for the purposes of its application, as is made clear in para 1.1(7). Both forms of organization enable the participators to operate a business or profession without incurring full personal liability for the firm's debts. Limited liability, in effect, triggers the stewardship question. We shall not therefore look at the general problem of insolvent partnerships (governed generally by the Partnership Act 1890), which are subject to specific regulation in the Insolvent Partnerships Order 1994 (as amended).[19] For similar reasons we will not consider governance issues in relation to limited partnerships registered under the Limited Partnerships Act 1907 because the general partners do not enjoy limited liability and the limited partners are not allowed to manage (see s. 6(1) of the 1907 Act). That said, comparable insolvency procedures and the company directors' disqualification regimes are often made available to such firms.

Our study will also seek to pay particular attention to the position of SMEs, though not exclusively so. On a definitional point, the Companies Act 2006 characterizes SMEs in broad terms – so, for instance, under s. 382 a small company is defined as one in which two of the following three factors are present – turnover of less than £6.5 million, balance sheet total below £3.26 million and fewer than 50 employees. A medium-sized enterprise must, according to s. 465, manifest two of the following three criteria – turnover less than £25.9 million, balance sheet total less than £12.9 million and fewer than 250 employees. Although there is no formal legal definition, we should also note the importance of micro-businesses, which typically have fewer than 10 employees. It is clear that many thousands of businesses will fall within these catchment areas. It has been estimated that some 20 per cent of the companies currently experiencing financial distress are micro companies.

We shall focus our study on companies that operate for profit, though it cannot be denied that many of the issues under examination are relevant to

[2012] 3 WLR 10 where he held at para [213] that members of LLPs do not (in the absence of express provision) owe fiduciary duties inter se, but rather to the firm itself. This point was confirmed by Hamlen J in *Brown v InnovatorOne plc* [2012] EWHC 1321 (Comm) at para [1304] – leave to appeal has been granted – see [2012] EWCA Civ 1587.

18 [2012] BPIR 409.

19 SI 1994/2421. See A. Bacon (1994) 10 IL & P 166, S. Frith and B. Jones (1995) 11 IL & P 14.

those many charitable undertakings that experience financial distress.[20] As a former director of such a social undertaking, I can attest to that.

There is some evidence that small firms have a greater propensity to fail than larger concerns.[21] Within the EU we find quoted a 50 per cent failure rate in the first five years of corporate existence. The reasons for this relatively high mortality rate are varied. Commentators point to initial undercapitalization, a lack of managerial experience and the 'barriers to entry' into a market presented by competition from larger established firms as significant elements featuring in this high failure rate. There is no doubt that new companies face particular difficulties in their early years of operation. Large public companies tend to be established businesses with well-qualified managers and access to expert professional advice in a range of areas covering marketing, finance and IT. A distressed larger venture may present opportunities for restructuring – this is often less likely the case at the SME end of the spectrum, where the options are more constrained. It may simply be easier to let such companies fail and (assuming there has been no managerial misbehaviour) for the entrepreneurs involved to try again with a new business armed with the benefits of a tough experience.

1.4 'DIRECTORS'

One of the central players in our study will be the company director. The director is the essential element in the running of a modern limited liability company. Historically the footprint of directors can be traced back to the earliest days of company law, but in reality they are a nineteenth-century entrant to the scene. They have their own representative organizations,[22] which are effective lobbyists. Many MPs are, or will have been, or will become, company directors and this fact tends to reinforce their voice in policymaking. A few initial points of clarification are in order. First, under English law a

---

[20] So the Charity Commission produced a booklet in 2000 entitled *Managing Financial Difficulties and Insolvency in Charities*. For legislative provision specifically directed towards the winding-up of charities, see Charities Act 2011 s. 113. The link with company law is enhanced with the introduction by the 2011 Act of charitable incorporated organizations, to which many of the standard insolvency provisions were applied by SI 2012/3013.

[21] On this phenomenon see D. Milman and G. Cook [2002] 34 Manag Fin 34 and the material cited therein. There is a useful discussion provided by Y. Rotem in [2011] 20 IIR 131.

[22] Such as the Institute of Directors (1903) and the Confederation of British Industry (1965) (which arose out of a merger of existing representative bodies).

company director may surprisingly be another corporate entity.[23] This is unusual in world corporate law systems, where the norm is to permit only natural persons to act in that capacity.[24] This latitude on our part does cause some difficulties in practice where the law seeks first to identify and then affix a natural person with real legal responsibility. So, in the past, we have seen the syndrome of offshore companies acting as sole directors of English companies, thereby making a nonsense of domestic corporate regulatory policy. Even where there is no offshore element at work, the use of corporate directors in any stewardship model can cause problems for the regulators. Witness the case of *HMRC v Holland*,[25] where the UK Supreme Court felt constrained to hold that an individual who was a director of a corporate director of Company A could not *ipso facto* be treated as a de facto director of Company A.[26] Some 50 years ago the Jenkins Committee[27] recommended that corporate directors should be prohibited in English Law. The difficulties posed by corporate directors have eventually led Parliament to enact through the medium of s. 155 of the Companies Act 2006 a compromise[28] requirement that a company must have in addition at least one natural person acting as a director, though the possibility of having corporate directors still remains available. By way of comparison, it should also be noted that a partnership cannot be appointed as a company director,[29] though there is no objection to a limited liability partnership assuming that role as it enjoys separate legal personality. We could complete the circle here by pointing out that a company can be a partner, a member of an LLP or a limited partner in a limited partnership (see s. 4(4) of the 1907 Act).

---

23 See *Re Bulawayo Markets and Office Ltd* [1907] 2 Ch 458 and Companies Act 2006 s. 164 (which implicitly confirms the point). It follows therefore that a corporate director can be disqualified – see *Official Receiver v Brady* [1999] BCC 258. For the implications of the disqualification of a corporate director, see the comments of Floyd J in *Secretary of State for BIS v Gifford* [2011] EWHC 3022 (Ch).

24 See for example the prohibition imposed in Ireland – see *Re Worldport Ltd* [2009] 1 IR 398. Bizarrely, it seems that a company can be a shadow director in Ireland. The Irish prohibitive position mirrors that found in Australia, Malaysia, New Zealand, Singapore and South Africa. Developing jurisdictions such as Kazakhstan operate similar bars. But France appears to permit corporate directors as does The Netherlands to a limited extent.

25 [2010] UKSC 51, [2011] BCC 1. For comment see L. Sealy [2011] 287 SMCLN 1.

26 See also *Re Hydrodan (Corby) Ltd* [1994] BCC 161. Note also s. 251(3) of the Companies Act 2006.

27 (1962, Cmnd 1749) para 85(d).

28 Similar compromises have been made in Hong Kong – see J.L. Yap [2012] JBL 579 at 581.

29 On this see *Commercial Management Ltd v Registrar of Companies* [1987] 1 NZLR 744.

There are other points to note. Company directors must be of a certain age of responsibility; a minimum age of 16 is now being specified by s. 157 of the Companies Act 2006 – why this is not fixed at 18 is hard to justify. But it is a move in the right direction as previously no minimum age was fixed.[30] Indeed, formal educational/vocational qualifications are not required. Undischarged bankrupts are automatically disqualified by virtue of s. 11 of the Company Directors Disqualification Act 1986, though this disqualification has lost some of its bite with the progressive reduction of bankruptcy periods to a current maximum of one year. Similar bars contained in s. 11 apply to persons subject to debt relief orders, debt restriction orders or debt restriction undertakings. Such automatic disqualifications, although reinforced with criminal liability,[31] are unlikely to fall foul of the European Convention on Human Rights.[32] But there is no means test in operation linked to personal resources and no need to provide a minimum capital requirement in order to gain access to limited liability. Many private companies have share capital of less than £100.[33] Some 372 500 of the 426 500 new incorporations in 2011–12 featured such minimally capitalized enterprises according to Table B1 of the Companies House Annual Statistics for that year. There is no need to show experience in business, though banks asked to provide business finance might be interested in that matter. English law permits the most unskilled of persons to become a company director and then criticizes them if things do not work out.[34] Gender, until recently, has not been seen as an issue – with the result that the overwhelming majority of directors of public companies are male.[35] There is no

---

[30] See *Marquis of Bute's case* [1892] 2 Ch 100.

[31] See *R v Doring* [2002] EWCA Crim 1695, [2002] BPIR 1204.

[32] See *Michael v Official Receiver* [2010] EWHC 2246 (Ch).

[33] Hence the tendency towards 'incorporation tourism' as supported by the European Court of Justice in *Centros (C212/97)* [2000] Ch 446. This particular ruling led to hundreds of EU firms relocating their place of incorporation to the UK whilst continuing to trade with limited liability in their 'home' jurisdiction. This in turn led to a 'race to the bottom' in terms of a reduction of the minimum share capital requirement in Germany, France and Denmark for private companies. One wonders whether corporate stewardship in the EU has suffered here as part of the price of regulatory competition and the operation of the market in corporate charters.

[34] See *Re HHO Licensing Ltd* [2007] BPIR 1363 and *Re DKG Contractors Ltd* [1990] BCC 903.

[35] This has been criticized by Lord Davies in his report *Women on Boards* (February 2011). See editorial in [2011] 291 SMCLN 1. There has been some impressive scholarship on this broad issue – see for example M. McCann and S. Wheeler (2011) 38 Jo of Law and Soc 542. The DBIS has produced an update with the focus on the Voluntary Code of Conduct agreed with recruitment agencies – see BIS Press Notice 24 July 2012. Figures released in late 2012 suggest that for FTSE 100 companies the number of female directors is just over 17 per cent – see the *Guardian*, 1

licensing system for company directors, though informal trade associations exist. It also follows that there is no in-house disciplinary model – the sanctioning of directors is a matter for the general law of the land and, in particular, for the shareholders themselves. Moreover, there is no need for a director of a UK company to have British nationality, or indeed to be resident in the jurisdiction.[36] That said, the register of directors must by virtue of s. 163(1) of the Companies Act 2006 disclose details of nationality and residence. This disclosure is repeated in the context of the annual return by s. 855A of the 2006 Act. As is the case with corporate directors, this latitude has the potential for posing difficulties for national regulatory policy.[37] On the other hand, it at least avoids any clash with EU Law and the principle of free movement of services.[38] Finally, we should note that the number of directorships one can hold is not capped by English law, though the courts will treat with some circumspection an assertion that an individual can give proper attention to a large number of companies under his stewardship.[39]

When we talk about directors, we need to distinguish *three* legally distinctive[40] categories that are formally recognized in most corporate law jurisdic-

---

December 2012. This issue is now attracting the attention of EU regulators, where the issue of quotas has been raised. The Commission put a proposal for a 40 per cent quota to be introduced by 2020; we await developments in the EU as there is some opposition to a binding quota-based reform from a range of Member States. Certainly, there are unlikely to be EU-wide sanctions introduced for failure to comply. See Editorial [2012] 325 SMCLN 1.

[36] A survey in 1996 showed that nearly 20 per cent of directors were non-resident. A number of wanted fraudsters, terrorists and war criminals are also apparently registered as company directors – see *The Times*, 21 February 2008 (p. 28). It was quite common in the past to find residents of Sark (which at that time had no system of company law itself) taking up UK company directorships in huge numbers – this was the so-called Sark Lark which featured in the judgment of Blackburne J in *Official Receiver v Vass* [1999] BCC 516, where the individual at the time held some 1313 directorships in UK companies. For background details, see the *Independent*, 27 June 1999. As a result of a crackdown in Guernsey, the offshore nominee director phenomenon has simply moved offshore to various sites in the Caribbean and Indian Ocean. There is a residence requirement in Ireland but that can be waived in a range of circumstances.

[37] For a sensible response by the English courts see *Re Seagull Manufacturing Co Ltd* [1993] BCC 241.

[38] See TFEU Art 56 and cases such as *Commission v Spain (C114/97)* [1999] 2 CMLR 701 and *Commission v Belgium (C355/98)* [2000] 2 CMLR 357.

[39] See the comments of the court in *Re Kaytech International Ltd* [1999] 2 BCLC 351.

[40] As to whether they are mutually exclusive there is some dispute. For instance in *Re Mea Corp Ltd* [2006] EWHC 1846, [2007] 1 BCLC 618 Lewison J opined at para [89] that the categories of de facto and shadow director were not mutually exclusive. Other judges have been more sceptical.

tions. Before doing that we should observe that a person is characterized (rather than defined) as a director in English law by reference to *functions* discharged and not by reference to title.[41]

The ***de jure*** director is the director who has been properly appointed to that position and is officially recorded as holding that status. That status is not affected by a relative lack of visibility or any degree of inactivity.

Second, a **de facto** director[42] is a person (in the fullest sense of the word) who acts from the viewpoint of the outside world as if appointed as a *de jure* director. The functional element is apparent in this context. Visibility is also clearly relevant here. A useful indicator was suggested in *Re Mumtaz Properties Ltd*,[43] where the court asked the question whether the individual could be said to be part of the governance structure. As always, there are fine lines to be drawn here. So a consultant who is clearly operating as an independent contractor providing managerial consultancy input is unlikely to be labelled a de facto director.[44]

Third, we have the mysterious category of the **shadow** director.[45] First appearing in 1917 via the Companies (Particulars as to Directors) Act of that year, this is a person in accordance with whose instructions the directors are accustomed to act.[46] Professionals acting solely within their professional capacity are not thereby deemed to be shadow directors.[47] So a gatekeeper who is advising the directors in times of corporate financial stress can do so without being enmeshed in the fate of the company. This is important to ensure that professionals can provide professional guidance in situations of corporate

---

41 See Companies Act 2006 s. 250, Insolvency Act 1986 s. 251 and Company Directors Disqualification Act 1986 s. 22(4).

42 On the identification of de facto directors see *Gemma Ltd v Davies* [2008] 2 BCLC 281, *Apax Global Payment and Technologies Ltd v Morina* [2011] EWHC 2983 (Ch), *Re Mumtaz Properties Ltd* [2011] EWCA Civ 610, [2012] 2 BCLC 109 and *Re Snelling House* [2012] EWHC 440 (Ch). For a penetrating discussion of the concept of a de facto director see C. Noonan and S. Watson [2008] JBL 587.

43 *Re Mumtaz Properties Ltd* (supra).

44 *City of London Group plc v Lothbury Financial Services Ltd* [2012] EWHC 3148 (Ch).

45 See S. Griffin (2003) 54 NILQ 43 and his later piece in [2011] 24 Ins Intell 44. Note also C. Noonan and S. Watson [2006] JBL 763. For an Australian perspective see M.R. Hobson [1998] 10 Bond Law Rev 184. The South African position is reviewed by K. Idensohn in [2010] 22 SA Merc LJ 326.

46 Companies Act 2006 s. 251(1), Insolvency Act 1986 s. 251, Company Directors Disqualification Act s. 22(5). The Irish definition mirrors this terminology – Companies Act 1990 s. 27. For recent discussion by David Richards J see his preliminary observations in *McKillen v Misland (Cyprus) Investments Ltd* [2012] EWHC 521 (Ch) and his judgment in [2012] EWHC 2434 (Ch) at paras [592]–[602].

47 Companies Act 2006 s. 251(2), Insolvency Act 1986 s.251, Company Directors Disqualification Act 1986 s. 22(5).

crisis so that distressed companies are not left to face ruin without the prospect of assistance. Creditors using standard monitoring procedures would also appear to fall outside this shadow director status. This latter issue has been discussed in English law for some time[48] and the banks (after initial concerns were expressed on their behalf[49]) now seem to know how far they can go before crossing the Rubicon.[50] However, if creditors exceed normal levels of control there must be a risk of a shadow directorship issue arising.[51] In Australia the New South Wales Court of Appeal has supported monitoring rights in *Buzzle Operations Pty v Apple Computer Australia Pty Ltd.*[52] As far as shareholders are concerned, Lewison J suggested in *Re Mea Corp Ltd*[53] that a majority shareholder in an SME could easily be viewed as a shadow director. In general the test for shadow directorship seems to be whether the alleged shadow director exercises *real influence* over the company's management.[54] It is not necessary to prove that a person is continually issuing instructions to the board,[55] nor is it essential to show that the alleged shadow director has real influence over *every aspect* of management.[56] But control over a majority of board members is a precondition.[57] Essentially, all relevant factors are to be taken into account when determining whether a shadow directorship has arisen. A holistic perspective is required.

Why do these three categories matter? Well, they are relevant to the issue of stewardship and in particular to the enforcement of legal responsibilities. So, for instance, a de facto director can be disqualified from future office.[58]

---

48 See *MC Bacon Ltd* [1990] BCC 78, *Re PFTZM Ltd* [1995] 2 BCLC 354. Note also Lord Millett's *ex cathedra* statement on the subject published in [1991] Insolv Pract 14.

49 See F. Bartlett (1994) 10 IL & P 52. Note also the Financial Law Panel's *Shadow Directorships* paper published in 1994.

50 It is interesting in the Farepak case that there was no argument that the bank (which was criticized by Peter Smith J when the disqualification proceedings against the directors were discontinued) was a shadow director. That is probably because its role was largely passive.

51 This seems to have been accepted in principle by Knox J in *Re A Company (005009 of 1987)* [1988] 4 BCLC 424.

52 [2011] NSWCA 109 – discussed by A. Burrow in [2011] Jo of Law Soc of Scotland 50, N. Jamieson and K. Hughes in [2012] Butt Jo of Int Bank and Fin Law 364.

53 [2006] EWHC 1846 (Ch), [2007] 1 BCLC 618 at paras [90]–[91].

54 See *SoSTI v Deverell* [2001] Ch 340.

55 But see *Re Unisoft Ltd (No. 3)* [1994] 1 BCLC 609 (a single act will not suffice).

56 *Ultraframe (UK) Ltd v Fielding* [2005] EWHC 1638 (Ch).

57 *Kuwait Asia Bank v National Mutual Life Nominees* [1990] BCLC 868, *Re Unisoft Ltd (No. 2)* [1994] BCC 766.

58 See *Secretary of State for Trade and Industry v Becker* [2003] 1 BCLC 555.

Shadow directors are subject to a wide range of responsibilities.[59] For someone (such as a liquidator looking to apportion blame for a corporate failure) they offer a range of targets of opportunity for recovery litigation. That is particularly important when a well-to-do entrepreneur has elected to use an undercapitalized limited company as the chosen business vehicle and (in order to further distance himself from liability) has declined to assume a formal position as director.

Moving away from formal legal differentiation, there is also the nominee director to note.[60] This phenomenon can cause problems for corporate governance, particularly where the nominee is a multiple repeat player merely offering a service to an investor who wishes to remain off the radar.[61] Some jurisdictions have formal rules dealing with such a status. Other jurisdictions prefer to leave this to jurisprudence of the common law. The main point to note is that a nominee director does not escape the fundamental responsibilities of stewardship simply by virtue of being a nominee of a major stakeholder. Seeking an indemnity before accepting appointment is thus important.

We should also note the position with regard to non-executive directors (NEDs). As far as the law is concerned, these do not form a legally distinct category of director. The Hampel Committee in 1998 looked at NEDs and opposed the establishment of a lesser duty of care.[62] It is clear that in terms of definition that we are not looking at a term of art. Indeed, the courts[63] have indicated the difficulty in defining such a person. In spite of this the non-executive director is well recognized in practice, particularly in the listed

---

[59] Some of these are mapped out by legislation; others have been the subject of judicial suggestion. The full range is not clear. So in *Ultraframe (UK) Ltd v Fielding* [2005] EWHC 1638 (Ch) Lewison J opined that the standard fiduciary duties do not apply. This has been questioned. See also *Re Mea Corp* [2006] EWHC 1846 (Ch), [2007] 1 BCLC 618. But see Companies Act 2006 s. 170(5), an unhelpful provision that leaves the question of which duties apply to the underlying common law. We do know that s. 214 of the Insolvency Act 1986 applies to shadow directors, as do the requirements laid down in SIP 13. Companies Act 2006 s. 858 also applies. On the applicability of s. 190 of the Companies Act 2006 see *Re Unigreg Ltd* [2005] BPIR 220. Generally see Appendix I of this work.

[60] For an excellent review see D. Ahern (2011) 127 LQR 118.

[61] This situation was the subject of a major exposé in the *Guardian* on 26 November 2012 and followed up by a BBC *Panorama* programme broadcast on the same evening.

[62] See Hampel Committee, *Committee on Corporate Governance: Final Report* (1998) at 3.3. Previously the Cadbury Committee (1992) made the point that all directors (including NEDs) are stewards (see para 1.8). See also *Equitable Life Assurance Society v Bowley* [2003] EWHC 2263 (Comm) at para [35] per Langley J.

[63] See *Re Langreen Ltd* (21 October 2011, unreported) per Registrar Derrett at para [84].

company environment. As to what is expected of a non-executive director, there is no comprehensive statement in law, though Park J did observe in *Re Continental Assurance Co of London plc*[64] that it would be unrealistic to expect them to overrule a specialist director (such as a finance director).

Before leaving this discussion of the family of directors, it is worth noting that in English Law there is no concept of an 'apparent director' or a 'director by holding out'[65] under which a person who does not purport to be a director is represented as such by some other party – this differentiates company law from partnership law.[66]

1.5 OTHER PLAYERS

Up to now our focus has been exclusively upon company directors. But our corporate governance system casts its net wider, both linguistically and pragmatically. So, for instance, some statutory provisions have as their target a group designated as company 'officers'. In Appendix I of this work we identify some of these provisions. We can assume from the wording of s. 1173 of the Companies Act 2006 and its equivalents in the Insolvency Act 1986 (s. 251) and Company Directors Disqualification Act 1986 (s. 22C) that company directors would fall within this grouping, but presumably senior executives outside the board might also qualify. All of these provisions referring to officers include managers and secretaries within their catchment area. Certainly, where statutory provisions refer to persons being concerned in the management of a company, an assumption that non-directors are encompassed is irresistible. There is a fair amount of case law arising in a variety of contexts and dealing with who might be seen as a manager,[67] but it is regrettable that a degree of uncertainty persists in this regard.

1.6 'INSOLVENCY'

Increasingly, English law, like other corporate systems, views the use of

---

64 [2001] BPIR 733 at para [399]. For judicial views on the role of NEDs in Australia see *ASIC v Healey* [2011] FCA 717.

65 This might explain the generous ruling in *Gemma Ltd v Davies* [2008] 2 BCLC 281.

66 See Partnership Act 1890 s. 14.

67 See for example *Re A Company* [1980] 2 WLR 241, *R v Campbell* [1984] BCLC 83, *Re Clasper Group Services Ltd* [1989] BCLC 14 and *Re Market Wizard Systems Ltd* [1998] 2 BCLC 282. For illuminating discussion see T. Clench (2012) 25 Ins Intell 28.

solvency tests as an important ongoing protection for creditors. This is particularly true in the area of transactions relating to the share capital of a company. So, for example, under Companies Act 2006 s. 642, a declaration of solvency is required to enable a private company to reduce its share capital. Ultimately, whether a company enters members' voluntary liquidation or creditors' voluntary liquidation will depend on whether the directors can vouch for its solvency (see Insolvency Act 1986 ss. 89 and 90).

English law employs *two* tests to determine whether a company is insolvent. Historically, for these purposes it has utilized the cash flow or liquidity criterion.[68] A company is insolvent in this sense according to s. 123(1) of the Insolvency Act 1986 if it cannot, or will not, pay its debts as they fall due. Thus, an asset-rich company that wilfully refuses to pay an undisputed debt can find itself being characterized as insolvent under the law, even though it is manifestly in rude financial health.[69]

As a result of reforms enacted in 1985, we now also use a balance sheet criterion, which prima facie involves a mathematical comparison of assets and liabilities, including contingent liabilities. This criterion to measure insolvency is now to be found enshrined in s. 123(2) of the Insolvency Act 1986. Recent consideration to this test was given by the Court of Appeal in *BNY Corporate Trustee Services Ltd v Eurosail-UK 2007-3BL plc*.[70] Here Lord Neuberger MR stressed that this test is to be applied in a flexible fashion and should not be seen as a purely mathematical exercise. Commercial common sense should be taken into account. Whilst this approach is commendable for its realism and for taking a number of firms outside insolvency territory, practitioners are concerned that it has generated uncertainty.[71] The moment a company can be said to be insolvent can be critical in determining the applicable duties of directors and the nature of the professional advice given to such directors. The case in question is awaiting the outcome of a further appeal to the Supreme Court and it will be interesting to see if these concerns are addressed.

We should enter a note of caution here. Both tests are not employed in every instance where issues of directorial liability fall to be determined. Thus, Professor Goode has pointed out[72] that it is only the balance sheet test that has any relevance for determining wrongful trading liability. That may be the subject of a range of opinions but the general point made is accurate – each situation needs to be reviewed on its individual basis.

---

68 *Re Patrick and Lyon Ltd* [1933] Ch 786.

69 See *Cornhill Insurance plc v Improvement Services Ltd* [1986] BCLC 26.

70 [2011] EWCA Civ 227, [2011] BCC 400. See also *Re Cheyne Finance* [2007] EWHC 2402 (Ch), [2008] BCC 182.

71 See D. Henderson (2011) 24 Ins Intell 54.

72 See [1989] JBL 436.

We should also observe that prospective insolvency may be relevant in some contexts. So the court can place a company into administration using the Insolvency Act 1986 Schedule B1 para 11 procedure if the company is *likely* to become insolvent. The courts are quite receptive on friendly applications to reach such a conclusion; less so where the application may be construed as hostile.[73]

There are other tests for what constitutes insolvency for the purposes of particular pieces of legislation. Thus there is a test under s. 183 of the Employment Rights Act 1996[74] and one for the purposes of the Pensions Act 2004.[75] Within the European Union we could also note Art 2 of the EC Insolvency Directive (2008/94).

Looking beyond legislation, commercial documentation may employ a customized definition of what constitutes an insolvency event for the particular relationship – for example one finds such definitions in contractual break clauses or in a finance agreement.

1.7 INSOLVENCY PRACTITIONERS[76]

Apart from directors, the other human actors that will be the primary focus of our attention are insolvency practitioners. We stress the human characteristic here; English law does not permit a firm, whether corporate or not, to hold an insolvency office.[77] The post of liquidator, etc, must be held by a natural person.[78] Although there are clear benefits[79] flowing from this idea of an ad personam appointment, this can cause practical difficulties, particularly as the

73 See the case of *Re Colt Telecom (No 2)* [2002] EWHC 2815 (Ch), [2003] BPIR 324 – decided under the old administration order regime but still relevant for these purposes.

74 See *Secretary of State for Trade and Industry v Key* [2004] BPIR 214.

75 Section 121 – see the discussion in *Re Olympic Airlines SA* [2012] EWHC 1413 (Ch), [2012] BPIR 1163.

76 See D. Milman [2012] 321 SMCLN 1 for a review of current issues. Excellent background on the regulatory context can be gleaned from the pieces by V. Finch in [1998] JBL 334 and [2012] JBL 645.

77 This is not the position overseas. Indeed, within English law it is possible to cite stewardship examples where a corporate body can act – witness Trustee Act 1925 s. 68.

78 The one exception is the official receiver – see Insolvency Act 1986 ss. 399–401. It is interesting to compare this insistence on human agency with the more liberal approach to the appointment of trustees – see Trustee Act 1925 s. 68.

79 See *Reid and Stephen, Noters* [2010] CSOH 138 where the court observed that an office-holder cannot simply walk away from the responsibility whilst leaving matters in the hands of a co-appointee.

reality is that the appointment is managed by an insolvency firm, of which the appointee is but a member. If an insolvency practitioner dies in post, or retires, or leaves the firm to move to fresh pastures, there will be a need for replacement. As individual office-holders invariably hold multiple offices concurrently, the replacement problem is magnified. In response to these inevitable facts of life, the law has had to introduce mechanisms to deal with 'block transfers' of insolvency offices.[80] The overriding imperative here is that the insolvent estate should not bear the cost of this change of stewardship – see Insolvency Rule 7.10D(4). The courts will also be careful to examine the circumstances behind the block transfer and will not simply rubber stamp the nomination of the outgoing office-holder.[81] The views of the relevant recognized professional body (RPB) may be taken into account when any substitution is being considered.

Holding office as an insolvency office-holder is something that needs careful regulation. So under s. 164 of the Insolvency Act 1986 it is an offence to offer bribes to procure appointment as a liquidator. If, in spite of this, a liquidator has improperly solicited appointment, any claim to remuneration will be jeopardized (Insolvency Rule 4.150).

One problem we have in dealing with the law on insolvency practitioners is the profusion of official terms that can be used to describe them. So in s. 388 the term 'insolvency practitioner' is used. We then have the category of 'office-holders' as defined somewhat confusingly in different ways in ss. 230–37 of the Act. There is then the common-law idea of 'officers of the court', which is wider than we might anticipate. Finally we have the very broad designation of 'appointee' as used under the *Practice Direction on Insolvency Proceedings*.[82] If we take administrative receivers as an example, we find that they are insolvency practitioners and office-holders (for some purposes) but are not officers of the court nor appointees.

The insolvency profession itself is a late nineteenth-century professional manifestation.[83] The profession grew in importance throughout the twentieth century. That said, it only assumed the mantle of a fully fledged profession[84]

---

80 The courts lead the way with a number of significant authorities – see *Donaldson v O'Sullivan* [2008] EWCA Civ 879, [2009] BCC 99. There is now specific treatment of this issue in Insolvency Rules 7.10A–7.10D as inserted by Insolvency (Amendment) Rules 2010 (SI 2010/686).

81 See *ACCA v Koumettou and Morfakis* [2012] EWHC 132 (Ch) and *ICAEW v Webb* [2009] EWHC 3461 (Ch). Compare *Re AJ Adams Builders Ltd* [1991] BCC 62.

82 [2012] BPIR 409 para 1.1(11).

83 For a historical perspective see J. Flood and E. Skordaki, *Insolvency Practitioners and Big Corporate Insolvencies* (1995) (ACCA Research Report No. 43). Note also V.M. Lester, *Victorian Insolvency* (1995).

84 See G. Borrie [1984] JBL 111 at 113 for comment.

with monopoly standing in the wake of the implementation of the Cork Report (1982).[85] It successfully rebranded[86] itself in the latter half of the 1990s so as to have an explicit focus on business recovery. One can see the public relations advantages in this marketing strategy. Turnaround is clearly an important goal (and one that few people will criticize), but the less glamorous liquidation role still retains its importance, as all of the statistical evidence on UK corporate insolvencies confirms. There are more insolvent liquidations annually than all other corporate insolvency regimes combined together. Moreover, many administrations (and CVAs) are little more than disguised liquidations. That is particularly so since administration was remodelled by s. 248 of the Enterprise Act 2002.[87] Business rescue in reality is the exception rather than the rule. There is nothing unusual about this; it is the pattern replicated across the globe. Furthermore, there are a number of businesses where rescue has been but a temporary stay of execution.[88] To associate insolvency with 'rescue' may therefore be an illusion. This may present an uncomfortable truth for policy-makers and the insolvency profession who have invested heavily in the idea of business rescue, even to the point of rebranding their professional association.[89] Devotees of the potential of creative destruction would not be alarmed by the failure of the law to rescue distressed firms – the economic opportunity could be exploited by a new market entrant.

The Office of Fair Trading (OFT) Market Study Report[90] in 2010 is valuable in placing the different insolvency regimes in context. From that report we find out in para 3.8 that some 50 per cent of fee income is derived from administrations. We also learn that 29 per cent of administrations have a CVL outcome. This report also produces the impressive statistic that insolvency practitioners realize some £5 billion in assets every year at a cost of £1 billion.

There are surprisingly few insolvency practitioners who take office. Current figures suggest that there are at present only some 1800 insolvency

---

85 Cmnd 8558. For contemporary analysis see D.M. Hare and D. Milman (1983) 127 Sols Jo 230–335 seriatim.

86 The key representation organization is the Association of Business Recovery Professionals (or R3). Up to 2000 it was called the Society of Practitioners of Insolvency (which more accurately represented its remit).

87 But there are still important differences between these two regimes – see the comments of David Richards J in *Heis v MF Global Inc* [2012] EWHC 3068 (Ch) at para [52]. For analysis of the 2002 Act see V. Finch [2003] JBL 527, J. Armour, A. Hsu and A. Walters [2008] 5 ECFLR 148. The Insolvency Service also published a survey on the impact of this legislation in 2008.

88 See L. Lo Pucki and J.W. Doherty, *Professional Fees in Corporate Bankruptcies* (2011) where it is pointed out (at 6) that 26 per cent of US companies undergoing Chapter 11 are required to seek a further restructuring within five years.

89 See the marketing article by W. Black in [2012] (Autumn) Recov 28.

90 See *The Market for Corporate Insolvency Practitioners* (2010) (OFT).

practitioners in the country and of these only 1341 are active.[91] With the high number of insolvencies occurring each year, this can lead to the phenomenon of multiple posts in respect of many companies being held concurrently by the same individual. Accordingly, critics[92] have suggested that more competition is needed in the market for insolvency services and that this might be achieved through an increase in the number of insolvency practitioners. Clearly the bulk of licensed insolvency practitioners are associated with the large firms of accountants[93] and the impact of 'bank panels' should be noted, but there is a healthy group of smaller firms who have developed niche specialisms. Another strategy has been to introduce turnaround specialists into the market, such as company doctors into the field, but these still cannot hold a formal insolvency office as a liquidator, administrative receiver or administrator. The Insolvency Act 2000 made strides in this direction by introducing through s. 4(4) a new s. 389A into the Insolvency Act 1986, but such individuals still cannot take formal appointments as this provision has not been brought into force. The problem seems to be that the legislation does not contemplate selective authorization of permitted roles. Consequently, their role is restricted to advising distressed firms in the hope that formal insolvency can be avoided. We will examine the consequences of this role later.

There is also a gender gap phenomenon that should be confronted. Current estimates suggest that only 21 per cent of insolvency practitioners are female[94] – this compares unfavourably with female representation in similar allied professions, such as law and accountancy. The gender issue is being taken seriously by the insolvency practitioner profession and also by the Insolvency Service, which publishes data on its own gender profiling.[95]

In terms of regulation we are faced with a balkanized structure with no less than eight regulators playing a role. There are seven recognized professional bodies (RPBs),[96] plus the Insolvency Service, which still retains a direct

---

91 *2011 Insolvency Service Annual Report on IP Regulation* (2012) at 4. In 1994 it was calculated that the figure was 1925 – see J. Flood and E. Skordaki, Insolvency Practitioners and Big Corporate Insolvencies (1995) (ACCA Research Report No. 43).

92 This concern seems to be implicit in the setting-up of the 2010 OFT Market Study review.

93 This potentially could raise issues of conflict of interest – the effective use of so-called 'Chinese walls' could be important here – see *Bolkiah v KPMG* [1999] 2 AC 222.

94 See R3 publication *The Value of the Insolvency Industry* (2008) at pp. 3 and 24. In the mid-1990s the figure was estimated to be as low as 5 per cent. All of the evidence suggests travel is being made in the right direction.

95 See the Diversity and Equality heading on the Insolvency Service website, where details of an annual data survey appear.

96 See Insolvency Act 1986 s. 391.

licensing role. This situation has attracted criticism but there are some powerful players at work here who are reluctant to cede territory in a turf war. The role of the Insolvency Service in terms of authorization is likely to be reviewed in the future as it does represent an anomaly.

The profession is well represented by trade bodies such as R3 and the ILA. These are influential pressure groups. Their impact can be attested by the speedy enactment of the Insolvency Act 1994 and in their efforts to restrict the reforms in the Enterprise Act 2002, particularly with regard to administrative receivership. They serve the public interest in disseminating valuable information about current insolvency developments. The R3 Technical Bulletin celebrated its 100th edition in October 2012. In so doing, these organizations inform both their members and benefit the public at large.

1.8 'STEWARDSHIP'

A 'steward' is defined in Jowitt's *Dictionary of English Law*[97] as a ward or keeper, or a person appointed in the stead of another. The term stewardship can be applied to a multiplicity of legal relationships.[98] Ideas of stewardship are very much in vogue at present across a diverse range of contexts.[99] We are all familiar with situations of stewardship arising in English law. The trustee acting under a trust on behalf of beneficiaries is perhaps the most obvious scenario. But there are others: for instance, guardians acting for wards, those representing persons lacking mental capacity, and personal representatives of the deceased. These are all general forms of stewardship. A more specialized and attenuated variant is found in the law of bailment, where a bailee is responsible for the safe custody and transmission of goods entrusted to its care by the bailor.

In stewardship situations it is not uncommon to find the steward invested with the legal title of property held for the benefit of the protected party – e.g. in the classic trust scenario. But this is not an absolute prerequisite – both directors and insolvency practitioners are indisputably stewards, but it would be unusual to find them holding the legal title of property belonging beneficially to the company.[100] What matters here is the de facto control of property.

---

97 3rd ed., 2010. Vol 2. See also S. Ali [2012] Jo of Fin Crime 207.

98 Soren Holm mentions 13 possible meanings of the word 'steward' in his piece in [2011] 62 NILQ 617.

99 Witness the special issue of the *Northern Ireland Legal Quarterly* in 2011 (vol 62 part 5) devoted to stewardship in the medical context.

100 So for instance the controller of a company can steal company property (*Attorney General's Reference (No. 2 of 1982)* [1984] QB 624) and has no insurable

What we will seek to do in this study is to locate the position of the company director and insolvency office-holder within that broad stewardship tradition and to examine the extent to which general principles of stewardship (if any such exist) apply. We shall also note situations where stewardship responsibilities towards the company (however defined) may come into conflict with stewardship responsibilities owed to other stakeholders.

1.9 STAKEHOLDER GROUPS

In our definition of governance we introduced the term 'stakeholder'.[101] This again is an example of modern terminology. Clearly, it encompasses shareholders but it goes beyond that. A perusal of the minutiae of s. 172 of the Companies Act 2006 will provide a sense of how expansive this concept has become with business counterparties, local communities and the environment being potential candidates as stakeholders.

Creditors today are indisputably viewed as stakeholders, whether the company is solvent or not. That was not always so – in the past they were denied the opportunity to challenge *ultra vires* business activities.[102] Things have moved on. Indeed, as the company degenerates, they become *the* dominant stakeholders. Accordingly, their consent will be required for any sort of restructuring – see Companies Act 2006 s. 899. Creditors may be contractual counterparties or involuntary creditors such as tort victims or the revenue authorities. We need to be careful here in placing all creditors into a single class. This note of caution is reinforced when one considers the statement that English law can be viewed as 'pro creditor'. That is a puzzling statement when one considers the poor returns enjoyed by unsecured creditors on corporate insolvency. What this statement really implies is that English law is pro secured creditor. That is true, though there has been some withdrawal from that sectarian position in the wake of the Enterprise Act 2002.

Employees fall within the stakeholder group. Their rights as suppliers of labour may be protected on a restructuring and they enjoy the right, through their representatives, to be consulted on any potential job losses.[103]

---

interest in company property (*Macaura v Northern Assurance Co* [1925] AC 619). This separation of ownership and control of company property is a central governance issue – see Chapter 2.

[101] See Will Hutton, *The Stakeholding Society* (1999).

[102] *Mills v Northern Rwy of Buenos Aires* (1870) 5 Ch App 621.

[103] I reviewed this issue in 'From Servant to Stakeholder: The Employee Interest in Company Law', Chapter 8 in D. Feldman and F. Meisel, *Corporate and Commercial Law: Modern Developments* (1995).

1.10 THE PUBLIC INTEREST[104]

The material covered in this study will be primarily within the domain of private law in that private interests are to the fore. But that is not to say that the element of public interest is irrelevant. In a capitalist society there is a clear public interest in encouraging enterprise and responsible risk-taking. Limited liability is essentially available as a matter of public policy choice, with that choice being made critically by the UK Parliament in 1855. A public policy choice engages public interest. Limited liability therefore needs to be monitored by the state: any suggestion of abuse of this economic concession might result in an informal investigation under s. 447 of the Companies Act 1985 (reconstituted by s. 21 of the Companies (Audit, Investigations and Community Enterprise) Act 2004).[105] Cooperation by company officers with such an investigation is compulsory.[106] In the wake of such a gathering of evidence a petition may be presented under s. 124A of the Insolvency Act 1986 for a winding-up in the public interest.[107] According to Insolvency Service Annual Report,[108] this power was exercised on 355 occasions in the year 2011–12 (for perspective, compare this statistic with the 2.5 million registered companies on the register in that same year). The primacy of the public interest was confirmed recently in *Secretary of State for Business, Innovation and Skills v Top Choice Wholesale Ltd*,[109] where the court confirmed that a s. 124A petition could be presented notwithstanding an extant winding-up petition presented by a creditor. The power can be exercised not merely against limited companies but also against LLPs.[110] Such a form of liquidation does not however come within the embrace of the EC Regulation on Insolvency Proceedings (1346/2000).[111] As winding-up is a draconian step, there is the possibility of the concerns being addressed through the acceptance of formal undertakings about the future business operations of the company.[112]

---

104 See Cork Committee (Cmnd 8558, 1982) Chapter 43.

105 Minor amendments were made by s. 1038 of the Companies Act 2006.

106 See Companies Act 1985 s. 453C and *Secretary of State for BIS v Scaggs* [2012] EWHC 3120 (Ch) where proceedings for contempt followed acts of non-cooperation.

107 See V. Finch [2002] Ins Law 157, A. Keay [2000] 51 NILQ 509.

108 See *Insolvency Service Annual Report and Accounts 2011/12* (HC 358) at p. 32.

109 [2012] EWHC 1262 (Ch). See also *Re PGMRS Ltd* [2010] EWHC 2983 (Ch), [2011] BCC 368 and *Re Treasure Traders Ltd* [2005] EWHC 2774 (Ch). Under para 82 of Sched B1 of the Insolvency Act 1986 a company in administration can still be wound up in the public interest.

110 *Re Inertia Partnership LLP* [2007] EWHC 539 (Ch), [2007] BCC 656.

111 *Re Marann Brooks CSV Ltd* [2003] BCC 239 per Patten J at para [34].

112 See *Bell Davies Trading v SoSTI* [2004] EWCA Civ 1066, [2005] BCC 564.

There is a public interest involved when one calculates the costs to the national exchequer in protecting society from the harm that can be caused by unfit directors.[113] The director disqualification regime, especially where there is a disqualification based upon s. 8 of the Company Directors Disqualification Act 1986, is posited upon the protection of the public, rather than on penalizing errant directors. There is a clear public interest at stake when one takes into account the financial costs of taking measures to combat errant directors. The public interest element in liquidation was stressed by Lord Millett in *Official Receiver v Wadge, Rapps and Hunt*[114] when characterizing the essence of the liquidation process. The role of the official receiver in winding up hopeless cases where the private sector is not interested could be mentioned here. But we must be careful when discussing public interest as what constitutes public interest is not always the subject of consensus – witness the different interpretations in *Whitehouse v Wilson.*[115]

Conversely, the state has an interest in trying to ensure that companies in difficulty survive, because of the negative impact upon employment where a business fails (thereby causing further indirect loss to the exchequer). Companies are major tax-gatherers for the state, which therefore has a creditor stakeholder interest in every company. This on average amounts to nearly 25 per cent of the unsecured debt. The desire on the part of the state to preserve companies is manifested in a range of contexts. For example, under s. 17 of the Company Directors Disqualification Act 1986, a director of a failed company who has consequently been disqualified can apply for special leave to remain as director of another solvent company.[116] In making such an application it is not uncommon for the applicant director to argue that this second concern would also fail without his/her input.[117] In granting leave under s. 17, the public interest can be protected by the introduction of an upgraded corporate governance regime.[118] The courts have shown themselves receptive to

---

113 Hence the National Audit Office Reports in the 1990s investigating the costs of the court-based director disqualification regime. See for analysis A. Hicks, *Disqualification of Directors: No Hiding Place for the Unfit?* (1998) (ACCA Research Report No. 59).

114 [2003] UKHL 49, [2004] 1 AC 158. Lord Millett was merely reiterating the views he expressed a decade earlier as Millett J in *Re Barlow Clowes (Gilt Managers) Ltd* [1991] BCC 608 at 616–17.

115 [2007] BPIR 230.

116 See generally T. Clench (2008) 21 Ins Intell 113, A. Belcher [2012] 16 Edinburgh Law Rev 386. A similar provision can be found in Ireland in s. 160(8) of the Companies Act 1990.

117 See for example *SoSTI v Barnett* [1998] 2 BCLC 64 (where the sob story failed).

118 See for example *Re Gibson Davies Ltd* [1995] BCC 11 (some nine conditions were attached to the leave).

such an argument. Any leave granted under s. 17 may be general or simply a specific authorization to exercise certain directorial powers (for example instructing solicitors to act on behalf of the company[119]). Leave applications under s. 17 are few in number when compared with the overall number of disqualifications, a point disclosed in a recent study by Alice Belcher.[120]

Again, in *R v Cotswold Geotechnical Holdings Ltd*,[121] Field J in the Crown Court noted that, under sentencing guidelines, fines imposed for a conviction for corporate killing under the Corporate Manslaughter and Homicide Act 2007 should not be so great as to put a company out of business. That said, if a terminal fine was appropriate, that sanction should not be eschewed. The £385 000 fine imposed by Field J, which was upheld on appeal,[122] contributed to the demise of the offending company, which went into liquidation shortly thereafter.

The public interest is not merely protected by traditional legal institutions. It is a vital function of the role of RPBs – this point was stressed by Lord Slynn in *ICAEW v Customs and Excise*.[123]

1.11 CHANGING TECHNOLOGIES[124]

One problem that both directors and insolvency practitioners have had to grapple with has been the changing technological climate in which they have to operate in. This is particularly true of the revolution in communications technology over the past two decades. The paper-based system for communication, upon which the 1986 regime was modelled, has become an anachronism with the widespread use of modern communications technology in business. To what extent can directors and insolvency office-holders take advantage of such changes in conducting their stewardship of a limited company in a more efficient manner and thereby save administration costs? Caution is the key word here. Although the courts might be prepared to stretch the meaning of a statutory provision to reflect technological evolution,[125] there is no guarantee that

---

[119] See *Re Portland Place Historic House Ltd* (unreported, 20 June 2012).

[120] See [2012] 16 Edin Law Rev 386.

[121] [2011] All ER (D) May 100.

[122] [2011] EWCA Crim 1337.

[123] [1999] UKHL 19, [1999] STC 398.

[124] For general background see D. Milman, *National Corporate Law in a Globalised Market* (2009) at 57.

[125] See *R v Taylor* [2011] EWCA Crim 728, [2011] 1 WLR 1809, where the concept of 'books or paper' when used in the context of s. 206 of the Insolvency Act 1986 was held to include computer records. A similarly flexible approach was taken by HHJ Purle in *Re Advent Computer Training Ltd* [2010] EWHC 459 (Ch), [2011] BCC

they will always be so accommodating. That said, the legislature has shown itself increasingly willing to embrace new technology to facilitate the stewardship role. So, from the viewpoint of directors, s. 360A of the Companies Act 2006 permits remote company meetings. As far as insolvency practitioners are concerned, there were a raft of reforms introduced by the Insolvency (Amendment) Rules 2010[126] and the Legislative Reform (Insolvency) (Miscellaneous Amendments) Order 2010[127] designed to make greater use of electronic communication during the conduct of the administration of an insolvency. So, for instance, remote attendance of creditors may be permitted in s. 246A of the Insolvency Act 1986 and an insolvency practitioner may make use of websites to communicate with stakeholders under the provisions in s. 246B of the Act. It is too early to determine how widely these concessions are being used, but contacts with IPs suggest that this has been a positive move.

Technological change may not simply be a matter of easing burdens. So, for instance, the Companies (Trading Disclosure) (Insolvency) Regulations 2008[128] *increased* the disclosure obligations of insolvency practitioners where websites and electronic means of communication were being used to deal with customers.

44. In *Re Sporting Options plc* [2004] EWHC 3128 (Ch), [2005] BPIR 435, one gets the feeling that Mann J was trying to be helpful but nevertheless felt constrained by the law.

126 SI 2010/686.

127 SI 2010/18.

128 SI 2008/1897.

2. The relevance of corporate governance theory and related issues

2.1 BACKGROUND

This chapter will feature a brief discussion of general corporate governance theories, but only insofar as they are relevant to our proposed study. There is a vast literature on corporate governance in general and, inevitably, there is a limited supply of fresh insights.[1] But this chapter will highlight the relative lack of significant scholarly attention paid by legal writers and policymakers to the governance of companies in financial difficulty and also the paucity of academic input to the particular perspective of SMEs (which make up the overwhelming majority of firms[2]). The 'think small first' mantra, which has been so influential in shaping recent substantive corporate law reform in the UK, as is evidenced by the focus placed upon it by the Company Law Review, should be applied with equal vigour to the SME constituency in the wider governance debate. As far as UK corporate law is concerned, this new philosophy has left its mark on the law relating to company accounts (see for example s. 380 and Part 15 of the 2006 Act) and has led to the removal of a requirement for a company secretary in private companies (s. 270 of Companies Act 2006). But if we move to the core provisions on company directors, there is little evidence of variation,[3] and the same is true when we look at the regulation of corporate insolvency. In the latter regard we could note by way of exception the modified CVA procedure outlined in Schedule A1 of the Insolvency Act 1986, which does only apply to SMEs – but as this regime is hardly ever used,[4] it is difficult to treat it as of any great importance,

---

1 A rare exception is A. Keay, *The Corporate Objective* (2008).

2 From DBIS statistics it appears that more than 99 per cent of the 2 663 100 registered companies in England and Wales are listed as private (source: *Companies Annual Report 2011/12* Table A2). But not all private companies are SMEs – there are some substantial private undertakings operating in the UK corporate sector.

3 One might point to CA 2006 s. 656 (obligation to call an EGM in the event of serious capital loss), which applies only to public companies.

4 This may be gleaned from the empirical study carried out by Adrian Walters and Sandra Frisby, which was outlined to the Annual ILA Academic Group meeting in Oxford in March 2011. Details on this research can be found in S. Frisby [2011] 64 CLP 349.

apart from the fact that it does signify a departure from the norm in the way that it offers differential options for SMEs.

2.2 THEORIES OF CORPORATE GOVERNANCE[5]

Corporate governance scholarship has mushroomed over the past four decades to the point where the law of diminishing returns applies. The term 'corporate governance' appears to have first surfaced in US circles in the early 1960s,[6] a jurisdiction where the first tentative moves towards the development of a governance code emerged in the late 1970s,[7] but, as far as the UK is concerned, it was very much a topic for discourse from the late 1980s onwards. The late John Parkinson played a formative role here.[8]

One initial question that invites discussion is why corporate governance as a subject of legal debate did not emerge for more than 100 years after the introduction of the limited liability company. The first recorded usage of the phrase is credited to Richard Eells in his 1960 monograph *The Meaning of Modern Business: An Introduction to the Philosophy of Large Corporate Enterprise*. Cynics might say that it is just a modern soundbite that has no real substance or practical consequence to it. Such critics point to the continuing wave of business failures where corporate governance lapses are all too apparent. Decades of corporate government 'wisdom' do not appear to have changed much on the ground. That negative view would be an uncharitable stance to adopt. One issue that may have been instrumental in the relatively late arrival of corporate governance was the emergence of the law and economics school in the USA.[9]

Whatever one thinks about the practical relevance of corporate governance theory, it is a reality for UK company law – particularly so since the publication of the Cadbury Report in 1992.[10] The Companies Act 2006 now includes

---

[5] For an excellent up-to-date review see I.G. MacNeil, *An Introduction to the Law on Financial Investment* (2nd ed., 2012), Chapter 9.

[6] See R.S.F. Eells, *The Meaning of Modern Business: An Introduction to the Philosophy of Large Corporate Enterprise* (1960).

[7] The American Law Institute, after years of deliberation, finally produced its code in 1992. For the background of this venture see W.J. Carney [1988] 66 Wash Law Q 239.

[8] See the tribute published in *Global Governance and the Quest for Justice: Vol 2 – Corporate Governance* (2006).

[9] For critical analysis see N. Duxbury, *Patterns of American Jurisprudence* (1995) (Clarendon Press) at Chapter 5. See also D. Campbell (2010) 73 MLR 305 for an acerbic criticism of a number of aspects of law and economics thinking.

[10] *The Financial Aspects of Corporate Governance* (1992).

explicit provisions relating to corporate governance standards in the context of issuers.[11] The UK Corporate Governance Code,[12] which first appeared in 2010 and was updated in September 2012, is an important benchmark, although it had well-developed predecessors in the UK. Although clearly intended for listed companies, its general principles and more specific code provisions are likely to be influential in the years to come. Thus, we see a clear emphasis on leadership, the obligation to devote appropriate time to the discharge of duties, and the need for proper induction and continuing education. Non-executive directors are expected to play a constructive and challenging role. The courts increasingly refer to corporate governance practices when handing down judgments relating to the performance of corporate management, but it is still the case that corporate governance codes are not legally binding in the formal sense of the concept.[13] Soft law it may be, but irrelevant it is not.

Much of our corporate governance thinking has originated from the USA.[14] There is no denying that some valuable insights have crossed the Atlantic. In particular, we note the recognition of the reality in widely held companies of the separation of ownership and control,[15] the concept of agency costs[16] and the risk of managerial opportunism as highlighted in agency theory discourse, the idea of disciplining management through the 'market for corporate control',[17] the reassuring corporate social responsibility[18] initiative, and the new emphasis on the significance of 'path dependency' in terms of the history and evolution of corporate law.[19] The widely accepted notion of 'comply or explain' (so central to the UK Corporate Governance Code) has its origins in North America. The debate over the trend towards the potential for the convergence[20]

---

11 See Companies Act 2006 s. 1269.

12 Available on the Financial Reporting Council website. For analysis see J. Lowry and A. Reisberg, *Pettet's Company Law: Company Law and Corporate Finance* (4th ed., 2012) at 215–24.

13 See *Re Astec plc* [1999] BCC 59. See also *Re Macro (Ipswich) Ltd* [1994] 2 BCLC 354.

14 For an excellent survey of this tradition see the collection of essays included in B. Cheffins (ed.), *The History of Modern US Corporate Governance* (2011).

15 A. Berle and G. Means, *The Modern Corporation and Private Property* (1932).

16 On agency costs see M.C. Jensen and W.H. Meckling (1976) 3 Jo of Fin Econ 305.

17 See H.G. Manne (1965) 73 Jo of Pol Econ 110, C. Bradley [1990] 50 MLR 171.

18 See I. Lynch-Fannon [2007] 58 NILQ 1 and J. Zhao, [2012] 12 JCLS 163 (a Chinese perspective on this subject).

19 See M. Roe, *Political Determinants of Corporate Governance* (2003) at 151.

20 See A. Dignam and M. Galanis, *The Globalisation of Corporate Governance* (2009). I deal with this issue in Chapter 9 of *National Corporate Law in a Globalised Market* (2009).

of corporate law systems kicked off in the USA. More recently, the development of what might be termed 'leximetric' analysis under which corporate law systems are scored against each other by reference to particular criteria (a methodology which again originated in the USA) has offered a new way to evaluate different corporate law systems.[21] A similar numerical scoring method is used for investment purposes by models such as Deminor ratings, which weigh up the strength of corporate governance protection in different jurisdictions. Such ratings are a particularly important source of reference for large institutional investors, such as CalPERS (Californian Public Employees Retirement Scheme).

This fertile American tradition does however present some difficulties for us and, in truth, for many other corporate law systems across the globe. These challenges are reinforced by a healthy chauvinistic scepticism as to the potential for (and benefits of) a total convergence in corporate law. First, there are significant differences between the US and UK corporate scenes, particularly with regard to the role played by private companies in this country. Second, we must never forget that we are part of the European Union and that our commitments to the EU in terms of corporate law harmonization are legally binding by virtue of TFEU Art 50(2)(g). But, as things stand at present, those commitments bear down primarily upon public companies, with only belated attention now being paid to the position of SMEs.[22] Taking together all of these points, and adding in the fact that the English judiciary are reluctant to refer to theory when formulating judgments, there must be a suspicion that the corporate governance rhetoric with its focus on large corporations is perceived to be of limited practical relevance from the perspective of the vast majority of UK companies. Whether that is a fair perception remains to be seen; what is clear is that it certainly does not justify a position of complete dismissal of corporate governance theory.

One current area of heightened discourse in connection with corporate governance is the important issue of gender diversity and the potential impact upon business performance of a lack of diversity. Figures for female boardroom presence are a matter of heightened interest, with a statistic of 17.4 per cent now being quoted for FTSE 100 companies in 2012. There is a school of thought that by encouraging female participation at boardroom level, this will

---

21 This approach was first used by the La Porta team – see [1998] 106 Jo of Pol Econ 1113. It has been evaluated by P. Lele and M. Siems in a study in (2007) 7 JCLS 17.

22 This newfound interest is reflected by the so-called Private Company ('SPE') Initiative and the putative Small Business Act (see editorials in [2008] 235 SMCLN 1 and [2008] 236 SMCLN 1). The 2012 Company Law Action Plan announced on 12 December 2012 indicates that there will be a follow-up to this initiative.

somehow enhance corporate performance. It is suggested (by a process of intuition) that females are more risk averse than males in taking commercial decisions. It is hard to produce conclusive supporting evidence to this effect, but there clearly is a constructive debate to be had here.[23] Moreover, there are legal obligations to note in connection with this question. As a company director will usually be an employee,[24] there must be the risk of a potential sex discrimination claim under the Equality Act 2010 where a decision to appoint a new member to a board is seen to be unjustifiable.[25] Equally, the introduction of a mandatory quota system for female directors would not be beyond legal challenge. It would certainly be resisted by the business community if it was made a legal imperative, as is clear from the public discussion of this idea in recent months.[26] The bottom line is that any director irrespective of gender can be removed by shareholders under s.168 of the Companies Act 2006. Would we wish the exercise of that power to be challenged on gender grounds? Hopefully, a working compromise can be arrived at.

2.3 CENTRAL GOVERNANCE COMPONENTS

The basic conundrum, therefore, in many firms, particularly large public companies, is the mismatch between the ownership of the firm (which is vested in the shareholders) and the day-to-day management (which is the responsibility of the directors). We can refer here to the so-called managerial prerogative. This is reinforced by Art 3 of the new Model Articles applicable to private and public companies post 2006 Companies Act.[27]

The potential problems posed by any such separation of ownership and control are addressed by a number of core mechanisms in corporate law:

---

23 See M. McCann and S. Wheeler (2011) 38 Jo of Law and Soc 542. The authors cannot find evidence to support the business case but they argue that improved female participation rates at board level are justified on the grounds of social justice.

24 *Secretary of State for BERR v Neufeld* [2009] EWCA Civ 280, [2009] BCC 687.

25 The same could be said of the denial of entry into a partnership (Equality Act 2010 s. 44) or membership of an LLP (s. 45) where sex discrimination has played a part.

26 On 14 November 2012 the European Commission put a proposal to the European Parliament calling for a 40 per cent female quota on the boards of listed companies to be achieved by 2020, but it significantly left the issue of sanctions for non-attainment of this target to the national authorities. See Editorial [2012] 325 SMCLN 1.

27 Companies (Model Articles) Regulations 2008 (SI 2008/3229).

1. The imposition on corporate managers of duties of competence and of ethical obligations in the form of fiduciary duties.
2. The requirement for independent audit of the firm's finances (first introduced in 1844). There is no doubting that the audit plays an important role, but the use of independent auditors are not a foolproof mechanism for protecting against abuse of limited liability for a variety of reasons. Common-law developments have hardly added lustre to this mechanism.[28] Audit firms can now cap their potential liability to the company under s. 534 of the Companies Act 2006. Some 71 per cent of small companies are also audit exempt within the meaning of s. 477 of the Companies Act 2006.
3. The use of disclosure via mandatory filing[29] of key information in a public registry to ensure transparency. Figures from the Companies House Annual Statistics for 2011–12 suggest an impressive 99 per cent compliance rate (see Table A7), though that still left some 169 531 companies in default to some degree or another (Table A8). We note that for SMEs a relaxed disclosure regime operates.
4. The adherence to a democratic principle (especially susceptibility of removal of directors by shareholders under Companies Act 2006 s. 168[30]).
5. The existence (in some cases) of internal supervision of the board (e.g. through use of non-executive directors (NEDs), and audit/remuneration committees).[31] This is an optional requirement in SMEs.[32]

---

[28] See *Re Kingston Cotton Mill Ltd (No. 2)* [1896] 2 Ch 279, *Caparo Industries plc v Dickman* [1990] 2 AC 605, *Stone and Rolls v Moore Stephens* [2009] UKHL 39, [2009] 1 AC 1391. The professional regulators have played an important role in imposing sanctions for audit failings in a number of high-profile collapses. Most recently, the Financial Reporting Council has lodged a formal complaint with regard to a number of aspects of the audit of the Farepak accounts – see FRC Press Notice PN022 (15 November 2012). Incidentally, the FRC is also pursuing an accountant/director in the aftermath of the Farepak affair – see FRC Press Notice PN026 (10 December 2012).

[29] See Companies Act 2006 ss. 441 (accounts) and 854 (annual return). Failure to file accounts can lead to a company being struck off the register and sanctions can be visited upon the directors – ss. 451 and 858. See Table D2 of the *2011/12 Annual Companies Statistics* where we find 2051 convictions recorded for breach of s. 441 and 1121 convictions for breach of s. 858.

[30] This is a corporate law standard across the globe – see Corporations Law 2001 ss. 203C and 203D (Australia), New Zealand Companies Act 1993 s. 156. The democratic principle can be bargained away in private companies that are SMEs – see *Bushell v Faith* [1970] AC 1099.

[31] It is a requirement for listed companies – see UK Corporate Governance Code (2010) (FRC). The example in February 2011 of Lloyds Bank clawing back bonuses from executives of Lloyds in the wake of the PPI mis-selling affair offers a rare example of such internal monitoring flexing its muscles.

[32] Private companies are also no longer required to have a company secretary –

We should stress that the aforementioned components are based upon the dominant Anglo-American unitary board model applying. Other systems use different tools, such as the two-tier board model based upon the German philosophy towards corporate governance.[33] Works councils can also be traced back to that continental source of inspiration. Research shows that diversity in any governance policy is an important consideration.

2.4 MONITORING

The activities of those who occupy a stewardship role in relation to the operation of companies are subject to various forms of *monitoring*. We have dealt with internal monitoring above, but we should say a word about other forms of monitoring.

Monitoring may be concurrent or retrospective. Retrospective or *ex post facto* monitoring may be carried out by successor managers, or in our context by insolvency office-holders. This latter form of monitoring may be applied not merely to directors of companies which fail, but also to initial office-holders whose actions fall to be reviewed by subsequent insolvency practitioners. This latter phenomenon is becoming quite marked these days, with certain insolvency practitioners pursuing fellow professionals with great zeal. Such a vigorous pursuit of fellow professionals should drive out 'cowboys' and drive up professional standards.

What about *external* monitoring? Such outside monitoring might be conducted by a significant creditor (such as a bank) which, in effect, has the power to require a distressed company to behave in a certain way[34] or even to call in investigating accountants.[35] In the past doubts have been raised as to

---

Companies Act 2006 s. 270. This particular deregulation removes a potential check on directorial abuse in private companies.

[33] For discussion see A. Dignam and M. Galanis, *The Globalisation of Corporate Governance* (2009).

[34] The role of the bank in the Farepak case came in for criticism from Peter Smith J in his statement in open court in the wake of the collapse of the disqualification proceedings in Farepak (see statement 21 June 2012 available on HM court website). Stung by this criticism, the bank provided an additional ex gratia payment of £8 million to be used to compensate those members of the public who had purchased food hampers that were not supplied by the time the company became insolvent – see *The Times*, 7 July 2012. For comment see A. Walters (2013) 34 Co Law 1.

[35] This is a vexed area, particularly where the investigating accountants recommend an insolvency appointment with such appointment being taken up by the same firm of accountants – on this see *Huxford v Stoy Hayward* [1989] 5 BCC 421. The consensus seems to be that (in the absence of contractual restriction) it is not improper or indeed unethical for an insolvency practitioner to investigate and then take up the

whether banks have effectively exploited their power to monitor, relying instead upon their relatively safe status as a secured creditor.[36] In the current lending climate and in an era where secured creditors no longer have total protection in the event of debtor default,[37] things may be different. On the other hand, major creditors may also be concerned about the risk of being labelled as shadow directors (see Chapter 1 above) and this may impel them to keep their distance.

The firm's professional advisers might in some senses be seen as external monitors. John Coffee famously labelled them as 'gatekeepers'.[38] Unfortunately, their performance as monitors in a number of high-profile corporate collapses might suggest that they are not particularly efficient in that stewardship role. The fundamental problem is that professional advisers have a nasty habit of telling dominant executives what they think they would want to hear. Retaining a fee-paying client in the short term often trumps the long-term reputational interests of the advising firm. We have here a new spin on the idea of 'regulatory capture'. When they do point out that a particular course of action is not appropriate, such advisers sometimes fail to ensure that such a message is then acted upon. There is also the problem that many gate-keeper firms are very large enterprises in their own right and it is difficult to ensure that high in-house professional standards filter down to all levels of the firm. Some commentators have argued that the introduction of LLP status in the UK in 2001 via the Limited Liability Partnerships Act 2000 might also serve to weaken internal supervision within gatekeeper firms by engendering a false sense of security generated by the newly available protection of limited liability.

The HM Revenue and Customs (HMRC), which will be a major unsecured creditor of all limited companies, is increasingly[39] taking a more proactive role in commencing insolvency proceedings against debtor companies. It has

---

recommended insolvency appointment. Indeed, it may be economically efficient to have such a succession. That said, whether it is sensible practice, is open to debate. See *Lloyds Bank v Lampert* [1991] BCC 507. The underlying dispute in this case still smoulders on – see the litigation featuring in *Lampert v Lloyds Bank* [2012] EWHC 2312 (Ch).

36 See the discussion in J. Day and P. Taylor [2001] Ins Law 97.

37 Witness the advent of the reserved fund for unsecured creditors in 2003 – s. 176A of the Insolvency Act 1986 and the Insolvency Act (Prescribed Part) Order 2003 (SI 2003/2097). This fund derived from a Cork Committee recommendation (1982, Cmnd 8558 paras 1538–49).

38 J. Coffee, *Gatekeepers: The Professions and Corporate Governance* (2006).

39 With the abolition of Crown preferential claim status by s. 251 of the Enterprise Act 2002 with effect from 15 September 2003, it seems that the HMRC is less content to sit tight secure in the knowledge that it would be well placed in the order of distribution.

always been a major factor in winding-up petitions and that position remains the case. This 'hardball' approach is best reflected by its actions in dealing with football clubs where tax arrears are outstanding.[40]

External monitoring may also be manifested by the growing pressure being placed upon institutional investors to ensure that their power as internal monitors is being fully exploited.[41] That pressure centres on the notion of stewardship of those trusted to invest beneficiary funds.

External bodies such as the Department for Business, Innovation and Skills (DBIS) might exercise their power under s. 447 of the Companies Act 1985 to make informal investigations into companies and then take follow-up action, possibly in the form of disqualification proceedings instituted under s. 8 of the Company Directors Disqualification Act 1986.[42] Alternatively, some external regulatory body might intervene in the way an insolvency practice is being run, if concerns are raised.[43]

Finally, we should note the growing influence of monitoring by the media/public opinion. This has over the past year had a marked impact on the reward packages claimed by directors of high-profile companies, particularly where there has been significant state investment. We saw this with regard to the public outcry over the RBS pay package of Stephen Hester.[44] State investment is not a prerequisite in this climate – witness the voting down of the Aviva[45] directors' pay package in May 2012. This element of monitoring, now

---

[40] So in February 2012 the HMRC were key players in initiating the administration of Portsmouth FC in England and Rangers FC in Scotland. The proposed CVA of Rangers was voted down by HMRC with the result that the club went into liquidation. HMRC famously challenged the football creditor rule thereby producing a highly particularized judgment from David Richards J in *HMRC v The Football League* [2012] EWHC 1372 (Ch), [2012] BPIR 812. This anomalous rule survived this challenge, though one suspects that its days are numbered. For criticism of the rule, which is often seen as promoting poor governance, see S. Fennell [2012] (Autumn) Recov 32.

[41] So the Financial Reporting Council in July 2010 produced a set of Stewardship Guidelines designed to ensure that institutional investors flexed their muscles as shareholders – see L. Roach [2011] 11 JCLS 463, A. Reisberg [2011] Jo of Fin Crim 126.

[42] These do not always succeed, as is attested by the Farepak debacle – for the official post-mortem see *Review of Disqualification Proceedings Taken in the Case of European Home Retail plc and Farepak Food and Gifts Ltd* (December 2012) (Insolvency Service).

[43] The Joint Insolvency Monitoring Unit (JIMU) played a leading role here in the decade 1994–2004. JIMU folded when some of the leading RPBs decided to take back in house the investigatory function. JIMU had attracted some criticism for conducting what were seen as box-ticking exercises.

[44] In January 2012 the media reported that the package was declined by Stephen Hester.

[45] See *The Times*, 4 May 2012.

characterized as 'the shareholder spring', however, is only likely to be relevant to those larger listed businesses that are well known to the public at large. We also need to be aware of the dangers of misconception peddled by the media, where the evidence forensically examined does not match up to the image that is being conveyed to the public.[46] For private companies we have to rely on legal constraints to control executive pay and on their strong desire in some instances to save the firm through personal sacrifice.

2.5 THE PARTICULAR PROBLEMS OF SMES

As far as the governance of small and medium-sized enterprises are concerned, there are a number of distinctive characteristics to note.

First, many of the corporate governance codes apply only to listed companies. It was only in late 2010 that the Institute of Directors produced a code specifically designed for non-listed companies.[47] This is a welcome initiative not least because of the focus it places in Principle 9 on the particular governance issues that can arise in family firms.

Second, there will often be no major separation between ownership and control. The managers of the company will in many cases be the only, or at least the majority, shareholders. This can take the sting out of the issue of executive remuneration. But in times of financial stringency, from the perspective of creditors this may be a worry by removing a potential counterbalance to executive shortcomings.

Third, such firms typically will not have independent non-executive directors. Again, this presents a potential cause of concern from the wider stakeholder perspective.

Fourth, such companies are more likely to finance their activities through private family wealth or through bank borrowings. We should note here that LLPs can borrow on the security of a floating charge.[48] There is less scope for fundraising through the issuing of share capital to the public at large. The

---

[46] The Farepak affair (discussed in Chapter 3) provides a perfect example of a media-inspired witch hunt where the correct facts were often ignored in the interests of a good story. A parallel may be found a decade ago in the high-profile Maxwell receivership costs case where at the end of the day some 99 per cent of the costs of the insolvency office-holders were found to be justified when taxed (assessed) – see [1999] BCC 684 and the discussion in Chapter 4 below.

[47] See *Corporate Governance Guidance and Principles for Listed Companies in the UK* Institute of Directors (2010) at p. 34.

[48] See G. Morse (ed.) *Palmer's Limited Liability Partnership Law* (2nd ed., 2011) at A1.67.

downside here is that many SMEs are undercapitalized,[49] which can play a key role in their lack of sustainability.

Fifth, the rules on share capital maintenance[50] operate more generously for SMEs – this means that other protective mechanisms become doubly important.

Sixth, and this point is particularly relevant to professional firms using the LLP format, external monitoring by professional regulatory bodies may play a greater role in governance. Such bodies often have formal powers of intervention[51] that one does not find in the PLC context, except when a DBIS investigation takes place.

Finally, we should recognize that many SMEs are family-owned enterprises.[52] The family relationship, particularly where it is based on a culture in which family ties are especially strong, can cause additional difficulties in applying general governance principles.[53] Agency theories stress the opportunistic tendencies of corporate managers and the need to combat these. Stewardship theory,[54] on the other hand, suggests that many managers have a strong affinity for the organization. This must be particularly true of family companies where the managers are family members. By implication this might suggest a lower level of regulation is necessary. But one of the most common problems here in the family business is the reliance on informality instead of strict compliance with corporate law requirements. This was well reflected in *Re Mumtaz Properties Ltd*,[55] where there was scant disregard for fundamental matters of governance, such as who actually was a company director in the family firm. Where the interests of a range of stakeholders are at risk, this tendency must be carefully watched.

[49] See A. Atherton [2012] 18 Int Jo of Entrepreneurial Beh and Research 28 for a valuable discussion of finance-related issues.

[50] See E. Ferran (1999) 20 Co Law 314, J. Armour (2000) 63 MLR 355, F. Ewang (2007) 21 Aust Jo of Corp Law 1.

[51] See Solicitors Act 1974 s. 35 (as amended) and the many provisions in the Legal Services Act 2007, for example.

[52] On the importance of family firms globally, see La Porta et al. [1999] 54 Jo of Fin 471. But family firms may not always be the most efficient of enterprises – see the recent study carried out by N. Bloom, C. Genakos, R. Sadun and J. van Reenen at the LSE Centre for Economic Performance for the DBIS, *Managerial Practices Across Firms and Countries* (December 2011, Discussion Paper 1109).

[53] Witness the role of the patriarch in *Re Harmer Ltd* [1959] 1 WLR 62. One can also appreciate the plight of the sisters in *Lex Holdings v Luqman* [2009] EWCA Civ 117, [2009] BCC 716. Cultural factors should not be underestimated.

[54] See L. Donaldson and J.H. Davis (1991) 16 Aust Jo of Man 49, J.H. Davis, M.R. Allen and H.D. Hayes [2010] Entrep Theory and Practice 1093.

[55] [2011] EWCA Civ 610, [2012] 2 BCLC 109.

2.6 COMPARATIVE PERSPECTIVES

There will be in Chapter 5 a discussion on the contrasting approaches to governance of distressed companies both under the Anglo-American model and under the institutional architectural structures favoured in Europe. Other common-law jurisdictions will also be referred to. That section will cover comparative discussion of the substantive aspects dealt with in Chapters 3 and 4 below. For present purposes we merely note the global spread of corporate governance codes, most of which have a close linkage to the Anglo-American approach.[56]

2.7 IS THERE A LINK BETWEEN GOVERNANCE FAILURES AND FINANCIAL DISTRESS?

Intuition might suggest the answer to this question must be in the affirmative.[57] But we need to be careful here – a well-managed firm can fail for reasons that have nothing to do with internal governance and everything to do with the external business environment in which the firm operates. The so-called 'domino effect' is well known to seasoned observers – the failure of a debtor to pay up can have a knock-on impact on the creditor firm by eliminating anticipated income and driving that business into insolvency. That was never more true than it is today. R3 has done some valuable work here over the years through a number of valuable surveys carried out on its behalf.[58] Latest R3 figures attribute business failure in some 56 per cent of cases to management inefficiencies.

This particular research question has attracted some scholarly effort.[59] So, for example, Argenti[60] analysed the causes of business failure nearly 30 years ago and his research still holds up to scrutiny. Those working with this issue have noted that common causes of business failure where the finger of blame can be pointed at management include overreaching, failure to maintain liquidity, high gearing and failure to recognize the early warning signs of distress. This latter point is important as there is a consensus that rescue is not

---

56 For the potential dangers in exporting corporate governance in this way see A. Dignam (2000) 21 Co Law 70.

57 See M. Charkham, *Keeping Better Company* (2nd ed., 2005) at 25.

58 See for example the study recounted by W. Black [2010] (Autumn) Recov 38.

59 There is a balanced discussion to be found in K. Gugler (ed.), *Corporate Governance and Economic Performance* (2001).

60 See J. Argenti, *Corporate Collapse* (1976).

a viable option if it is left too late. The New Zealand Law Commission[61] also looked at this issue as part of a preliminary study underpinning reform which informed the Companies Amendment Act 2006.

One related problem in this area concerns the question whether insolvency can be *predicted* scientifically.[62] Various models[63] have been put forward with this aim in mind and it may well be that they do have a role to play in predicting the fate of a larger corporation. But when we move towards the SME sector we find a lack of awareness of such diagnostic tools and a reluctance to employ them to constructive effect. The courts would be cautious about judging a director's conduct by using such a tool and there is scant evidence of expert evidence being used to this end, save in the case of the demise of the larger corporations – much more prosaic measuring tools tend to be used for such purposes in the SME context.

Notwithstanding these points, it is clear that an overbearing (albeit charismatic) style of management is not conducive to effective governance because it denies the company the benefit of constructive criticism. We saw this negative phenomenon at work in the UK in the controversial corporate career of the late Robert Maxwell.[64] Other examples of this syndrome have attracted judicial comment[65] and academic attention.[66] Moving to the present day, the financial difficulties of the financial institution RBS, although undoubtedly triggered by adverse global factors, may also be attributed in part to the influ-

---

[61] See Chapter 7 of Study Paper 11, *Insolvency Law Reform: Promoting Trust and Confidence* (2001).

[62] See T.E. Cooke and A. Hicks [1993] JBL 338, A. Belcher (1991) 7 IL & P 64.

[63] See for example E. Altman [1968] 23 Jo of Fin 589.

[64] Maxwell was described in the 1970s as a man not fit for the stewardship of a public company – see the DTI Inspectors' Reports on Pergamon Press (1971–73) and also the reported litigation in *Re Pergamon Press Ltd* [1971] Ch 388 and *Maxwell v DTI* [1974] QB 523. Yet Maxwell was able to assume that position in relation to a major enterprise with disastrous results in the 1990s – see the DTI Inspectors' Report on Mirror Group Newspapers (2001). For a useful summary of the Maxwell affair and other high-profile scandals where dominant personalities were key factors, see J. Farrar, *Corporate Governance* (2008). See also *Bishopsgate Investment Management v Maxwell (No. 2)* [1994] 1 All ER 261 for an indication of how the board became subservient to Robert Maxwell.

[65] See for example the comments of the court in *Re Polly Peck International plc (No. 2)* [1994] 1 BCLC 574. Asil Nadir, who headed Polly Peck, having returned to the UK was convicted of theft and handed a heavy 10-year sentence of imprisonment – see *The Times*, 24 August 2012. He was also made subject of a £5 million compensation order in October 2012.

[66] See R. Wearing, *Cases in Corporate Governance* (2005), where useful summaries are found of a number of high-profile corporate collapses involving a dominant figurehead.

ence of a dominant chief executive.[67] The fundamental problem in many cases is that having a dominant personality at the helm can be a positive characteristic in times of plenty, but can be a major impediment when alternative (and unpalatable) strategies have to be deployed.

The courts have noted the presence of what are essentially governance or management failings when companies have run into difficulties. So, in *HMRC v Rochdale Drinks Distributors Ltd*,[68] this particular factor was highlighted by the Court of Appeal when ordering that a company be placed into provisional liquidation.

---

[67] See FSA Board Report, *The Failure of RBS* (December 2011) and FSA Press Notice 110/2011. For analysis see I. MacNeil [2012] 6 LFMR 1.

[68] [2011] EWCA Civ 1116, [2011] BPIR 1604 at para [100] per Rimer LJ.

3. Governance in the twilight zone[1]

3.1 INTRODUCTION

The basic theme of this chapter will be to examine how the aforementioned general principles of corporate management/governance mutate once a firm becomes insolvent (or doubtfully solvent), even though no formal insolvency proceedings have actually been commenced in respect of it. Particular emphasis will be placed upon the implications of the introduction of s. 172 of the Companies Act 2006 (an innovation in UK corporate law) into this environment.

3.2 GOOD STEWARDSHIP

Tradition has it that directors are not, as a matter of general principle, trustees.[2] Increasingly, however, one finds the language of trust being used to analyse the conduct of directors. So, for instance, in *GHLM Trading v Maroo*,[3] Newey J stated that directors are obliged to explain the fate of company property in much the same way as if they were trustees of it. Whatever, directors of limited liability companies, whether such companies are solvent or not, have certain basic husbandry obligations under English law.[4] One of the most important of

---

1 See generally D. Milman [2004] JBL 493. For a non-legal perspective see S. Slatter and D. Lovett, *Corporate Turnaround: Managing Companies in Distress* (1999). An interdisciplinary treatment is found in D. Milman and G. Cook [2002] 28 Manag Fin 34.

2 *Re Lands Allotment Co* [1894] 1 Ch 616 at 631 per Lindley LJ. But see *Re Faure Electrical Accumulator Ltd* (1889) 40 Ch D 141, where Kay J raised the trust possibility. See L.S. Sealy [1967] CLJ 83 for analysis of the early authorities on this subject.

3 [2012] EWHC 61 (Ch), [2012] 2 BCLC 369 at para [148]. See also *Re Snelling House Ltd* [2012] EWHC 440 (Ch).

4 It must be remembered that the basic duties of directors are determined by the place of incorporation – *Base Metal Trading Ltd v Shamurin* [2004] EWCA Civ 1316, [2005] BCC 325. Though if they relocate the company so that it is liquidated in English law, specific provisions such as wrongful trading will kick in – *Re Howard Holdings Inc* [1998] BCC 549. For discussion see B. Jones (2004) 17 Ins Intell 81.

these is the duty to maintain accurate and informative management accounts.[5] Proper management is not possible without an awareness on the part of the directors of the current financial position of the company. Such accounts, which are a standard feature of stewardship, are also important as evidential records if a post-mortem is required as to the appropriateness of managerial conduct.

It can also be said with some confidence that there is a duty on directors to be attentive to the affairs of the company.[6] Certainly, a director cannot escape this responsibility by wholesale reliance on the substituted input of others.[7] Where a delegation of managerial responsibility has taken place (which is still permitted under English law), the delegating director must still monitor the actions of the delegate.[8]

There is also a duty not to improperly diminish the share capital of the company by an illegal return of share capital[9] or by payment of an improper dividend.[10] Ignorance of the technical rules of company law here is no defence in law if improper distributions are made.[11] The thinking of the policymakers here, although heavily compromised by the failure to prescribe a minimum share capital for private companies, is that the share capital fund acts as a reserve guarantee for unsecured creditors. This share capital maintenance theory (which has been noted above in Chapter 2) is best seen as a quid pro

5 See Companies Act 2006 ss. 386, 387. Note also Insolvency Act 1986 s. 206 – it is an offence to falsify company records. These records now probably include electronic records – see *R v Taylor* [2011] EWCA Crim 728, [2011] 1 WLR 1809. Under s. 388 of the Companies Act 2006 company records must be preserved for six years in the case of a PLC and three years for a private company.

6 The old authority of *Marquis of Bute's case* [1892] 2 Ch 100 must be treated with some caution these days.

7 *Re F Options Ltd* [2011] EWHC 3325 (Ch), [2012] BPIR 113 at para [10] per Charles Hollander QC. The more relaxed statement of Romer J in *Re City Equitable Fire Insurance Co* [1925] Ch 407 must be treated with some caution.

8 On this see *Re Westmid Packing Services Ltd* [1998] 2 All ER 124.

9 This is a general duty at common law – for discussion see *Progress Property Co Ltd v Moorgarth Group* [2010] UKSC 55, [2011] BCC 196 and is reinforced by statutory procedures applicable in the event of a return of capital – see Companies Act 2006 ss. 641–53.

10 See now Companies Act 2006 s. 830. For recent examples where improper dividends have been paid out by distressed firms see *It's a Wrap (UK) Ltd v Gula* [2006] EWCA Civ 544, [2006] 2 BCLC 634. This obligation was extended to CVA supervisors in *Re TXU Europe Group plc* [2011] EWHC 2072 (Ch), [2012] BCC 363, where a surplus was arrived at once CVA creditors had been paid off in full. Newey J held that the supervisors could not return this surplus to shareholders. Such a return would only be possible if the company was placed into liquidation.

11 See *It's a Wrap Ltd v Gula* (supra).

quo for limited liability. Its effectiveness is open to question[12] and a number of jurisdictions have moved away from it, preferring instead to use solvency-based tests as a precondition for a range of transactions. English law appears also to be moving in that direction.

Other more mundane (but no less important) duties of directors under UK corporate law include:

- the duty to insure the company's property[13]
- the duty to respect the constitution of the company[14]
- the duty to act in the interests of the particular company of which they have been appointed as director. Directors are fiduciaries and this obligation is best seen as an aspect of their fiduciary status.[15] This is particularly important in the group context.[16]

The position here seems to be that a director can take into account group interests when carrying out his role as a director of a group member, but not to the point of subordinating the interests of his company to the interests of the group as a whole. More of this later.

These basic responsibilities have been further supplemented by statute. So, for instance, since 1980 directors have been obliged to convene a shareholder meeting (formerly designated an EGM) in the event of a serious loss of assets.[17] Presumably, this meeting should then be followed up by a proposal

---

12 Even in Europe its value is now contested – see the comments of the European Court of Justice in *Centros (C212/97)* [2000] Ch 446 and the watering down of the Second Company Law Harmonisation Directive (77/91) by Amending Directive (2006/68).

13 See *Re D'Jan of London Ltd* [1993] BCC 646. The policy must be in the name of the company because the directors (or controlling shareholders) have no insurable interest in the company's property – *Macaura v Northern Assurance* [1925] AC 619.

14 This duty is significant when directors seek to make a Sched B1 para 22 appointment of an administrator. Failure to use the correct constitutional procedures has triggered repeat litigation at first instance with a sharp divergence of views on the part of the courts being manifested – see the discussion at para 3.5.

15 For a recent judicial exploration see *Weavering Capital (UK) Ltd v Peterson* [2012] EWHC 1480 (Ch). Another aspect is the obligation not to fetter the exercise of directorial powers. But this is not an absolute duty: some fetters may be acceptable if in the broad interests of the company – see *Fulham FC v Cabra Estates* [1992] BCC 863. Although directors are fiduciaries they are not in any sense trustees for their shareholders.

16 See S. Wheeler and G. Wilson, *Directors' Liabilities in the Context of Corporate Groups* (1998).

17 See now Companies Act 2006 s. 656. On the implications for directors of a failure to observe this obligation, see *Re Samuel Sherman plc* [1991] BCC 699.

to reduce share capital or for some other form of reconstruction, perhaps under Part 26 of the Companies Act 2006. Other jurisdictions are more directive in this situation and some specify that trading *must* cease or else the shield of limited liability is removed. Statute (in the form of Companies Act 2006 s. 190) also requires any substantial property transactions between a director and the company to be approved by shareholders. That said, the fact of shareholder approval is no guarantee that the sale will stand up to challenge if it is later impugned as a transaction at an undervalue contrary to s. 238 of the Insolvency Act 1986.[18] The statutory provisions here represent *cumulative* hurdles to be overcome if the transaction is to stand up to scrutiny.

Statute has since 1908 also provided for mitigation in the event of breach of duty owed to the company. Thus, provided a director has acted honestly, reasonably and ought fairly to be excused, the court can under s. 1157 of the Companies Act 2006 relieve such director of liability in whole or in part.[19] Such instances of relief being granted are rare[20] simply because it is difficult for a director having been found in breach of duty to establish *all* three of the statutory mitigating factors. Note that under subs (2) of this provision, advance clearance from the court may be obtained;[21] but this form of comfort is rarely applied for. What often happens is that legal advice, even to the point of obtaining counsel's opinion, is sought by directors, but this does not offer the absolute degree of protection that is available from the court. It should also be pointed out in fairness that the court is uneasy about any form of advance clearance as there may be many uncertain factors involved and it does not wish to create too many hostages to fortune.[22]

---

18 See *Re Conegrade Ltd* [2002] EWHC 2411 (Ch), [2003] BPIR 358.

19 The stewardship link is evident here – compare Trustee Act 1925 s. 61. For general discussion see L. Linklater [2002] 3 SMCLN 1, R. Edmunds and J. Lowry (2003) 66 MLR 195.

20 See *Re D'Jan London Ltd* [1993] BCC 646 for a rare such instance. This reluctance to grant relief was apparent in *Towers v Premier Waste Management Ltd* [2011] EWCA Civ 923, [2012] BCC 72. See also *Tayplan Ltd v Smith* [2011] CSIH 8, [2012] BCC 523 and *Re Oxford Pharmaceuticals Ltd* [2010] BCC 834. Judicial pardons are also not available to defend against claims for wrongful trading (*Re Produce Marketing Consortium (No. 1)* [1989] 1 WLR 745) or liability under s. 216 IA (*First Independent Factors Ltd v Mountford* [2008] EWHC 835 (Ch), [2008] BPIR 515) or liability for breach of s. 15 of the Company Directors Disqualification Act 1986 (*IRC v McEntaggart*) [2006] BPIR 750.

21 See *Re Home Treat Ltd* [1991] BCC 165 for an example in effect of an advance clearance application under this provision. The relieving provision does not need to be specifically pleaded in order to rely on it – see *Re Kirby's Coaches Ltd* [1991] BCC 130, where great reliance was placed upon the mirror provision of s. 61 of the Trustee Act 1925.

22 See *Equitable Life Assurance Society v Bowley* [2003] EWHC 2263 (Ch) at

Although the court has the power to mitigate liability, UK company law traditionally has set its face against the contractual exclusion of liability. Witness s. 232 of the Companies Act 2006, which represents the latest iteration of a longstanding prohibition dating back to 1929 in this regard. Clauses seeking to exempt directors from liability for breach of duty to the company are banned. There are differences here with trust law, where the position is less dogmatic.[23] This strict approach towards the exclusion of directorial liability is also in stark contrast to the situation in the US state of Delaware, where capping liability via corporate statutes is now an option (see Delaware Corporations Act s. 102(b)(7)). One concession available in English law to alleviate risk, however, should be noted. It has been possible since 1989 for companies to take out indemnity insurance to protect directors against liability for breach of duty to the company. It is clear from s. 233 of the Companies Act 2006 that this would enable the company to pay the premiums on any such policy. Such policies, however, cannot protect against liability to third parties, or indeed against liability for either fraudulent or wrongful trading. In the latter instances, to allow such an indemnity as this would be contrary to public policy. The Companies (Audit, Investigations and Community Enterprise) Act 2004 amended the position further by enabling companies to offer indemnities to directors to cover certain litigation risks where litigation is instituted against them by third parties – see now s. 234 of the 2006 Act. The rules on charity trustees are similar to those described above (see Charities Act 2011 s. 189).

3.3 MODIFIED DIRECTORIAL RESPONSIBILITIES IN SITUATIONS OF BUSINESS DISTRESS

The primary focus of this section will be on how regulatory systems seek to control the actions of directors who manage distressed companies in the 'twilight zone'.[24] Regulatory mechanisms here include those available under both common law and statute. The use of *ex post facto* regulation (such as the imposition of wrongful trading liability and disqualification) will also be considered. The importance of taking and following professional advice during this transitional period will also be discussed.

para [45] per Langley J. On this problem generally see *Hunt v Harb* [2011] EWCA Civ 1239, [2012] 1 WLR 317.

[23] *Armitage v Nurse* [1998] Ch 241. For background discussion see A. Hudson, *Equity and Trusts* (7th ed., 2012) at 883–4.

[24] The 'twilight zone' is now accepted terminology across the globe to describe this context – see INSOL Report, *Directors in the Twilight Zone* (now in its 3rd edition). See also D. Milman [2003] Ins Law 147 and D. Milman (2008) 21 Ins Intell 25.

3.3.1 Common Law

The focus of the common law (in the widest sense of the term) when developing duties for directors was always on the solvent company. The fiduciary duties, typical features of stewardship, emerged first in the early days of company law in the nineteenth century. Fiduciary duties are notoriously strict.[25] These were then followed by the slow evolution throughout the twentieth century of a duty to take reasonable care.[26] These duties are now consolidated in the Companies Act 2006 (ss. 170–77 and s. 182).[27] The aim of this consolidation is to enlighten the community of directors and possibly to promote better standards of stewardship.[28] There is a clear educational purpose at work here.

When a company was solvent any duties would in effect be owed to the shareholders, but could only be enforced by the company.[29] Shareholders as individuals could not police duties owed by directors. The unsecured creditors certainly had no independent right of enforcement,[30] though of course they could take action against the company in the form of a winding-up (and, more recently, an administration) petition. Things began to change in the 1970s and 1980s with a recognition that the common law should address the all too familiar managerial dilemma when a company became doubtfully solvent. In a clutch of cases the Commonwealth courts[31] began to develop the idea that in such a scenario the directors should be expected to husband the remaining assets for the benefit of creditors. Basically the idea of the 'company' had been transformed from a simple substitute for shareholders now to a synonym for creditors. Some courts characterized this as part of the fiduciary obligation to

---

25 See *Towers v Premier Waste Management* (supra).

26 Significant benchmarks in the process of evolution would be *Re City Equitable Life Insurance Co Ltd* [1925] Ch 407, *Dorchester Finance v Stebbing* [1989] BCLC 498 and *Norman v Theodore Goddard* [1991] BCLC 1028. This duty is now framed in Companies Act 2006 s. 174 – see the discussion in *Weavering Capital (UK) Ltd v Peterson* [2012] EWHC 1480 (Ch). For general background see S. Worthington (2001) 64 MLR 439.

27 For discussion see J. Birds [2007] 49 Manag Law 13.

28 See the observation of Lord Hope in *Eastford v Gillespie* [2009] CSOH 119 at [9]. For discussion see D. Ahern [2012] 128 LQR 114.

29 See *Multinational Gas and Petrochemical Co Ltd v Multinational Gas and Petrol Services Ltd* [1983] Ch 258. *Percival v Wright* [1902] 2 Ch 421 makes it clear that there is no legally enforceable duty owed to individual shareholders as such.

30 *Mills v Northern Rwy of Buenos Aires* (1870) 5 Ch App 621.

31 See the view of Mason J in *Walker v Wimborne* (1976) 50 ALJR 446 (highlighted in English law by the piece by R. Barrett in (1977) 40 MLR 226) and the comments of Cooke J in *Nicholson v Permakraft Ltd* [1985] 2 NZCLC 99. This development is expertly documented by A. Keay in [2002] JBL 379.

act in the best interests of the company, but more recent pronouncements on the subject have questioned this characterization.[32] Whatever, this idea finally took root in English law in the Court of Appeal decision in *West Mercia Safetywear Ltd v Dodd.*[33] It is now well established and in effect this common-law duty is recognized by s. 172(3) of the Companies Act 2006 on the basis that it is a 'rule of law' to which the primary statutory obligation in s. 172 is subject. The importance of this ruling from the Court of Appeal is that this is still seen as a duty owed to the company and therefore it can be enforced by a liquidator[34] through the pursuit of misfeasance proceedings conducted under s. 212 of the Insolvency Act 1986. In such a scenario any limitation period runs from the date of breach of duty and not from the appointment of the liquidator.[35] It should also be remembered that individual creditors can enforce a breach of duty by using s. 212, but equally it is clear that directors do not as a rule owe enforceable obligations to individual creditors.[36] Although this duty is now recognized, it is not an absolute obligation, but rather one consideration amongst many, a point that can be taken from the comments of Hoffmann J in *Re Welfab Engineers Ltd.*[37]

What might this common-law duty require of directors? This practical question has caused some difficulties, but a perfect illustration is provided by the facts of *Colin Gwyer and Associates Ltd v London Wharf (Limehouse) Ltd*,[38] where the focus was upon the voting responsibilities of directors at board meetings. Here it was indicated by Leslie Kosmin QC (sitting as a Deputy Judge of the High Court) that for a board of directors to casually surrender a potentially valuable legal claim which the company may have

---

32 See for example *Peoples Department Stores v Wise* [2004] SCC 69 in Canada and *Spies v The Queen* [2000] HCA 43 in Australia. R. Flannigan effectively demolishes the idea that this duty is fiduciary in nature in his article in [2004] JBL 277 at 301.

33 [1988] 4 BCC 30. See also *Winkworth v Baron Developments* [1986] 1 WLR 1512 at 1516 per Lord Templeman. This area of law was recently considered by Newey J in *GHLM Trading Ltd v Maroo* [2012] EWHC 61 (Ch), [2012] 2 BCLC 369. See also the comment of Toulson LJ in *Rust Consulting v PB* [2012] EWCA Civ 1070 at para [25]. Note also Insolvency Act 1986 s. 206, which seeks to protect company property in the run up to liquidation. These records now include electronic records – see *R v Taylor* [2011] EWCA Crim 728, [2011] 1 WLR 1809.

34 Creditors can also invoke this procedure but strangely it is not available to administrators – *Irwin v Lynch* [2010] EWCA Civ 1153, [2011] 1 WLR 1364, [2011] BPIR 158.

35 *Re Eurocruit Europe Ltd* [2007] EWHC 1433 (Ch), [2007] BCC 916.

36 *Yukong Lines of Korea Ltd v Rendsburg Investment Corporation* [1998] 1 WLR 294. For criticism see T. Ogowewo [1999] Ins Law 106.

37 [1990] BCLC 833.

38 [2003] 2 BCLC 153. See also the discussion of Lord Hodge in *Eastford Ltd v Gillespie* [2010] CSOH 132 at para [22].

against a third party, without even taking advice on the matter, could potentially breach this duty.

Beyond this, one can envisage other forms of behaviour that might be seen as contravening this husbandry duty. For instance, allowing third parties to claim unjustified payments from the company or to make improper withdrawals from company coffers.[39] Asset-stripping the company or allowing asset-stripping to take place[40] would also clearly breach this duty and could be remedied via a misfeasance claim.

Conversely, it would be a clear indication on the part of directors that they were taking this duty to creditors seriously if they were to set up a protective trust to protect advance payments (such as deposits for future goods or services to be supplied) received from customers.[41] Such an arrangement (often described as a 'twilight trust'[42]), which in most areas of business is not mandatory,[43] is unlikely to be challenged with any degree of success under insolvency law as a preference[44] unless the company attempts to convert customers who are already owed an unsecured debt into beneficiaries of a subsequent trust. This benevolence might be seen as breaching the general anti-avoidance principle in insolvency law. A trust scheme might also fail if the 'three certainties' of a trust are not present.[45] The downside to such a strategy is that such funds would become unavailable to service the day-to-day needs of the company and any attempt to use them for such purposes would place the director in real personal jeopardy if the company subsequently failed. The irony therefore is that by protecting certain creditors the company might fail, thereby causing loss to a wider pool of creditors. A utilitarian observer

---

39 See *Re Mumtaz Properties Ltd* [2011] EWCA Civ 610, [2012] 2 BCLC 109. Note also *Re Kudos Business Solutions Ltd* [2011] EWHC 1436 (Ch), [2012] 2 BCLC 65.

40 Even after the company has been dissolved in the wake of a striking-off for non-filing of accounts – *Re Transocean Equipment Manufacturing and Trading Ltd* [2005] EWHC 2603 (Ch), [2006] BPIR 594.

41 Along the lines of the arrangement in *Re Kayford Ltd* [1975] 1 WLR 279.

42 See T. Pritchard (2007) 23 IL & P 112 and M. Ellis and L. Verrill (2007) 20 Ins Intell 151.

43 Witness the Farepak affair once again where there were real difficulties in determining if trusts existed largely because of the role of intermediary agents. See *Farepak Food and Gifts Ltd* [2006] EWHC 3272 (Ch), [2008] BCC 22 and *Farepak Food and Gifts Ltd (No. 2)* [2009] EWHC 2580 (Ch), [2010] BCC 735 for how the litigation proceeded. The Cork Committee (Cmnd 8558, para 1056) felt that the introduction of wrongful trading liability would encourage directors to make greater use of such trusts.

44 See *Re Chelsea Cloisters Ltd* (1981) 41 P & CR 98, *Re Lewis of Leicester Ltd* [1995] BCC 514 and *Re ILG Travel Ltd* [1996] BCC 21.

45 See *Re Holiday Promotions* [1996] 2 BCLC 618.

might find this outcome unattractive. Indeed, this very scenario might well serve to explain the abortive disqualification proceedings[46] in the Farepak affair.

What does seem clear is that to confer a fixed-charge security on a bank (which previously may have been unsecured) as part of an arrangement to buy more time for the company would neither breach this duty (nor s. 239 of the Insolvency Act 1986) in spite of the fact that the effect of such actions would be to greatly marginalize the position of trade creditors.[47] Such behaviour also seems immune from attack as a transaction at an undervalue under s. 238 of the Insolvency Act 1986 (because it is said not to diminish the value of the company's assets) or under s. 245 (which applies only to floating charges). The inability of the law to counter this practice of topping up security is something to which we shall return later, as it does have important implications for governance.

One issue that is still unresolved with regard to the common law is whether the duty to have regard to creditors is only triggered when the company is insolvent or whether it applies in cases of doubtful solvency. Various linguistic formulations have been used to characterize this latter scenario[48] but precise identification of the tipping point remains a significant problem in practice. The better view is that the duty to creditors should also apply in cases of doubtful solvency,[49] but in such situations clearly the interests of shareholders will still have to be weighed up alongside the interests of creditors. In other words, we are not looking at a black and white transition of legal responsibilities, but at subtle shades of grey in this twilight period.

---

[46] Instituted as *Secretary of State for BIS v Fowler* (unreported), which was the litigation that was discontinued before Peter Smith J on 21 June 2012. For the official post-mortem see Insolvency Service, *Review of Disqualification Proceedings Taken in the case of European Home Retail plc and Farepak Food and Gifts Ltd* (December 2012).

[47] See *Re MC Bacon Ltd* [1991] Ch 127. For a comparable Irish authority see *Re O'Connors (Nenagh) Shopping Centre Ltd* [2011] IEHC 508.

[48] I am indebted to Andrew Keay for pointing this out in his paper presented at the ILA Academic Colloquium at Luton Hoo on 21 March 2012. Phrases used include 'in financial difficulties' – *Re MDA Investment Management Ltd* [2003] EWHC 2227 (Ch), [2004] 1 BCLC 217 at para [70] per Park J; 'near insolvency' – *Liquidator of Wendy Fair Ltd v Hobday* [2006] EWHC 5803 at para [66] per Peter Smith J, 'borderline solvency' – *Eastford Ltd v Gillespie* [2011] CSIH 12, [2012] BCC 303 at para [15] per Lord Hardie and 'doubtful solvency' per Proudman J in *City of London Group plc v Lothbury Financial Services Ltd* [2012] EWHC 3148 (Ch) at para [54].

[49] This would appear to follow from *Colin Gwyer* (supra) and the comments of Park J in *Re MDA Investment Management Ltd* [2003] EWHC 2227 (Ch), [2004] 1 BCLC 217 at para [70].

We should also note that the courts are reluctant to rely too heavily on hindsight when judging any potential misfeasance.[50]

The common law has another role to play in offering constructive guidance to directors. Normally, directors can shelter behind the separate personality of the company and thereby avoid personal liability to third parties for their actions. This protection is supported on grounds of public policy[51] but it is, however, not an absolute rule. This was reflected in *Contex Drouzhba Ltd v Wiseman*,[52] where a director, in his eagerness to maintain the supply of essential raw materials to the company, put himself out on a limb by making representations as to the creditworthiness of his company, with serious personal consequences for himself. Attempts to escape this form of liability by seeking the protection of s. 6 of the Statute of Frauds Amendment Act 1828 have proved unsuccessful.[53] To assume personal responsibility for corporate obligations, even though no legally enforceable guarantee is given, is a risky strategy for any director to pursue.

3.3.2 Fraudulent Trading[54]

It has long been recognized that a limited company could be used as a tool of fraud. Accordingly, in 1929 we saw the advent through legislation of the concept of fraudulent trading.[55] A company that was set up or managed in order to defraud creditors should not be permitted to operate as such under English law. Under this principle, if fraudulent trading could be established, *any person*[56] who was party to the fraud would be stripped of the benefit of

---

[50] See Scott VC *in Facia Footwear Ltd v Hinchcliffe* [1998] 1 BCLC 218. Finlay Geoghegan J made the same point in the Irish case of *Re Derbar Developments Ltd* [2012] IEHC 144 at para [21].

[51] See the comments of the court in *Williams v Natural Life Health Foods Ltd* [1998] 1 WLR 830.

[52] [2008] EWCA Civ 1201, [2008] BCC 301. See also *Lindsay v O'Loughnane* [2010] EWHC 529 (QB), [2012] BCC 153.

[53] See for example *Roder (UK) Ltd v Titan Marquees Ltd* [2011] EWCA Civ 1126, [2012] 3 WLR 469.

[54] For discussion see J. Farrar [1980] JBL 336 and *Sealy and Milman's Annotated Guide to Insolvency Legislation* (15th ed., 2012) Vol. 1 at 207–9.

[55] Companies Act 1929, s. 275. This provision was recommended by the Greene Committee (Cmnd 2657) in 1926. See B. Wortley [1934] 50 LQR 405. Fraudulent trading liability was extended to sole traders by the Fraud Act 2006 s. 9.

[56] The provision originally applied only to directors. Its ambit was extended to any person in s. 332 of the Companies Act 1948. It is now possible in theory for a parent company to be held liable in respect of fraudulent trading carried out by a subsidiary – see the discussion of this by Hoffmann J in *Re Augustus Barnett Ltd* [1986] BCLC 170.

limited liability and could, alternatively,[57] be held criminally responsible. This duplication of forms of liability for what was essentially the same conduct has had unfortunate consequences as we shall see shortly.

If a *prosecution* for fraudulent trading is undertaken, a heavy burden of proof must be discharged beyond any reasonable doubt. If fraudulent trading can be established, under s. 993 of the Companies Act 2006 a maximum penalty of 10 years' imprisonment may be imposed. Official figures from 2005–06 suggest that there were 25 prosecutions in that year resulting in some 7 convictions. This gives some idea of the difficulties here. A convicted individual might then presumably find the provisions of the Proceeds of Crime Act 2002 being brought into play against him to recover any illicit gains.

Where *civil* proceedings are taken under s. 213 of the Insolvency Act 1986 there is also an onerous burden of proof on the liquidator,[58] which in this instance must be satisfied on the balance of probability. In addition, a number of de facto defences operate. The first of these is linked to the mental element, which requires proof of actual dishonesty.[59] Proving dishonesty in an entrepreneurial risk-taking context is difficult. As a result of this requirement for proof of dishonesty it became common for directors to concede that they were incompetent, but in the same breath to deny they were fraudulent. This strategy of self-deprecation has proved effective. A similar ploy has been to deny dishonesty but to concede over-optimism.

Second, there was the question of inertia. Under established case law[60] it would appear that liability under this provision required some form of active participation in the fraud. Mere passivity would not apparently suffice. It is difficult to see how this view squares with notions of proactive stewardship in general and one wonders whether the case law here is ripe for revision in the light of modern developments in governance discourse where a lack of curiosity is often castigated.

A person who may be held liable under this provision does not count as a 'contributory', as s. 1170B of the Companies Act 2006 makes clear.

Fraudulent trading only provided a means of combatting the most egregious examples of corporate managerial misbehaviour, such as asset-

---

[57] We could also note that s. 10 of the Company Directors Disqualification Act 1986 could come into play, though it is clear from Companies House statistics for 2011–12 that its usage is minimal.

[58] This is apparent from *Atkinson v Corcoran* [2011] EWHC 3484 (Ch), where Bean J was at pains to stress the difference in terms of burden of proof between a claim based upon s. 213 and one based upon s. 239 (where often the burden switches back onto the defendant).

[59] See *Re Patrick and Lyon Ltd* [1933] Ch 786.

[60] *Re Maidstone Buildings Provisions Ltd* [1971] 1 WLR 1085, *Re Peake and Hall Ltd* 1985 PCC 87.

stripping.[61] Accordingly, reported successful civil litigation and criminal prosecutions are not common. This downbeat assessment may be evidenced by the relative scarcity both of prosecutions and of successful civil cases.[62]

3.3.3 Wrongful Trading[63]

In view of the clear limitations of the fraudulent trading mechanism, the Cork Committee recommended[64] that it should be supplemented by the concept of wrongful trading. Fraudulent trading should be retained, but only in its criminal law dimension. Accordingly, s. 214 of the Insolvency Act 1986 was enacted – it was only to have a civil law dimension and in this sphere it was to operate *in addition to* fraudulent trading. The statutory provision is complex and lacking in some clarity,[65] but the essential elements of the prohibition may be teased out:

- liability for wrongful trading is purely civil (though a disqualification order may also be imposed[66])
- we are looking at a new form of liability that is only triggered if the company goes into insolvent liquidation[67]
- only the liquidator can pursue proceedings[68]
- whether the company was considered to be insolvent is to be viewed objectively (s. 214(2), s. 214(4))
- standards of competence are to be determined again by using objectivity[69]

---

61 See *Carman v The Chronos Group* [2005] EWHC 2403 (Ch), [2006] BCC 451, where the conduct complained of allegedly took place *after* the company had been struck off the register for filing defaults.

62 For a rare modern example of a successful claim see *Re Overnight Ltd (No. 2)* [2010] EWHC 613 (Ch), [2010] BCC 796. Compare *Morphitis v Bernasconi* [2002] EWCA Civ 289, [2003] Ch 552.

63 An early study is to be found in C. Williams and A. McGee, *A Company Director's Liability for Wrongful Trading* (1992) (ACCA Report No. 30). For a recent overview see R. Werdnick (2012) 25 Ins Intell 81. A useful analysis of the application of this provision was provided by M. Simmons in (2001) 14 Ins Intell 12.

64 Cmnd 8558 Chapter 44. This supplemental feature is explicit in s. 214(8).

65 See L. Doyle (1992) 13 Co Law 96.

66 Under s. 10 of the Company Directors Disqualification Act 1986 – see *Re Idessa UK Ltd* [2011] EWHC 804 (Ch), [2011] BPIR 957.

67 See *Re Howard Holdings Inc* [1998] BCC 549. A director subject to this form of liability is not classed as a 'contributory' – see Companies Act 2006 s. 1170B.

68 In recent years the Insolvency Service has raised the possibility of extending this right of action to administrators, but such a reform has not materialized.

69 See *Re Kudos Business Solutions Ltd* [2011] EWHC 1436 (Ch), [2012] 2 BCLC 65.

but factoring in subjective considerations (such as the professed expertise of the director)

- once, on an objective basis, it should have been recognized that the company was destined for insolvent liquidation, the directors must take every step to minimize loss to creditors[70]
- inertia is no defence[71]
- the provision applies to shadow directors.[72]

The fundamental difference between fraudulent trading and wrongful trading civil liability is the use of *objective* standards of stewardship in sanctioning the latter.

Although statistically the number of successful wrongful trading claims is miniscule[73] as compared with disqualifications (see below), there have been a number of significant reported authorities on wrongful trading, with a relative spike in reported successful claims in recent years. If we return to our point about how the law impacts differentially upon SMEs, we should note that virtually every case involving wrongful trading involves a private company where the (mis)behaviour of the directors has been relatively unsophisticated.[74] Rather than simply recounting the facts of these reported cases, we shall attempt to highlight the general lessons for management to be derived from these authorities. These would include:

- the need for the keeping of proper management accounts[75]
- the obligation to keep oneself properly informed about the company's affairs[76]
- the advisability of the exercise of personal austerity in difficult financial times for the business[77]

---

70 It seems likely that we are talking about reasonable steps – s. 214(3).

71 Insolvency Act 1986 s. 214(5).

72 Ibid s. 214(7).

73 A rough estimate might suggest 20. This figure could be obtained by looking at the number of reported cases and working on the assumption that there are few unreported decisions in this area because of the prestige factor resulting from getting a successful case reported. This figure might be 0.1 per cent of the total of disqualifications obtained in the same period.

74 The exception that proves the rule is *Re Continental Assurance Co of London plc* [2001] BPIR 733, where the directors of a large insurance company were held by Park J not to be liable for wrongful trading. This case is important for several other reasons – such as the light cast upon the position of NEDs, why ceasing to trade might not always be the best option and on the measure of liability.

75 See *Re Purpoint Ltd* [1991] BCLC 121.

76 See *Re Landhurst Leasing Ltd* [1999] 1 BCLC 286. It is arguable that there is in effect a duty to exercise curiosity.

77 *Re Purpoint Ltd* (supra), *Re Kudos Business Solutions Ltd* (supra). One could

- the desirability of taking, and then following, professional advice[78]
- the absence of a requirement for an immediate cessation of trade
- the obligation not to asset-strip the failing company[79]
- the fact that directors are to be judged individually; there is no automatic collective responsibility principle at work[80]
- the confirmation that lax standards of stewardship traditionally operate in a particular industry is not an excuse[81]
- the requirement that any person appointed to a board must display minimum standards of stewardship[82]
- the directors are to be judged by reference to what they should have understood the position to be at a particular point in time[83]
- judicial hindsight must be exercised with extreme caution[84]
- that liability for wrongful trading is compensatory and not punitive[85]
- but that the extent of any liability for wrongful trading must be assessed in the light of any other form of liability (e.g. for misfeasance).[86]

There are clearly problems with the financing of a wrongful trading claim to a successful conclusion.[87] Public funding is generally not available.[88] These

---

also add that arranging for the transfer of company assets at an undervalue might indicate wrongful trading – see *Valentine v Bangla TV* [2009] EWHC 1632 (Ch), [2010] BCC 143.

78 *Re Brian Pierson Contractors Ltd* [1999] BCC 26.

79 On this see the discussion in *Re Bangla Television Ltd* [2009] EWHC 1632 (Ch), [2010] BCC 143.

80 *Re Continental Assurance Co of London plc* [2001] BPIR 733 – discussed by A. Walters in [2001] Ins Law 211. But see the qualifying comments of Lord Glennie in *Secretary of State for BIS v Khan* [2012] CSOH 85, 2012 SLT 1090 at para [13].

81 *Singla v Hedman* [2010] 2 BCLC 61.

82 Note the position of the wife in *Re DKG Contractors Ltd* [1990] BCC 903. The Irish courts have also taken an equally harsh view of the passive wife acting as a company director – *Re Hunting Lodges Ltd* [1985] ILRM 75 per Carroll J.

83 Thus the liquidator should plead a specific date (or possibly an alternative date). Using a multiplicity of dates is not to be recommended because this might suggest uncertainty as to the liquidator's case. Equally undesirable is a late change of highlighted date – see *Re Hawkes Hill Publishing Ltd* [2007] BCC 937. There is a valuable discussion on this question provided by A. Keay in (2006) 19 Ins Intell 132.

84 See *Re Hawkes Hill Publishing Ltd* (supra).

85 *Re Idessa UK Ltd* [2011] EWHC 804 (Ch), [2011] BPIR 957. Also liability is capped by reference to the increase in the deficiency during the period in question – without such an increase there cannot be wrongful trading according to the court in *Re Marini Ltd* [2004] BCC 172. This authority is not without its critics.

86 *Re Idessa UK Ltd* (supra), *Re Kudos Business Solutions Ltd* [2011] EWHC 1436 (Ch), [2012] 2 BCLC 65.

87 *Re Oasis Merchandising Services Ltd* [1998] Ch 170.

88 But see the curious one-off case of *Official Receiver v Doshi* [2001] 2 BCLC 235.

difficulties and resulting options for liquidators will be considered more fully in Chapter 4. But, that said, very often the mere threat of a wrongful trading claim (with its associated stigma for any career-minded director) can produce a settlement which is of benefit to creditors.[89] Such settlements are not publicized, so we are in the dark as to how common they are. That said, discussions with practitioners over the years suggest that they are quite common.

A more fundamental problem with wrongful trading is that very often we are dealing with a business judgement par excellence with regard to the decision on continued trading rather than a straightforward issue of breach of duty or not. One consequence of this broad dilemma is the marked reluctance of the courts to accede to a wrongful trading claim on a summary application where all of the evidence and possible justifications for trading on cannot be properly aired and then evaluated.[90]

The Cork Committee (Cmnd 8558) favoured (at para 1798) the introduction of an anticipatory declaration procedure designed to reassure directors worried about the risk of wrongful trading liability. This recommendation was not enacted. This in some respects is a pity, but at the end of the day one wonders how many directors would have taken advantage of this mechanism. In practice, seeking an authoritative legal opinion can achieve almost as good reassurance.

3.3.4 Guidance on Acceptable Stewardship from the Disqualification Regime[91]

The director disqualification regime serves a dual purpose in the context of the present debate. It informs future generations of managers (or more likely their advisers), through reported case law, as to good and bad practice, and it temporarily eliminates from the limited liability game those directors whose conduct has shown them to be unfit as stewards. Without doubt, it has been the dominant strategy used by successive governments to improve standards of stewardship in the past 40 years. Since its introduction a conservative and rough 'guestimate' might indicate that at least some 30 000 directors have been disqualified, though in many instances such disqualifications will now have lapsed with the passage of time.

---

[89] But this ploy needs to be carefully monitored – see *Re Langreen Ltd* (2011, an unreported decision of Registrar Derrett delivered on 21 October 2011).

[90] On this see *Liquidator of Wendy Fair Ltd v Hobday* [2006] EWHC 5803 (Ch) and *Singla v Hedman (No. 1)* [2009] EWHC 3510 (Ch), [2010] BCC 674.

[91] See generally R. Williams [2007] 7 JCLS 213 and his monograph *Disqualification Undertakings* (2011). Note also D. Milman [1992] 43 NILQ 1.

There are various bases for disqualification but the overwhelming majority (perhaps as much as 90 per cent) are on the ground of 'unfitness' within the s. 6 regime. The procedure for the disqualification of unfit directors was introduced in the Insolvency Act 1976, but the major change came with the enactment of the Company Directors Disqualification Act 1986, which is supported by secondary legislation.[92] The 1986 legislation removed the precondition for the director to have been involved in multiple insolvencies[93] and crucially introduced a statutory whistleblowing duty for insolvency practitioners.[94] The tool used to report the names of directors to the authorities is the 'D Report'. Judicial discretion was also circumscribed.[95] Disqualifications can be directed to last for periods of between 2 and 15 years. Statistics[96] show the average disqualification imposed to be approximately 5.9 years.

Under the 1986 model the disqualification of unfit directors of insolvent firms became a major issue, with the courts being swamped with applications. Such was the success of the 1986 regime that it placed great strains on the public exchequer[97] and cost saving alternatives had to be considered. So, under s. 6 of the Insolvency Act 2000, the use of binding undertakings given outside the court became an option; these days this is the most common method of arranging a disqualification.[98] Court proceedings tend to be reserved for test cases or instances where the allegations of unfitness are being contested.[99]

---

92 See Companies (Disqualification Orders) Regulations 2009 (SI 2009/2471). Note also *Practice Direction: Directors Disqualification Proceedings* [2007] BCC 862.

93 The '2 in 5 year' rule which prevented a finding of unfitness in relation to a first corporate collapse was thus abolished.

94 Company Directors Disqualification Act 1986 s. 7(3).

95 So where unfitness was established a minimum two-year disqualification had to be imposed by the court – s. 6.

96 See *Insolvency Service Annual Report and Accounts 2011–12* (HC 358) at 30. The figure for 2010–11 was 6.1 years.

97 As evidenced by the attention paid by the National Audit Office to this matter – see its reports in 1993 (*Company Director Disqualification*) and 1999 (*The Insolvency Service Executive Agency – Company Directors Disqualification: A Follow-up Report*). For comment see A. Hicks (1999) 15 IL & P 112.

98 Statistics from the *Insolvency Service Annual Report and Accounts 2011/12* (HC 358) show that of the 1151 disqualifications made in 2011–12 some 80 per cent were implemented through the undertakings procedure – see p. 30. The total number of disqualifications is down from 1437 in the previous year and this has worried practitioners.

99 As in Farepak, where the authorities in the light of the evidence put before the court decided to discontinue the proceedings. This drew an unusual response from Peter Smith J, who, on 21 June 2012, made a statement in open court explaining how this situation had come about. For discussion see A. Walters (2013) 34 Co Law 1. Note also the Insolvency Service assessment of the debacle – *Review of Disqualification Proceedings Taken in the Case of European Home Retail plc and Farepak Food and Gifts Ltd* (December 2012).

A disqualification extends beyond holding a directorship and covers any sort of participation in the management of a limited company. Directors who breach such a disqualification run risks. These risks are exacerbated by the existence of the Enforcement Hotline, which is advertised in prominent fashion on the Insolvency Service website. A director who is found to have continued to act in breach of a disqualification could be held personally liable for corporate debts (Company Directors Disqualification Act 1986 s. 15)[100] or be convicted of a criminal offence (Company Directors Disqualification Act 1986 s. 13). This criminal dimension then opens up the possibility of the Proceeds of Crime Act 2002 coming into play.[101] This bar cannot be avoided by putting a directorship in the name of a family member because that could also trigger sanctions against such person. This point is particularly relevant in the context of small family firms.

Because of the severity of the potential consequences for a respondent director, the provisions of ECHR are engaged, particularly Art 6, which requires the proceedings to be concluded within a reasonable time.[102]

This is not the place to evaluate the disqualification mechanism in the round. Rather we should use the guidance in Schedule 1 of the Act and voluminous case law as a guide to identifying appropriate standards of stewardship. Sched 1 identifies a number of key indicia of unfitness. These might include responsibility for the company's insolvency (para 6), failure to supply promised goods or services (para 7) and the giving of preferences (para 8). From that mass of reported litigation certain lessons stand out:

- unfitness is not to be inferred from mere commercial misjudgement[103]
- conduct which is not in accordance with 'commercial morality'[104] will merit disqualification
- inactivity is no excuse to an allegation of unfitness[105]
- trading on Crown debts is evidence of unfitness[106]

---

100 For a rare case on this see *Re Prestige Grindings Ltd* [2006] BCC 421.

101 See *R v Seager* [2009] EWCA Crim 1303, [2012] BCC 124, *Hill v DBIS* [2011] EWHC 3436 (Admin), [2011] BCC 473.

102 See *Eastaway* [2005] 40 EHRR 17.

103 See *Re Lo Line Electric Motors Ltd* [1988] Ch 477.

104 Whatever that is.

105 *Re Lo Line Electric Motors Ltd* [1988] Ch 477, *Re Majestic Recording Studios Ltd* (1988) 4 BCC 519. Thus a failure to supervise co-directors may point to unfitness – *Secretary of State for BIS v Khan* [2012] CSOH 85, 2012 SLT 1090. See also *Secretary of State for BIS v Cork* [2012] EWHC 3284 (Ch), where reference was made to a lack of engagement.

106 *Re Sevenoaks Stationers (Retail) Ltd* [1991] Ch 164. For recent applications

- wrongful trading is a clear indicator of unfitness[107]
- agreeing to the payment of improper dividends is evidence of unfitness[108]
- continuing to trade knowing the precarious position of the company is not necessarily wrongful trading, particularly where it was done to minimize loss to creditors[109]
- failure to maintain proper financial records is evidence of unfitness[110]
- the giving of preferences suggests unfitness[111]
- discriminating against a particular creditor (such as the HMRC) might suggest unfitness[112]
- excessive pension drawings from the company might suggest a lack of fitness[113]
- fitness will be assessed in relation to a director's professed competence[114]
- although liability is to be determined ad personam, all directors have some degree of responsibility for the way a company is run[115]
- a mere breach of duty is not conclusive proof of unfitness[116]
- a director who acts on professional legal or accounting advice is in a strong position to rebut an allegation of unfitness[117]

---

see *Secretary of State for BIS v Khan* [2012] CSOH 85, 2012 SLT 1090 and *Cathie v Secretary of State for BIS (No. 2)* [2012] EWCA Civ 739. It is clear that this form of misbehaviour is on the increase, whereas other forms of misconduct are in decline – *Insolvency Service Annual Report and Accounts 2011/12* (HC 358) at p. 30.

107 See the discussion in *Secretary of State v Creegan* [2002] 1 BCLC 99.

108 *Re AG (Manchester) Ltd* [2008] EWHC 64 (Ch), [2008] BCC 497.

109 Witness Farepak again.

110 *Secretary of State for Trade and Industry v Ettinger* [1993] BCLC 312, *Secretary of State for Trade and Industry v Thornbury* [2007] EWHC 3202 (Ch), [2008] 1 BCLC 139.

111 See Sched 1 of the Company Directors Disqualification Act 1986.

112 See *Re Structural Concrete Ltd* [2001] BCC 578.

113 *Official Receiver v Stern (No. 2)* [2002] 1 BCLC 119.

114 *Re Cladrose Ltd* [1990] BCC 11. The fact that a director is professionally qualified might enable the court to take into account breaches of ethics prescribed by that particular profession.

115 *Secretary of State for BIS v Khan* [2012] CSOH 85, 2012 SLT 1090. But if the authorities unfairly pick on one director when there are others equally culpable the courts will raise concerns – see *DETI v Black* [2012] NI Master 1.

116 See *Re Stakefield (Midlands) Ltd* [2010] EWHC 3175 (Ch) at para [251] per Newey J.

117 See *Re Uno plc* [2006] BCC 725. Compare *Re GSAR Realisations Ltd* [1993] BCLC 409.

- when considering unfitness the court can look at a director's conduct after the commencement of formal insolvency proceedings (for example any failure to cooperate with the office-holder).[118]

3.3.5 Governance and Phoenixism[119]

A particular form of directorial abuse characterized as 'phoenixism' rose to prominence in the 1980s largely due to adverse media attention. This phenomenon involves the directors of a failed company setting up a successor company to take over the business and then continuing to abuse limited liability through that second vehicle, which often used a name suggesting an association with the former business. Goodwill was thus exploited and customers could be misled. Whilst the first company was in decline, business assets were often sold off to the successor firm at an undervalue. The Cork Committee recommended legislation to combat this syndrome.[120] Under s. 216 of the Insolvency Act 1986 a director or former director of a failed company cannot be involved in the management of a second company using the same or similar name for a five-year period. Breach of this prohibition results in personal liability for the debts of the second company.[121] Phoenixism, of course, might suggest unfitness meriting disqualification. It also involves the commission of a criminal offence of strict liability.[122] The Proceeds of Crime Act 2002 can once again come into play.[123]

This technical provision is not well known to the business community in general[124] and applies automatically, irrespective of any improper motive.[125]

---

[118] See Company Directors Disqualification Act 1986 Sched 1 para 10(g) and *Secretary of State for Trade and Industry v McTighe* [1997] BCC 244. On the costs implications of any failure to cooperate see *Hunt v Renzland* [2008] BPIR 1380.

[119] See D. Milman [1997] JBL 224 and [2001] Ins Law 199. See also S. Griffin [2002] CLP 377. Griffin's paper in Chapter 9 in J. de Lacy, (ed.) *The Reform of UK Company Law* (2002) is most illuminating. See also C. Werner (2009) 22 Ins Intell 105.

[120] Cmnd 8558 para 1827 – the recommendation was not clear cut and seems only to have been directed at SMEs (see para 1834).

[121] Insolvency Act 1986 s. 217.

[122] *R v Doring* [2002] EWCA Crim 1695, [2002] BPIR 1695. As the offence is one of strict liability, this mixture of sanctions does not produce the negative evidential consequences that one finds in fraudulent trading.

[123] See *R v Weintroub* [2011] EWCA Crim 2167, [2011] All ER (D) 126 (July). The court confiscated the entire sum earned by the defendant during the period of improper trading. See also *R v Neuberg* [2007] EWCA Crim 1994.

[124] Though it may have motivated the actions of the directors in *Morphitis v Bernasconi* [2002] EWCA Civ 289, [2003] Ch 552.

[125] See the harsh decision in *Ricketts v Ad Valorem Factors Ltd* [2003] EWCA Civ 1706, [2004] 1 All ER 894.

But it has been seized upon by opportunistic repeat creditors (such as HMRC,[126] local authorities[127] and even those debt factoring companies who have bought distressed corporate debt[128]) to ensure the recovery of a business debt from directors in circumstances where the second business is unlikely to pay up. The fundamental point to note is that the recovery claim is pursued by an individual creditor for its own benefit[129] and not by the liquidator for the collective benefit of creditors. Notwithstanding this, collective benefit may result because a major creditor is then removed from the list of creditors seeking to prove against the insolvent estate, leaving the possibility of a higher distribution for other creditors. Perhaps because of the highly technical nature of this matter and innocent parties can be caught out, the Insolvency Service operates an informal warnings system before matters get too serious – 85 such warnings were issued in 2011–12 according to official figures.[130]

The provision benefits in terms of its operational effectiveness from its purely objective nature. It does not require proof of dishonesty. It can, however, entrap an innocent director in circumstances where no blame can be attached to the first business failure and can be exploited by a creditor who is aware that the prohibition is being breached when credit is extended to the company. Opportunism of this nature is not a barrier to recovery.

There is, accordingly, flexibility written into the system. Exceptions are provided by Insolvency Rules 4.227–4.230.[131] Also, a director who would otherwise be caught by this provision can apply to the court for leave to act. This is implicit in s. 216(3) of the Act. The Cork Committee (Cmnd 8558, para 1831) was keen on this facility, but such applications are rare and the available court decisions are not entirely clear on the correct approach to be adopted.[132] One view suggests that additional precautionary measures can be imposed as a condition of leave, whereas the alternative approach suggests that this is not appropriate.

---

[126] See *IRC v Nash* [2004] BCC 150, *HMRC v Yousef* [2008] BPIR 1491, *Advocate General for Scotland v Reilly* [2011] CSOH 141.

[127] *Glasgow CC v Craig* [2008] CSOH 171, [2010] BCC 235.

[128] *First Independent Factors and Finance Ltd v Mountford* [2008] 2 BCLC 297.

[129] First recognized as a possibility in *Thorne v Silverleaf* [1994] 1 BCLC 637.

[130] See *Insolvency Service Annual Report and Accounts 2011/12* (HC 358) at p. 36.

[131] In the comparable provision in New Zealand these exceptions are sensibly contained in the primary legislation (ss. 386A–386E of the Companies Act 1993) and are thus more visible.

[132] Compare the approach of Morritt J in *Re Bonus Breaks Ltd* [1991] BCC 546 (where undertakings as to future conduct were required) with that adopted by Chadwick J in *Penrose v Official Receiver* [1996] 1 WLR 482 (where no undertakings were required).

There are certain weaknesses in the statutory regime as described above. These were identified by the Company Law Review in its Final Report of 2001.[133] One problem is that not all instances of phoenixism are bad.[134] As for reform, the Steering Group felt constrained by the fact that reforms to insolvency law were not part of its remit. It therefore settled on some modifications to the relating to substantial property transactions. It also made proposals to amend the position on obtaining leave, though it did not come in favour of the idea of automatic disqualification.

We mentioned asset-stripping in the context of phoenixism. At common law such behaviour would be seen as a breach of fiduciary duty and so could be challenged without recourse to specific provisions in the Insolvency Act 1986 (such as s. 238).[135] Very often the outcome is that the court orders the company which has received the assets to return them. The veil of separate corporate personality can be lifted to this end.[136]

3.3.6 Other Sources of Guidance on Stewardship in the Twilight Zone

Well-informed directors might also look to s. 121C of the Social Security Administration Act 1992 as providing guidance on how not to run the company. This provision, which harks back to a regime operated by s. 152(4) of the Social Security Act 1975 that was abolished by the Insolvency Act 1985,[137] was resurrected in 1998. It enables the tax authorities to serve a personal liability notice upon a director of a company that has failed to pay national insurance. A director can be liable under this provision where there is evidence of fraud or neglect. This terminology has been tested in the courts and surprisingly it has been held[138] in the most recent authority on the subject to require a subjective test to be satisfied as to the director's state of mind as this liability is akin to penal liability. On a strictly technical level, one has doubts about this generous interpretation, which appears to be inconsistent with the more draconian view taken in an earlier tribunal.[139] That said, it may

---

[133] URN 01/942 paras 15.55–15.77. For comment see D. Milman [2001] Ins Law 199.

[134] See the comments of Arden LJ in *ESS Print Ltd v Sully* [2005] EWCA Civ 554, [2005] BPIR 691.

[135] See *Anglo German Breweries v Chelsea Corp Inc* [2012] EWHC 1481 (Ch).

[136] See *Trustor AB v Smallbone (No. 2)* [2001] 1 WLR 1177.

[137] See Insolvency Act 1985 s. 235 and Sched 10. For guidance on this old regime see D. Milman (1984) 5 Co Law 91.

[138] *O'Rorke v HMRC* [2011] UKFTT 839 (TC) – see P. Ridgway (2012) 25 Ins Intell 106.

[139] *Inzani v Revenue and Customs Commissioners* [2006] STI 1354 – noted by A. Taylor in [2009] 22 Ins Intell 79.

reflect the spirit of the undertakings given by the government when the provision was enacted and the tone of information posted on the HMRC website. Nevertheless, greater clarity on the true extent of this potential liability would be welcomed here by the managerial community.

3.4 STEWARDSHIP WITHIN THE DISTRESSED GROUP[140]

Up to now the discussion has proceeded on the assumption that we have been considering stewardship responsibilities in the context of a single company. That is misleading in the sense that many companies (even in the SME context) operate in a group environment. This is a legitimate risk management strategy. How does that reality affect stewardship responsibilities of directors within the group?

The basic principle operating here is that the directors (even nominee directors) owe their duties to the company over which they have been appointed to act. They are the stewards of that company and it matters not that it is a subsidiary contained within a group of companies. One reason for this is that English law maintains that creditors are creditors of single companies within the group and not of the group as a whole.[141] Therefore the duty of husbandry discussed above is owed to the creditors of a particular company and not to group creditors.[142] We do not 'do' pooling, equitable subordination[143] nor substantive consolidation (unlike some other jurisdictions, which are considered in Chapter 5). But that principle is flexible and circumstances may apply that mean that acting in the interests of the group may in fact be in the long-term interests of the subsidiary. So in *Facia Footwear Co Ltd v Hinchcliffe*[144] Scott VC took account of the fact that there were group treasury arrangements in place and therefore the interests of group creditors became relevant when reviewing the behaviour of directors of a particular company within the group. It is possible in principle that directors of a parent company (or even the parent

---

140 See generally Cork Committee (1982) (Cmnd 8558, Chapter 51). Group issues were of course to the fore in the Farepak affair.

141 *Re Southard & Co Ltd* [1979] 1 WLR 1198.

142 See *Re Capitol Films Ltd* [2010] EWHC 2240 (Ch), [2011] BPIR 334. Note also the comments of Lewison J in *Re Mea Corp Ltd* [2006] EWHC 1846 (Ch), [2007] 1 BCLC 618.

143 That is treating intra-group finance as subordinated. This idea is used in the US in cases such as *Taylor v Standard Gas* (1939) 306 US 307. For discussion see E. Scherer and R.J. Schimmelpenninck (2004) 20 IL & P 54.

144 [1998] 1 BCLC 218.

company itself) may become de facto or even shadow directors of a subsidiary company, but the English courts have resisted drawing such a conclusion in the paradigm scenario.[145] One problem frequently encountered in English law is the informality in which some groups (particularly a group of family companies) operate; this laxity can come back to bite the directors if the business fails.[146]

Another authority of interest is *Nicholas v Soundcraft Electronics Ltd*,[147] where the court indicated that for a parent company to refuse to pay its debts to a subsidiary may raise the possibility of unfair prejudice contrary to s. 994 of the Companies Act 2006, but although the holding back of payments is undoubtedly prejudicial it is not necessarily unfair if the intention is to protect the integrity of the group of which the subsidiary is a member.

3.5 CONSTRUCTIVE OPTIONS

Bearing in mind the pressures faced by directors operating companies in the twilight zone and the inherent dangers of trading on, what are the remedial options if collapse appears inevitable?

Cutting and running through a well-timed resignation might be an option that would be considered by many a director of a distressed company. That is hardly exemplary behaviour in terms of stewardship, but we are all human. But great caution needs to be exercised here. Resignation does not protect against accrued liability for wrongful trading or a charge of unfitness; indeed it may exacerbate the situation. Another trap to be aware of is that if resignation is the selected option, a release must be obtained from any guarantee liability.[148]

One simple solution would be to get the members to resolve to put the company into CVL. Notice must be given to any qualifying floating charge holder under s. 84(2A) of any such proposed resolution to allow it to exercise its options as security holder. In such a case five business days' notice is required (s. 84(2B)). If a declaration of solvency cannot be made under ss. 89 and 90 of the Insolvency Act 1986, the liquidation will proceed as a CVL and the directors should call a meeting of creditors pursuant to s. 98 in order to determine choice of liquidator. Such meetings are feared by directors and there

145 See *Re Hydrodan (Corby) Ltd* [1994] BCC 161 and *HMRC v Holland* [2010] UKSC 51, [2011] BCC 1.

146 See the comments of Peter Leaver QC sitting in the High Court in *Re HHO Licensing Ltd* [2007] BPIR 1363 at para [71].

147 [1993] BCLC 360.

148 See *Goodman v First National Finance Corp* [1983] BCLC 203.

have been suggestions that that fear has fuelled an appetite for alternative options such as administration.[149] That said, the CVL option is a straightforward choice, but in many senses, unless one embraces the Schumpeterian ideas of creative destruction, it may be seen as a negative move.

In the real world things are often not so clear cut. A business may be distressed but there may be no certainty of failure. The important relationship between imposing liabilities on directors and offering them the opportunity to seek more constructive solutions to the firm's predicament will now be reviewed. This is the so-called 'stick and carrot' strategy favoured by the Cork Committee (1982).[150] The 'rescue culture'[151] is an important policy phenomenon that intersects with stewardship in many respects. Essentially a distressed firm that sees any hope of survival should consider either of *two*[152] formal restructuring options. Before discussing these we should not close our eyes to informal possibilities. These might involve the directors seeking to make an informal arrangement with the company's creditors. Such an approach is not without its problems because such informal arrangements may not always be legally enforceable because of the vagaries of English law of contractual consideration.[153] Another solution that is largely unregulated is to invite a turnaround specialist or company doctor to prescribe a remedy. From the viewpoint of the professional in this scenario, steps must be taken to avoid the shadow director attribution danger.[154]

First, the directors may approach an insolvency practitioner with a view to setting in place a company voluntary arrangement (CVA) under Part 1 of the Insolvency Act 1986.[155] Formal insolvency does not appear to be a prerequisite for going down this route. In so doing they must act honestly – it is an offence under s. 6A of the Insolvency Act 1986 to seek to procure a CVA by false representation. Under such an arrangement a period of grace for restructuring may be bought with the promise of better returns for unsecured creditors than would accrue on a liquidation. This prospect of a better return is not

---

149 See the discussion in A. Keay [2005] JBL 143.

150 See Cmnd 8558.

151 See M. Hunter [1999] JBL 491. Muir Hunter was a member of the Cork Committee and his insights are therefore particularly valuable.

152 There is a third, the scheme of arrangement under Part 26 of the Companies Act 2006. But this is not used extensively by SMEs. On the other hand, it is seen as very attractive by distressed firms incorporated abroad in jurisdictions which are seen to lack effective restructuring tools. For examples of foreign usage, see the discussion in P. Godfrey [2012] (Winter) Recov 8. See also Chapter 5.

153 See *Re Selectmove Ltd* [1994] BCC 349.

154 Witness *Re Tasbian Ltd (No. 3)* [1992] BCC 358.

155 Note SIP 3 here.

merely illusory; empirical research confirms it as a reality.[156] From the viewpoint of the directors, the great attraction of a CVA lies in the fact that they will remain in control of the firm, albeit subject to the obligations they have undertaken as part of the CVA. Thus, we have a rare example of a 'debtor in possession' feature operating in English corporate insolvency law. The trick here lies in getting the unsecured creditors onside by obtaining the necessary voting majority (75 per cent of the total debt and more than 50 per cent of the debt owed to independent creditors). The problem of classes of creditors (which bedevils schemes of arrangement) is not an issue. Once a CVA has been established a new dualist governance regime for the company will come into effect – more of this later. This type of procedure, although used to a limited extent, has proved to be popular with SMEs. Before leaving CVAs, we should note again that there is an alternative CVA model introduced under the Insolvency Act 2000 with effect from January 2003. This is only available to SMEs and suggestions that it should be made more widely accessible were rebuffed in 2010. However, this alternative has not been embraced[157] by either the managerial community or the insolvency profession and the instances of its usage are miniscule. We choose therefore to exclude it from our study. But before doing so we can at least observe that this is a rare example of specific provision being made for distressed SMEs. In that sense it is worthy of some praise.

The second, and more drastic, option would be to seek to put the company into administration. The procedures for doing this were considerably relaxed by the Enterprise Act 2002 with effect from 15 September 2003. Either the company, or its directors, can achieve this outcome by an out-of-court procedure laid down in para 22 et seq of Sched B1 of the Insolvency Act 1986.[158] Essentially what happens is that they file a notice of intention to appoint an administrator and then follow that up with an actual appointment within 10 days.[159] This procedure cannot be used if the company is facing a winding-up petition (see para 25(a) of Sched B1). If the directors take this step, it is important that they hold a meeting to resolve accordingly – although a majority vote will suffice, failure to hold a meeting may prove fatal. Proper notice must also

[156] See research carried out by D. Milman and F. Chittenden for the ACCA in the 1990s (*Corporate Rescue: CVAs and the Challenge of Small Companies*) (ACCA Research Report 44, 1995) and the more up-to-date survey conducted by A. Walters and S. Frisby, details of which are provided by S. Frisby in (2011) 64 CLP 349.

[157] See A. Walters and S. Frisby in their paper to the ILA Annual Academic Conference in Oxford in March 2011.

[158] Sched B1 was introduced via s. 248 of the Enterprise Act 2002 with effect from 15 September 2003.

[159] If they fail to take this second step within 10 days, they can file a second notice of intention – see *Re Cornercare Ltd* [2010] EWHC 893 (Ch), [2010] BCC 592.

be given to all prescribed parties, including the company itself. These points were made forcefully in *Minmar 929 Ltd v Khalatschi.*[160] It is evident that the lapses in procedure identified by Sir Andrew Morritt in that case were not an isolated instance.[161] That said, it is equally clear that the judges at first instance are split on how to resolve this procedural shortcoming.[162] One way out is for the court to retrospectively validate the administration,[163] but, if it decides to do this, it can only go back 12 months.[164] Furthermore, it is arguable[165] that it will have to be satisfied when the application is made to it that the administration was viable – hindsight can thus be used to block an administration. One consequence for IPs is that the actions of the administrator will be invalid unless para 104 of Sched B1 can be brought into play and judicial views on this have been divided.[166] The duty of directors to respect the constitution, which we noted above, thus has real currency in this context. Why are the courts so pernickety? Could it be latent fear of the spectre of prepacks, or even a desire to recover their former exclusive power to initiate administration? What makes some of the recent judicial rulings here more

---

160 [2011] EWHC 1159 (Ch), [2011] BCC 486. Followed by Henderson J in *Baker v London Bar Co Ltd* [2011] EWHC 3398 (Ch), [2012] BCC 69.

161 This is apparent from *Re Derfshaw Ltd* [2011] EWHC 1565 (Ch), [2011] BCC 635.

162 *Minmar* was followed by Warren J in *National Westminster Bank v Msaada* [2011] EWHC 3423 (Ch), [2012] BCC 226. A more flexible approach, which is typified by *Hill v Stokes plc* [2010] EWHC 3726 (Ch), [2011] BCC 473, found favour with Norris J in *Re Virtualpurple Professional Services* [2011] EWHC 3487 (Ch), [2012] BCC 254. This liberal view has also manifested itself in the judgment of Arnold J *Re Ceart Risk Services* [2012] EWHC 1178 (Ch), [2012] BCC 592, of Mann J in *Re MF Global Overseas Ltd* [2012] EWHC 1091 (Ch), [2012] BCC 490 and *Re BXL Services* [2012] EWHC 1877 (Ch), [2012] BCC 657 where HHJ Purle QC stated (perhaps optimistically) that the point was now the settled view at first instance. For a trilogy of excellent accounts of the current turmoil see J. Anderson [2011] 304 SMCLN 1, [2012] 309 SMCLN 1 and [2012] 320 SMCLN 1.

163 By relying on the precedent of *Re G Tech Construction Ltd* [2007] BPIR 1275. What is clear is that the saving provision in Insolvency Rule 7.55 does not come into play – *Re Frontsouth (Witham) Ltd* [2011] EWHC (Ch), [2011] BCC 635. But IR 7.55 was used to cure a different procedural defect in the appointment of an administrator in *Re Euromaster Ltd* [2012] EWHC 2353 (Ch), [2012] BCC 754 (appointment made one day after notice of intention to appoint had expired). Its applicability therefore is a matter of degree.

164 See *Re Frontsouth Ltd* (supra).

165 On the authority of *Re Care Matters Ltd* [2011] EWHC 2543 (Ch), [2011] BCC 957.

166 Compare the approach of Norris J in *Re Care Matters Ltd* [2011] EWHC 2543 (Ch), [2011] BCC 957 at paras [7] and [8] with the earlier approach of Hart J in *Re G Tech Construction Ltd* [2007] BPIR 1275 on this point.

surprising is the contrast here with regards to the more generous approach of the courts towards the appointment of administrative receivers.[167]

Putting a company into administration will ensure that a protective moratorium is placed around the company. Indeed, interim protection is activated the moment the directors file notice of intention to appoint an administrator.[168] This protection will enable a rescue package to be devised and put to creditors. The downside of administration is that the directors will lose control of the business during the period of administration. The administrator, a qualified insolvency practitioner, will hold the reins of power. Explicit power to remove the directors is conferred by para 61 of Sched B1, though this option is not always exercised. Powers of investigation are given to administrators so the directors cannot assume an easy ride, though they do avoid the trauma of having to attend a notorious s. 98 meeting, which would be required if they decided to put the company into creditors' voluntary liquidation. For many directors, fearful of facing their creditors, that appears to be an important consideration.

On the appointment of the administrator, a completely new governance model, that now post-2003 has much in common with liquidation, is triggered. This will be considered below in Chapter 4.

The existence of these constructive options should exercise the thought processes of directors of struggling firms. In theory the 'ostrich syndrome' (i.e. burying one's head in the sand and hoping that things will pick up) should no longer be encountered. Failure to access either the CVA or administration mechanisms may have damaging personal consequences if the directors decide to trade on and then the business fails, leaving unresolved debts.

In the context of the aforementioned scenario we should revisit our consideration of the role played by company doctors, turnaround specialists and other professional advisers in the period of twilight. A sensible director will take both legal and accounting advice in a situation of corporate distress. It is worth noting that legal professional privilege is preserved by s. 20A of the Company Directors Disqualification Act 1986.[169] If this course of action in seeking professional advice is adopted, it is even more important that the advice given is followed. Although following legal/accounting advice does not

---

167 Compare *Brampton Manor (Leisure) Ltd v McLean* [2007] BCC 640. Any abortive challenge may have consequences in costs – see for example *Brampton Manor (Leisure) Ltd v McLean (No. 2)* [2009] BCC 30 – even for a director who is not formally party to the challenge because s. 51 of the Senior Courts Act 1981 could come into play.

168 *Re Business Dream Ltd* [2011] EWHC 2860 (Ch), [2012] BPIR 490.

169 But if fraud is alleged (for example in the context of s. 423 of the Insolvency Act 1986), the court might be prepared to lift legal privilege – see *Barclays Bank v Eustice* [1996] BPIR 1.

guarantee immunity from sanctions,[170] it certainly places a defendant director in a much more comfortable position should litigation ensue.[171] Ignoring professional advice is certainly a recipe for disaster.[172] Where advice is sought it will have to be paid for. In seeking advice it is important to clarify whether it is the company or the directors personally who are seeking such advice.[173] If the advice is sought after a winding-up petition is presented against the company, any payment by the company to the professional adviser is void under s. 127 of the Insolvency Act 1986.[174] In such a scenario the directors may have to dip into their own pockets to fund the professional support. Going beyond the taking of advice, the directors may invite a firm of investigating accountants in to look at the company's finances and prospects. It is not uncommon to find the company's bank encouraging such a step. There is a trap to avoid here in that such an investigation may be a prelude to the bank opting for administration or administrative receivership. There may be a suspicion that a fee-conscious firm of professionals may be inclined to such a conclusion. To avoid this temptation a contractual provision[175] in the letter of engagement might be a wise precaution.

3.6 PROTECTING THE COMPANY FROM HOSTILE INSOLVENCY PROCEEDINGS

Directors may quite legitimately take the view that the activation of a formal insolvency regime is not in the best interests of the company. This may be a legitimate stance that should be recognized by the law. Where this position is arrived at, the directors will hardly seek a CVL or CVA or seek to put the company in administration. To what extent can a hostile insolvency regime (such as liquidation, receivership or even some form of administration) be foisted upon the company in the face of opposition from directors? What are the options of directors in that latter scenario?

---

170 *Official Receiver v Ireland* [2002] BCC 428, *R v Doring* [2002] EWCA Crim 1695, [2002] BPIR 1204.

171 See *Re Uno plc* [2006] BCC 725, *Re Continental Assurance plc* [2001] BPIR 733.

172 As was attested in *Re Brian Pierson Contractors Ltd* [1999] BCC 26 at 36.

173 See *Wade v Poppleton & Appleby* [2003] EWHC 3159 (Ch), [2004] 1 BCLC 674.

174 See *Re Ledingham-Smith* [1993] BCLC 635.

175 Such as was featured in *Sheppard and Cooper Ltd v TSB Bank* [1996] BCC 653, [1997] 2 BCLC 222.

It does seem clear that directors do enjoy residual power to challenge the hostile appointment of a receiver, administrator or liquidator.[176] This interpretation of the law must be correct or else the company would be left defenceless in the face of an aggressive creditor. Directors can oppose a winding-up petition and normally will do so safe in the knowledge that they will not be personally liable for the associated litigation costs should that opposition prove futile.[177] Such costs should be treated as part of the overall winding-up costs. However, if they are behaving unreasonably, or clearly out of self-interest, the sanction of an adverse costs order made against them personally should be borne in mind. A typical ground raised to oppose the petition is to argue that the alleged petition debt is disputed, in which case it will first have to be resolved by separate trial before the petition can proceed. Where there is no dispute the assumption is that the court will accede to the petition; they may do this because the stewardship role of the liquidator is seen as a way of guaranteeing the safeguarding of the interests of all parties.[178]

Directors may challenge the appointment of a receiver over the company's undertaking against their wishes, but the courts would normally dismiss such a challenge if the appointment was justified under the terms of the borrowing agreement. By creating security on terms the company has, in effect, rendered itself a hostage to fortune.

If directors are unwilling to accede to the appointment of an administrator, a bank with a qualifying floating charge might make such an appointment under para 14 of Sched B1, or an unsecured creditor might choose to apply to the court under para 11 for it to make the appointment. Attempts by directors to challenge the appointment of an administrator in such circumstances usually fail,[179] as is the case where a receiver is appointed in a hostile move.[180]

3.7 SHAREHOLDER RIGHTS

We have seen that under English law an essential aspect of the governance matrix is to be found in the fact that shareholders have rights enforceable

---

[176] *Re Union Accident Insurance Co* [1972] 1 WLR 640, *Elwick Bay Shipping Co v RBS* [1982] SLT 62, *Toynar Ltd v Whitbread Ltd* [1988] 4 BCC 6 and *Stephen Petitioner* [2012] CSOH 119, [2012] BCC 537.

[177] See the discussion in *Re North West Holdings plc* [2002] BCC 441. Compare *Re Aurum Marketing Ltd* [1999] 2 BCLC 498.

[178] See the comments of Laffoy J in the Irish High Court in *Re Albion Enterprises Ltd* [2012] IEHC 115 at para [10].

[179] See *Curistan v Keenan* [2011] NICh 23.

[180] See *Lloyds Bank v Lampert* [1991] BCC 507 and *Wade v Poppleton & Appleby* [2003] EWHC 3159 (Ch), [2004] 1 BCLC 674.

through litigation (e.g. by bringing a derivative claim or via an unfair prejudice petition). This contrasts with the continental corporate governance model where rights are protected by institutional structures, such as two-tier boards comprising management and supervisory components.

How are these shareholder rights affected by the decline into insolvency? The short answer is that these rights largely disappear with the solvency of the firm[181] and this has implications for stewardship. Their rights are residual, and in effect non-existent, unless the company turns out to be solvent at the end of the day (which can happen). Shareholders in those major distressed UK banks[182] that were in effect nationalized in 2009 via a taxpayer bailout found this out to their cost – they had lost any economic interest in those banks which, to add insult to injury, were now being propped up through their payments as taxpayers.[183] Their impotence in this situation has been rammed home by the European Court of Human Rights in *Grainger v UK (34940/10)*,[184] where the point was made that shareholders have no legitimate expectation that public money will be pumped into the company to save it.

This divestment of shareholder rights means that the right of shareholders to ratify[185] breaches of duty committed by directors will lapse once insolvency intrudes. This particular point was emphasized by Newey J in *Secretary of State for Business, Innovation and Skills v Doffman (No. 2)*[186] in the context of informal ratification using the well-known *Duomatic*[187] principle of unanimous assent in lieu of formal shareholder resolution.

Similarly, it was held in *Fargro Ltd v Godfrey*[188] that the right of a share-

---

181 So pre-emption rights under a shareholder agreement cannot be enforced – *Leedon Ltd v Hurry* [2010] UKPC 27, [2011] BCC 189. Equally in *Re Barings (No. 7)* [2002] 1 BCLC 401, the court held that the shareholders lacked *locus standi* to challenge the actions of the liquidator as they lacked a tangible interest in the company's assets.

182 A similar fate befell shareholders in Railtrack plc, which was placed in administration by the government in 2001 – subsequent legal action by disgruntled shareholders failed before Lindsay J in 2005. On this episode see *Weir v Secretary of State for Transport* [2005] EWHC 2192 (Ch).

183 See *R (on the application of SRM Global Master Fund) v Treasury Commissioners* [2009] EWCA Civ 788, [2010] BCC 558 as discussed by R. Tomasic [2009] 262 SMCLN 1. For an overview of this sorry saga see J. Gray and O. Akseli, *Financial Regulation in Crisis? The Role of Law and the Failure of Northern Rock* (2011).

184 [2012] ECHR 1675.

185 See generally S. Worthington (2000) 116 LQR 638.

186 [2011] 2 BCLC 54.

187 Named after *Re Duomatic Ltd* [1969] 2 Ch 365.

188 [1986] 1 WLR 1134. Note also *Watts v Midland Bank* [1986] BCLC 15, which is discussed by D. Milman in (1986) 7 Co Law 115. See also A. Keay (2008) 21 Ins Intell 49.

holder to pursue a derivative claim is lost once the company ceases to be solvent. Equally, the ability to make an application to the court under s. 994 of the Companies Act 2006 alleging unfair prejudice normally will be lost in these circumstances.[189] The courts might reason that with an independent professional in charge any unfair prejudice will cease. That said, it would follow from *Re Phoenix Contracts (Leicester) Ltd*[190] that if an unfair prejudice petition is properly brought the court can take into account any loss of value in the shareholding resulting from unfair prejudice where the company has been driven into administration after the petition was presented. It is also true to say that if a remedy is sought against a particular individual respondent, the insolvency of the company should not present an insuperable barrier to recovery.

Certainly, the drastic option of a shareholder seeking the winding-up of the company on the just and equitable ground under s. 122(1)(g) of the Insolvency Act 1986 will also disappear.[191] Conversely, it is doubtful if a contributory can appear to resist a creditor petition for winding-up.[192]

Shareholders have no rights to seek the disqualification of a director of an insolvent company.[193] Any financial loss they have suffered is merely a reflection of the damage done to the company and it will be for the office-holder to consider whether action should be taken to remedy that. If such action is taken and proves successful, it is highly unlikely that the shareholders will receive any of it.

Why is this loss of shareholder rights so pronounced? The short answer would appear to be that at this stage in the decline of the company's fortunes, the shareholders have no tangible interest in the company's assets which, by definition, are likely to be over-committed to satisfying creditor claims. If that is a valid justification, it is difficult to explain why shareholders have an apparent[194] right of veto over the CVA process, not that such a veto is ever

---

189 See *Re A Company (008126 of 1989)* [1992] BCC 542. But compare *Gamlestaden Fastigheter AB v Baltic Partners Ltd* [2007] UKPC 26. See also *Re Tobian Properties Ltd (Maidment v Attwood)* [2012] EWCA Civ 998.

190 [2010] EWHC 2375 (Ch).

191 See *Re Rica Gold Washing Co* (1879) 11 ChD 36, *Re Othery Construction Ltd* [1966] 1 All ER 145 and *Re Expanded Plugs Ltd* [1966] 1 WLR 514. This issue was recently discussed in the High Court in Ireland by Laffoy J in *Re La Plagne Ltd* [2011] IEHC 91.

192 See *Re Camburn Petroleum Products Ltd* [1980] 1 WLR 86, which is the exception that proves the rule. As to whether this rule should be applied in the LLP context, see Morritt C in *The Charity Email Technology Partnership v Vermillion International Investments Ltd* [2009] EWHC 388 (Ch), [2009] BPIR 762.

193 See *Re Adbury Park Estates* [2003] BCC 696.

194 This would seem to follow from a reading of ss. 3 and 4 of the Insolvency Act 1986.

exercised. Moreover, why the approval of shareholders to substantial property transactions carried out by receivers in favour of directors should be required is equally a mystery.[195] Logic would dictate that both anomalies be expunged from our law.

In spite of what has been said above, there is, however, one further shareholder right that is retained (and should be preserved) notwithstanding the decline of the company. It was held in *Re Sussex Brick Co*[196] that the right of an individual to seek a rectification of the share register (see now Companies Act 2006 s. 125) is preserved. This is important because on insolvency shareholders become 'contributories' within the meaning of s. 74 of the Insolvency Act 1986 and any existing liabilities owed to the company may be called in. Conversely, it should also be noted that any debts owed to them in their capacity as shareholders (e.g. unpaid dividends) will become deferred debts of the company (Insolvency Act 1986 s. 74).[197] It should also be borne in mind that shareholders as contributories can exercise inspection rights pursuant to s. 155 of the Insolvency Act 1986.

To complete this survey we note that under English law shareholders cannot compete with unsecured creditors in terms of asserting a claim to the company's assets on insolvent liquidation. This is a fundamental principle of English law.[198]

3.8 IMPACT OF SECTION 172 OF THE COMPANIES ACT 2006

Section 172 of the Companies Act 2006 requires the directors[199] to run the business in order to promote success of the company. In effect it reflects the orthodox idea of shareholder wealth maximization, but then insists that this is done in an enlightened way as described below. The obligation is imposed upon individual directors rather than the board collectively. The Interpretation

---

195 See *Demite Ltd v Protec Health* [1998] BCC 638. The key provision here is now found in Companies Act 2006 s. 190. Exceptions are created for liquidators and administrators, but not for disposals by receivers.

196 [1904] 1 Ch 598.

197 But the scope of s. 74 was restrictively interpreted by the House of Lords in *Soden v British and Commonwealth Holdings plc* [1997] 3 WLR 840.

198 The principle was challenged in Australia in the controversial ruling of the High Court of Australia in *Sons of Gwalia v Margaretic* [2007] HCA 1. See B. Mamutse [2011] 62 NILQ 65. The ruling of the High Court of Australia was overturned by legislation – Corporations Amendment (Sons of Gwalia) Act 2010, which amended s. 563A of the Corporations Act 2001. For discussion see J. Ward (2010) 23 Ins Intell 88.

199 Including nominee directors – see D. Ahern (2011) 127 LQR 118.

Act 1978 could be engaged to produce this conclusion. In theory, therefore, one board member may breach this duty, whereas other directors may be found to be compliant.

This new provision has, as of yet, not been tested in any significant way in the context of an insolvent company, but it has been the subject of judicial comment in disputes involving solvent companies[200] and has also attracted considerable academic debate.[201]

Some inkling of its significance might be gleaned from the experience with the now repealed s. 309 of the Companies Act 1985. This former provision is interesting because it has been effectively subsumed within the much wider parameters of s. 172 and was most likely used as a model for its drafting. Essentially, section 309 required the directors *to have regard to* the interests of employees when exercising managerial powers.[202] This is not an uncommon statutory formulation.[203] It must be remembered that there are comparable statutory obligations in employment legislation (such as the duty to consult on impending redundancies[204]). Nevertheless, s. 309, when introduced in 1980, was seen as an important symbolic act in a system of corporate law that up to then was viewed as manifestly capitalist in nature.[205] Critics viewed it as foreshadowing the arrival of socialism.[206] Its value in the context of a distressed business is borne out by the enlightened ruling of Hoffmann J in *Re Welfab Engineers Ltd.*[207] Here it was held that directors could take into account the interests of employees when determining a downsizing policy. They could thus sell a factory for a reduced price, where the purchaser gave certain under-

---

200 Typically in the context of derivative claims litigated under s. 260 of the Companies Act 2006 or unfair prejudice petitions based upon s. 994.

201 See A. Keay, *Directors' Duties* (2009) Chapter 6. For the copious periodical literature see A. Keay (2007) 28 Co Law 106, D. Fisher [2009] 20 ICCLR 10, S.F. Copp (2010) 31 Co Law 406, A. Keay (2010) 23 Ins Intell 129.

202 A comparable provision is to be found in s. 52 of the Irish Companies Act 1990, where the duty is described as fiduciary in nature.

203 See Legal Services Act 2007 s. 115 – Office of Legal Complaints must have regard to good corporate governance in carrying out its role.

204 See Trade Union and Labour Relations (Consolidation) Act 1992 s. 188. The parlous financial state of the company is no excuse for failure to consult – *Bakers Union v Clarks of Hove Ltd* [1978] IRLR 366.

205 The classic illustration of this pro-shareholder bias was found in *Parke v Daily News* [1962] Ch 927, a decision which itself was reversed by s. 74 of the Companies Act 1980. See now Companies Act 2006 s. 247.

206 The irony was that it actually aided the managerial class by extending their range of managerial options whilst imposing no enforceable obligations – see D. Milman Chapter 8 in D. Feldman and F. Meisel, *Corporate and Commercial Law: Modern Developments* (1995).

207 [1990] BCC 600.

takings about the retention of staff. This was justified even though it may not have been in the interests of unsecured creditors.

Returning to s. 172 of the 2006 Act, we find the same formula being used as the basis of the obligation. The provision commences by reinforcing the need to manage the company in the interests of shareholders but it then goes on with a nod towards the idea of corporate social responsibility to require that there is a duty *to have regard to* various stakeholder interests amongst other [unspecified] matters. This is enlightened shareholder philosophy at work. The subject matter of such concern is, however, much wider. It includes:

- employees
- the environment
- business reputation
- suppliers and customers
- local community.

There is no prioritization between these often competing stakeholder categories and these groups as such have no direct right of enforcement in their capacity as a stakeholder in that group – that is restricted to those claiming through the company.

An interesting authority that sheds some light on s. 172 is *Odyssey Entertainment Ltd v Kamp*.[208] Here the point was made by Simon Barker QC (sitting as a judge of the High Court) that a director who adopted too negative a view of the company's prospects and recommended its winding-down in circumstances where this may be unjustifiable could not be said to be complying with his duty to promote the success of the company. Undue pessimism is a bad thing.

Will this provision really change the way directors manage distressed firms? The short answer is probably not.[209] Many of these areas for attention were the subject of discrete legislative obligation before s. 172 was enacted. This is true in the spheres of employment law, environmental law, competition law and fair trading law. Other discrete matters covered by s. 172 have since attracted legislative action (see for example the Bribery Act 2010). But that does not mean the provision is worthless. It cannot be ignored or observed through mere lip service, as Mary Arden LJ has pointed out in a public speech.[210] It will ensure that a well-advised board keeps better records of

---

208 [2012] EWHC 2316 (Ch). The suggestion in the case was that the director may have been influenced by his own personal plans for the future which were not disclosed to the other less influential board members.

209 See N. Okoye (2012) 33 Co Law 15.

210 See [2010] 10 JCLS 1 at 7.

meetings. Under s. 417 of the 2006 Act the extent of compliance with s. 172 should be mapped out in the directors' report. It may, by requiring an act of reflection, encourage a more circumspect approach to situations of distress. We are all familiar with defensive thinking in our everyday lives – risk-averse thinking may put in an appearance in the conduct of business. That may, or may not, be a good thing. Many businesses have failed through over-ambition – others continue to prosper on that risk-taking philosophy.

We should also note s. 172(3) in this context. Its precise relationship with s. 172(1) is less than clear, but what it seeks to do is to preserve any common-law duty to creditors.[211] The duty remains a common-law obligation. It does this by displacing the general enlightened shareholder duty in subs (1) in circumstances where the common-law duty to creditors will apply. This particular duty was discussed above at para 3.3.1. The problem we have is the familiar question, which we have discussed above – i.e., when exactly does the duty to consider the interests of creditors kick in? The Explanatory Notes to the Companies Act 2006 refer to a situation where the company nears insolvency (see para 332). That clearly indicates a point in time when the company is not exactly insolvent, but, beyond that, it leaves matters vague. That state of affairs is not attractive to those practitioners advising directors who are looking for a clear steer.

3.9 STEWARDSHIP GOVERNANCE IN A GLOBAL BUSINESS WORLD

There is a natural tendency on the part of lawyers to consider stewardship issues in a purely national context. From a practitioner's perspective, that is perfectly understandable. But that ignores the reality of modern business, much of which has a truly global dimension. Regulators, in the widest sense of the word, must recognize this reality.

The courts have made positive steps here to respond to the challenge. They have allowed English law substantive provisions and procedures to be applied to directors who base themselves outside the jurisdiction. Thus, in *Re Seagull Manufacturing Co Ltd*,[212] procedures for the investigation and disqualifica-

[211] The discussion here draws upon the arguments put forward by Andrew Keay in his paper at the ILA Academic Group colloquium held at Luton Hoo on 21 March 2012. Further details can be found on the ILA website. For recent judicial discussion see *Re Bilta UK Ltd* [2012] EWHC 2163 (Ch), [2012] STC 2424 per Morritt C at paras [33] and [37].

[212] [1993] BCC 241.

tion[213] of company officers were made applicable to non-resident directors of an English company, who were based in a friendly jurisdiction. Again in *Re Howard Holdings Inc*,[214] the English courts held that wrongful trading proceedings could in principle be used against non-resident directors of a foreign company that was being wound up under English law. Disqualification measures can also be taken against a foreign company that is being wound up here.[215] This is an interesting development because the basic rule is that directors' duties are to be determined by the law of the place of incorporation[216] – but once a foreign company becomes subject to the English winding-up jurisdiction, new responsibilities can be generated. Key provisions, such as the sections on fraudulent trading[217] and transactional avoidance,[218] have been given extraterritorial effect.

There is also the related issue of ensuring that those who have shown themselves to be unfit as stewards do not simply move jurisdiction and perpetuate bad stewardship in another country. The Irish took prompt action to mitigate this threat in s. 42 of the Company Law Enforcement Act 2001 by providing for the disqualification in Ireland of individuals who had previously been disqualified in other jurisdictions.[219] In the UK the Companies Act 2006 addresses this issue in Part 40. So under s. 1184 of the Companies Act 2006 the Secretary of State can make regulations to disqualify in the UK a person who is subject to foreign restrictions as defined by s. 1182. It is stressed in s. 1187 that any such regulations may also deprive a person of the benefit of limited liability. This is a positive reform that ushers in a more harmonized approach towards those who abuse limited liability status.

3.10 STEWARDSHIP AND THE DISTRESSED LLP

This section looks at the responsibilities of those who manage distressed LLPs. The LLP first appeared in English law through the instrumentality of the Limited Liability Partnerships Act 2000.[220] According to official statistics,

---

213 *Re Seagull Manufacturing Co Ltd (No. 2)* [1993] BCC 833.

214 [1998] BCC 549.

215 See the *obiter* observations of Mervyn Davies J in *Re Eurostem Maritime Ltd* 1987 PCC 190.

216 *Base Metal Trading Ltd v Shamurin* [2004] EWCA Civ 1316, [2005] BCC 325.

217 *Re Bilta (UK) Ltd* [2012] EWHC 2163 (Ch), [2012] STC 2424.

218 *Re Paramount Airways Ltd (No. 2)* [1992] 3 WLR 690.

219 See A. O'Neill (2007) 18 ICCLR 166.

220 As supplemented by the LLP Regulations 2001 (SI 2001/1090). For an account see G. Morse (ed.) *Palmers Limited Liability Partnership Law* (2nd ed., 2011).

there are now some 49 000 LLPs operating in the UK, mainly in the professional services sector. We have had some 10 years of experience of LLPs and not surprisingly there have been a number of failures.[221]

The governance system for LLPs has been described as customized because of the flexibility offered by the LLP agreement.[222] That said, basic rules of stewardship as discussed above apply to a degree to those who manage LLPs. This is done by the legislative device of converting references to 'directors' to 'members'. We also have a concept of shadow members.[223] As a floating charge can be created by an LLP, there is the potential for banks to carry out a monitoring role similar to that undertaken (or some would say not undertaken) in relation to companies. These rules are made applicable to LLPs with suitable modification by virtue of the LLP Regulations 2001 (as amended).[224] However, the statutory list of duties demanded of company directors and found in ss. 170–77 of the Companies Act 2006 is not made applicable by the translational mechanism of the LLPs (Application of the Companies Act 2006) Regulations 2009 (SI 2009/1804). To some extent this is compensated for by applying certain partnership stewardship standards, but these have their limitations in the context of a modern business organization.[225] Moreover, any fiduciary duties owed by LLP members are owed to the LLP itself and not to fellow members, unless there is express provision imposing such fiduciary obligations.[226] One provision in the 2006 Act that does apply in amended form is s. 1157 – this is curious to say the least, but not entirely unexpected in view of the unsophisticated way in which companies legislation has been imported into LLP law.

So, for instance, in the context of wrongful trading s. 214 is modified by Reg 5 and Sched 3. The effect of this is to equate LLP members with the posi-

---

[221] For reported litigation in this context see *Feetum v Levy* [2005] EWCA Civ 1601, [2006] BCC 340 and *Re Halliwells LLP* [2010] EWHC 2036 (Ch), [2011] BCC 57.

[222] See *F & C Alternative Investments v Barthelemy (No. 2)* [2011] EWHC 1731 (Ch), [2012] 3 WLR 10 at [211] per Sales J.

[223] See Reg 2 of the 2001 LLP Regulations (SI 2001/1090).

[224] SI 2001/1090.

[225] For example there is no statutory duty to exercise reasonable care in management in partnership law and certainly no equivalent of the stakeholder duty found in s. 172 of the Companies Act 2006. The duty not to make a private profit is given a more generous interpretation in partnership law (*Aas v Benham* [1891] 2 Ch 244) as opposed to company law (*O'Donnell v Shanahan* [2009] EWCA Civ 751, [2009] BCC 822).

[226] *F & C Alternative Investments v Barthelemy* [2011] EWHC 1731 (Ch), [2012] 3 WLR 10 per Sales J at para [213], *Brown v InnovatorOne plc* [2012] EWHC 1321 (Comm) at para [1304] per Hamlen J. An appeal is pending in respect of this latter case – see [2012] EWCA Civ 1587.

tion of company directors under the unmodified version of s. 214. This provision also applies to shadow members of an LLP.

In addition, we have a discrete and novel provision in the form of s. 214A of the Insolvency Act 1986.[227] This provides a facility under which a liquidator of an insolvent LLP can claw back capital withdrawals (in any form) made within the two years prior to the commencement of the insolvent liquidation. As far as the author knows, there has been no reported instance of s. 214A being invoked with success.[228] One reason for this may be the fact that it requires the LLP to enter insolvent liquidation. Entry into administration will not enable a s. 214A claim to be brought, unless administration is then followed by liquidation.

Members of an LLP are also subject to the director disqualification regime as discussed above.[229]

---

[227] Introduced by Reg 5(2) and Sched 3 of the 2001 Regulations. See D. Milman [2001] Ins Law 178 and F. Payne (2005) 18 Ins Intell 104.

[228] There was speculation that the circumstances underpinning the widely discussed collapse of the major law firm Halliwells (which went into administration in 2010) might generate such a claim but, in spite of the company entering liquidation in late 2011, no such claim appears to have been made. The claims by the liquidators against certain LLP members seem instead to have focused upon alleged breach of duty. This may be because the contentious reverse premium transaction fell outside the timescale envisaged by s. 214A. Currently an attempt is being made to resolve these issues through a process of mediation. The Halliwells affair is covered widely in *The Lawyer*, with the most recent position with regard to the now adjourned mediation being outlined in its piece of 30 November 2012.

[229] For a customized account see Chapter 11 of G. Morse (ed.), *Palmer's Limited Liability Partnership Law* (2nd ed., 2011).

4. Governance post formal insolvency regime commencement

4.1 INTRODUCTION

This central chapter will consider the relationships that exist between insolvency practitioners (IPs), corporate management and various interested stakeholder groups once formal insolvency proceedings have commenced.

Mechanisms designed to control the actions of IPs will be evaluated in the light of the stewardship relationship created when an IP takes up office. These mechanisms include formal legal rules (whether imposed by statute, secondary legislation or created through common-law processes) and self-regulatory standards. The study will cover a wide range of aspects of corporate insolvency practice.

4.2 ADVENT OF INSOLVENCY: TRANSITIONAL ISSUES

Once a formal insolvency process commences, this will in effect involve a transfer of stewardship between the directors and the incoming insolvency practitioner(s). It has been said that a liquidator is in effect a substitute for the board of directors.[1] On one level, that is a fair characterization, provided it is understood that there are differences in the nature of the stewardship undertaken. These will be summarized in Chapter 6. What is clear is that in anticipation of this formal transition, the directors must not commence the process of winding up the company on an informal basis.[2] It is not the role of company directors to wind down an insolvent business; that is a matter for an independent professional with the appropriate experience. One ground for the judicial

[1] See *Re Berkeley Applegate Ltd (No. 2)* [1989] Ch 32 at 44 per Edward Nugee QC.

[2] *Re Ipcon Fashions Ltd* [1989] 5 BCC 733, *Re Perfectair Holdings Ltd* [1989] 5 BCC 837. See also the comments of Rimer LJ in the Court of Appeal in *HMRC v Rochdale Drinks Distributors Ltd* [2011] EWCA Civ 1116, [2012] BPIR 1604 at para [100].

criticism of the directors in *Macpherson v European Strategic Bureau*[3] was that they were in effect seeking to implement an informal winding-up of the company. It should also be made clear that entry into a formal insolvency regime could be important for stakeholders such as employees whose rights may well depend upon formal insolvency initiation.[4]

Once insolvency proceedings have begun the directors will be subject to an obligation to provide a statement of affairs[5] – this is both an important informational tool and a symbolic transitional benchmark that clearly indicates a change in the balance of power. A raft of criminal law obligations found in ss. 206–11 of the Insolvency Act 1986 are also triggered. So, for instance, under s. 208 of the 1986 Act there is a positive duty to provide information. As the court made clear in *R v McCredie*,[6] the duty to deliver up documents is not a once and for all requirement but a *continuing* obligation. The duty to cooperate is also reinforced by s. 235 of the Insolvency Act 1986.

The commencement of an insolvency regime has no effect on the legal personality of the company[7] – that will survive until the company is finally dissolved. Limitation of action issues can arise with regard to extant causes of action that may be available against the company, but the courts have successfully addressed these. The general position arrived at is that the clock stops on liquidation[8] as the leave of the court will be required to continue a claim once liquidation commences. But if the company is insolvent, to wait until the liquidation is completed seems a fruitless exercise. There is more uncertainty about the position on administration.[9] Equally the general rule is that company contracts survive this transition, with the exception perhaps of contracts of personal service.[10]

---

3 [2002] BCC 39 at para [48] per Chawick LJ.

4 See Employment Rights Act 1996 s. 183 and *SoS for BIS v Coward* [2011] BCC 712. Also see Pensions Act 2004 s. 121 and *Re Olympic Airlines SA* [2012] EWHC 1413 (Ch), [2012] BPIR 1163.

5 See for example Insolvency Act 1986 s. 131 (power of provisional liquidator to require statement). It is an offence to provide a false statement of affairs containing material omissions – ibid. s. 210. See also s.47 (administrative receivership) and Sched B1 para 48 (administration).

6 [2000] 2 BCLC 438.

7 See for confirmation Insolvency Act 1986 s. 87(2) and *Moss Steamship Co v Whinney* [1912] AC 263.

8 *Re General Rolling Stock Co* (1872) LR 7 Ch App 646.

9 In *Re Maxwell Fleet and Facilities Management Ltd* [1999] 2 BCLC 721 and *Re Leyland Print Co* [2010] EWHC 2105 (Ch), [2011] BCC 358 the courts ruled that the clock does not stop on administration. But both cases related to old-style administration and the reasoning placed great emphasis on the differences with liquidation. One wonders whether similar reasoning could be applied to new-style administration.

10 See *Chapman's Case* (1866) LR 1 Eq 346.

The switch towards a formal insolvency regime may also have certain implications for property ownership. By virtue of s. 144 of the Insolvency Act 1986, a liquidator is under a duty to take custody of company property. But, unlike in the case of bankruptcy law,[11] there is no automatic vesting of the legal title to such property in the liquidator. Vesting will only occur if the liquidator seeks that outcome under s. 145, but that rarely happens. In all cases, however, the liquidator is charged to perform the so-called statutory trust.[12] Similar arrangements operate in cases of company property on administration.[13] The liquidator will take possession of all company property (such as existing contracts) subject to any impediments.[14]

On receivership we see a firming-up of the latent equitable interest of the debenture holder, which was created when the security was given by the debtor company in return for finance.[15] A receiver will be installed as agent[16] of the company and thus there is no change in the occupation of its property, even if the company later goes into liquidation.[17] For CVAs there is no change in property ownership, though the terms of the arrangement may place certain assets in trust[18] for participating creditors and sums collected under the arrangement will normally be held on exclusively trust for such creditors[19] by the CVA supervisor.

In a compulsory liquidation the liquidator, who will be chosen by creditors, will be appointed after the winding order is granted.[20] Normally the official receiver (a public official) will be designated as the first liquidator,[21] with a private practitioner only being appointed if there is something of value in the estate to be realized. On the appointment of a liquidator the powers of directors cease.[22]

---

11 Insolvency Act 1986 s. 306.

12 *Ayerst v C & K Construction Ltd* [1976] AC 167. See R. Mokal (2008) 21 Ins Intell 129 and his article in [2008] 20 SAc LJ 495.

13 See Insolvency Act 1986 Sched B1 para 67 (duty to take custody).

14 *Quadmost Ltd v Reprotech (Pebsham) Ltd* [2001] BPIR 241.

15 Thus it is clear that the appointment of a receiver does not involve the disposition of company property for the purposes of s. 127 of the Insolvency Act 1986. Any such disposition would have occurred when the security was granted to the debenture holder – see *Sowman v David Samuel Trust Ltd* [1978] 1 WLR 22.

16 See D. Milman (1981) 44 MLR 658. For recent judicial consideration of the nature of this curious agency relationship see *Mills v Birchall* [2008] EWCA Civ 385, [2008] BCC 471, *Edenwest Ltd v CMS Cameron McKenna* [2012] EWHC 1258 (Ch).

17 See *Re Beck Foods Ltd* [2001] EWCA Civ 1934, [2002] BPIR 665.

18 See *Re Leisure Study Group Ltd* [1994] 2 BCLC 65.

19 *Re N.T. Gallagher & Sons Ltd* [2002] EWCA Civ 404, [2002] 1 WLR 2380, [2002] BCC 867.

20 Insolvency Act 1986 s. 139(3).

21 Ibid. s. 136(2).

22 See *Fowler v Broad's Patent Night Light Co* [1893] 1 Ch 724 and *Re Farrow's*

Indeed, the management powers of the directors may be sidelined at an earlier stage by the appointment of a provisional liquidator.[23] Such an appointment is possible under s. 135 of the Insolvency Act 1986 once the winding-up petition is presented. Although the courts have become more disposed towards this remedy in recent years, they are naturally reluctant to take this step, as it involves prejudging the outcome of the winding-up petition. In *HMRC v Rochdale Drinks Distributors Ltd*,[24] the Court of Appeal highlighted this reluctance, but still concluded that the appointment on the facts of that case was clearly the appropriate step. A provisional liquidator will be appointed where there is some suspicion of fraud or the assets of the company are perceived to be at risk.[25] The fact that the petition is disputed does not rule out a provisional liquidator.[26] An appointment may even be made on an *ex parte* basis, though this can trigger resentment.[27] The provisional liquidator in effect will perform an attenuated caretaking role focusing upon preservation of business and assets until the underlying petition is resolved.[28] No realization of assets is anticipated. The business may be continued by using a special manager.[29] Powers of investigation may be deployed. As an alternative to appointing a provisional liquidator, the courts might as a matter of general principle possibly instead accept legally binding undertakings from the directors as to future conduct. However, this less intrusive scenario is rarely

---

Bank Ltd [1921] 2 Ch 164. This is spelled out by legislation in the case of a CVL – s. 103 of the Insolvency Act 1986. In the case of a winding-up order, contracts of employment are automatically terminated – *Midland Counties District Bank v Allwood* [1905] 1 Ch 35.

23 *Re Mawcon Ltd* [1969] 1 WLR 78.

24 [2011] EWCA Civ 1116, [2011] BPIR 1604. See also *Re Highfield Commodities Ltd* [1984] 3 All ER 885, where the appointment was made on a public interest petition. In *SoS for BIS v Top Choice Wholesale Ltd* [2012] EWHC 1262 (Ch), a provisional liquidator was appointed by HHJ Hodge QC on a s. 124A petition notwithstanding an extant creditor petition. For another successful application for a provisional liquidator see *MHMH Ltd v Carwood Barker Holdings* [2004] EWHC 3174 (Ch), [2005] BCC 536, [2005] BPIR 601. Compare *Re Namco UK Ltd* [2003] EWHC 989 (Ch), [2003] BPIR 1170.

25 See generally Sealy and Milman's *Annotated Guide to Insolvency Legislation* (15th ed., 2012) Vol. 1 at 143.

26 *Re TAG Capital Venture* [2012] EWHC 1631 (Ch).

27 We might cite here the case of Abbey Forwarding, where the appointment of provisional liquidators on an *ex parte* basis has been the subject of considerable comment – see *Daily Telegraph*, 1 December 2012. See also the unsuccessful misfeasance claims against the directors – *Abbey Forwarding v Hone* [2012] EWHC 2029 (Ch).

28 See *Ashborder BV v Green Gas Power* [2005] EWHC 1031 (Ch), [2005] 1 BCLC 623.

29 See Insolvency Act 1986 s. 177. See *Re US Ltd* [1984] 1 BCC 98,985, *Re Highfield Commodities Ltd* (supra).

encountered. If there are serious doubts about the integrity of company management, this intermediate step is not likely to appeal to the court.

In order to prevent abuse in cases of CVL, s. 166(2) provides that the powers of a liquidator appointed by members are not fully operational until the creditors have made known their views on the choice of liquidator.[30] This provision is one of a number of mechanisms designed to discourage the abusive practice known as 'Centrebinding'.

Once an administrator is appointed, the managerial powers of directors are superseded.[31] They are not removed from office as such (unless the administrator so decides[32]), but are in effect rendered *functus officio*.

In cases of administrative receivership, although the directors are not formally displaced, they will be subordinated to the control of the receiver.[33] There has been some discussion as to whether any residual powers (such as the power to litigate on behalf of the company) survive[34] – the answer to this conundrum would appear to be that their powers do in theory survive,[35] though for all practical purposes it is the administrative receiver who is in the driving seat because such residual powers cannot be exercised if they might disrupt the conduct of the receivership. Such a receivership is seen as a form of prospective stewardship which the debenture holder bargained for when taking its security in return for the provision of finance to the company.

The position of directors under a CVA is different because of the unusual debtor in possession feature that is so characteristic of that particular corporate insolvency regime. They retain their day-to-day managerial powers, but manage the company subject to the terms of the CVA, which they have agreed with the creditors. This will usually only involve the making of regular payments to the supervisor, but other managerial restrictions may be imposed, for example salary curbs. On the other hand, the fact that a company is oper-

---

30 This is one of a number of provisions designed to combat the abuse of Centrebinding, named after *Re Centrebind Ltd* [1967] 1 WLR 377. Centrebinding involved putting insolvent companies into CVL without giving creditors their proper say in the appointment of liquidator and how the winding-up (particularly any disposition of assets) should be conducted.

31 This would seem to follow from Insolvency Act 1986 Sched B1 paras 64 and 68.

32 See ibid. Sched B1 para 61. Note *Newtherapeutics Ltd v Katz* [1991] Ch 226.

33 *Meigh v Wickenden* [1942] 2 KB 160.

34 Compare *Newhart Developments v Cooperative Commercial Bank* [1978] QB 814 with *Tudor Grange Holdings Ltd v Citibank NA* [1992] Ch 53. For the position in Ireland see *Lascomme v UDT Ireland Ltd* [1994] 1 ILRM 227. For discussion see M. Hemsworth [1999] Ins Law 92. The Cork Committee (Cmnd 8558) para 1730 favoured the continuance of residual directorial powers.

35 So for example that they can oppose a winding-up petition – *Re Reprographic Exports (Euromat) Ltd* (1978) 122 Sols Jo 400.

ating under the terms of a CVA is not publicly advertised. This lack of transparency is unusual in UK corporate insolvency law, where the public interest normally requires transparency. Furthermore, the supervisor will not wish to become too actively involved in the day-to-day management of the company for fear of incurring liability as a shadow director (see the discussion above in Chapter 1). In effect, the supervisor acts as an income collector and guardian of the CVA contract. That said, the nominee will have taken some responsibility for assessing the viability of what the directors are proposing to their creditors.[36] The role does not extend to seeking to obtain a deal for unsecured creditors, which is better than the one embodied in the CVA.[37] The court also cannot change the terms of a CVA.[38] A CVA supervisor is carrying out an agreed role and does not have general licence to champion the rights of unsecured creditors or to put pressure on directors to go beyond the terms of the agreed arrangement. The supervisor may be obliged to terminate the CVA if things are not working out.

4.3 PROFESSIONAL QUALIFICATION, APPOINTMENT, OFFICIAL GUIDANCE AND DISCIPLINE OF IPS

Until 1985 there was no formal legal requirement that all insolvency practitioners be professionally qualified. In fairness, in the context of stewardship relationships this apparent latitude was not uncommon. However, in the wake of a number of high-profile scandals involving misconduct by unqualified liquidators, the Cork Committee[39] called for the introduction of compulsory professional licensing. That recommendation was adopted by the Insolvency Act 1986 for most insolvency procedures.[40] Insolvency practitioners these days are members of recognized professional bodies. The introduction of this monopoly stewardship right has undoubtedly been of benefit to the profession; it has also led to improved standards of stewardship.

---

[36] See s. 2 of Insolvency Act 2000 amending various provisions in Part 1 of Insolvency Act 1986.

[37] On this limitation see *Appleyard v Ritecrown Ltd* [2007] EWHC 3515 (Ch), [2009] BPIR 235.

[38] See *Re Beloit Walmsley Ltd* [2008] EWHC 1888 (Ch), [2008] BPIR 1445.

[39] Cmnd 8558 para 758.

[40] But there is no need for a licensed insolvency practitioner to manage a Law of Property Act 1925 receivership, nor to implement a scheme of arrangement under Part 26 of the Companies Act 2006. In the latter instance, the company may not necessarily be insolvent. LPA receivers have their own professional organization which uses the acronym NARA (Non Administrative Receivers Association).

This is a twofold process that requires all IPs firstly to be qualified. The core provisions here are to be found in Part XIII of the Insolvency Act 1986 but are also scattered liberally across the Act (see for example para 6 of Sched B1). Under s. 396 an Insolvency Practitioners Tribunal is established to deal with disputes over licensing, but this rarely sits.[41] Note that under s. 389 it is a criminal offence to act if not qualified. Prosecutions are, however, rare. One advantage of this exclusive system is that insolvency practitioners are required to lodge a financial bond on taking up office.[42] Although there have been some difficulties recently concerning the timely provision of bonds,[43] this is in stark contrast to the latitude afforded to those individuals who assume the stewardship of a limited company in their capacity as a company director. No minimum capital needs to be put up by them. Insolvency practitioners are expected to undertake continuing professional development with the requirements here being spelled out by Sched 2 of the Insolvency Practitioners Regulations 2005 (SI 2005/524).

Corporations cannot by virtue of s. 390(1) be appointed as insolvency office-holders.[44] This may again be seen as a gesture towards accountability, but it does cause significant practical difficulties. Corporations are not banned from acting as trustees or even as charitable trustees (see Charities Act 2011 s. 251).

A bankrupt cannot act as an office-holder (see Insolvency Act 1986 s. 390(4)). Nor can a person who is the subject of a debt relief order or a bankruptcy restrictions order. But a person undergoing an IVA is not formally debarred under the Act, and this is one attraction of going down that particular personal insolvency route. However, the firm of which such individual is a member may have qualms about allowing such a person to take up insolvency office.

Banks play a role in the office-holder appointment regime by operating a panel system. Firms of insolvency practitioners may have to bid to be included on the panel. This may limit competition but may also serve both as a quality control tool and a way of keeping costs down.

---

41 See generally R. Clements and G. Broadbent (1987) 3 IL & P 34. According to a Freedom of Information request granted in July 2011, this tribunal had heard only one case in the previous five years.

42 See G. Todd and S. Dood (2006) 19 Ins Intell 129. For a more up-to-date survey note J. Tribe and S. Hunt (2012) 25 Ins Intell 37. For claims on bonds see *Hellard and Goldfarb v Money and Robbins* [2008] BPIR 1487.

43 See *2011 Annual Insolvency Service Report on Insolvency Practitioner Regulation* (2012) at p. 4.

44 See *Portman Building Society v Gallwey* [1955] 1 All ER 227. It follows therefore that a firm of insolvency practitioners is not the proper defendant to a claim arising out of the insolvency – *Ramsay and Maclaine v Leonard Curtis (A Firm)* [2001] BPIR 389.

In terms of the mechanics of appointment, that will depend upon the precise insolvency regime involved. If disputes arise as to rival nominees, in the absence of any factor disqualifying one nominee, the court will often support the nomination of the insolvency practitioner who enjoys greater creditor support. This eminently sensible 'tie breaker' solution was adopted by Morgan J in *Healthcare Management Services Ltd v Caremark Properties Ltd.*[45]

In addition, the regulated professional requirement exposes IPs to a regime of professional discipline. Each of the regulatory organizations will have its own set of professional standards, which will be strictly enforced.[46] Such disciplinary proceedings themselves may be subject to judicial scrutiny.[47] There are also guidelines and ethical codes which seek to eliminate significant conflicts of interest.[48] The Statements of Insolvency Practice (SIPs) produced by the Joint Insolvency Committee (which was set up in 1999 and comprises representatives of the RPBs and the competent authorities) provide a valuable structure highlighting good practice.[49] These SIPs are summarized in Appendix II of this work. Although not technically having the force of law, they do have a quasi-legal currency and certainly have relevance in any disciplinary context. For instance, a 'prepack' sale of assets (see later) conducted in compliance with SIP 16 is likely to get the green light from the court.[50] Conversely, where a prepack has been conducted without complying with SIP 16, the insolvency practitioner involved is exposed to criticism. The basic governance principle of 'comply or explain' will come into play.

Guidance on stewardship requirements can come from other sources. For example, for many years the Insolvency Service has produced hands-on advice on tricky issues through the medium of its 'Dear IP' communications published on the Insolvency Service website several times each year. So, for example, in Dear IP No. 55 of September 2012, insolvency practitioners are offered guidance on the ethics of seeking to obtain appointment through the

---

45 [2012] EWHC 1693 (Ch).

46 See the *Annual Review of Insolvency Practitioner Regulation* (2011), where a number of individuals are named and shamed.

47 See for example *R v ICA ex parte Eliades* [2001] BPIR 363 (disciplinary proceedings after JIMU visit), *Mond v ACCA* [2005] EWHC 1414 (Admin), [2006] BPIR 94 (flawed disciplinary proceedings).

48 For the IPA Code of Ethics and its treatment of conflicts of interest see the comments of Proudman J in *Doffman and Isaacs v Wood and Hellard* [2011] EWHC 4008 (Ch), [2012] BPIR 972 at para [25].

49 There are now 15 SIPs dealing with a wide range of operational matters. SIP 1 explains their overall purpose.

50 See for example *Re Halliwells LLP* [2010] EWHC 2036 (Ch), [2011] BCC 57.

use of online introducers. Organizations such as the HMRC[51] and the Pensions Regulator[52] sometimes weigh in with important guidance.

4.4 COMPLAINTS PROCEDURES AND OUTCOMES

This has become the focus of attention in recent times with the Insolvency Practices Council expressing some disquiet in its 2009 Annual Report. Insolvency legislation does not provide a self-contained complaints procedure as such, though it does make available mechanisms under which complaints about office-holders can be addressed through litigation – more of this angle later. There is, however, a possibility of pursuing complaints under the various self-regulatory regimes operated by the RPBs.[53] Valuable research on this regulatory aspect has been carried out on behalf of the Insolvency Practices Council[54] by Adrian Walters and Mary Seneviratne.[55] The main conclusions of these important studies are that the current system is uncoordinated, compares unfavourably with that operating in other professions and lacks adequate remedial mechanisms. In the light of these observations the call to revisit the possibility of an Insolvency Ombudsman was hardly surprising.

It must be remembered that many liquidations are managed by the official receivers acting out of the Insolvency Service. There is an in-house complaints procedure here involving an independent adjudicator. Full details are to be found on the Insolvency Service website. Ultimately, a complaint routed through this portal could end up before the Parliamentary Ombudsman. The author is aware of one or two such complaints of maladministration going to the Ombudsman, with one complaint being upheld in part.[56]

The 2011 Insolvency Service Report on the Regulation of Insolvency Practitioners provides a valuable indicator on how complaints are

---

[51] See for example the Crown Statement of 7 September 2005 post the ruling in *Nat West Bank v Spectrum Plus Ltd* [2005] UKHL 41.

[52] See for example the 'Nortel guidance' given on 26 July 2012.

[53] For an insider perspective on how this complaints procedure works see W. Trower [2009] (November) 3–4 Digest 24.

[54] Unfortunately, the IPC agreed to dissolve itself in 2012 in the wake of the Government's response to the Insolvency Service consultation on governance and regulation of the insolvency profession. See the IPC's letter to stakeholders dated 8 March 2012 and available in Dear IP 53.

[55] See *Complaints Handling in the UK Insolvency Practitioner Profession* (2008) – a follow-up report has also been published – *Complaints Handling by the Regulators of Insolvency Practitioners: A Comparative Study* (2009).

[56] See *Insolvency Service Annual Report and Accounts 2011/12* (HC 358) at 25.

handled.[57] Apart from naming and shaming those individuals who have fallen short of required professional standards, this report gives an indication of the range of sanctions that can be deployed by RPBs, though it is only the Insolvency Service that can remove a licence to act.

In general, however, there is, unfortunately, no Insolvency Ombudsman regime in place to deal with complaints against private sector practitioners, in spite of a recommendation from the Cork Committee[58] that one be established. We return to this lacuna in our concluding chapter.

4.5 STEWARDSHIP OBLIGATIONS OF OFFICE-HOLDERS AT COMMON LAW

It has long been recognized that those who control insolvent estates, and realize and then distribute[59] the proceeds, should be subjected to special stewardship obligations.

Many insolvency practitioners will have been appointed by the court and so become *officers of the court*. As such, they are subject to its inherent jurisdiction[60] and owe a general obligation to keep the court informed as to their handling of funds of an insolvent estate.[61] Indeed there is a general requirement to keep the court informed as to all relevant matters, as was emphasized by David Richards J in *Re TAG Capital Venture*.[62]

Perhaps the most obvious component flowing from court officer status is the requirement to act honourably. The honour principle emerged from the well-known bankruptcy precedent of *Ex parte James*.[63] The principle will apply in the case of corporate insolvency to liquidators in a compulsory liquidation[64] and administrators (who are deemed to be officers of the court, no

---

57 See also *OFT Market Survey* (June 2010) at paras 1.27 and 5.32, where the current complaints system is subject to critical analysis.

58 Cmnd 8558 para 1772.

59 On this distribution angle, see D. Milman, Chapter 8 in W. van Boom and J. Steele (eds), *Mass Justice: Challenges of Representation and Distribution* (2011).

60 On this see *Maltby Holdings Ltd v Spratt* [2012] EWHC 4 (Ch).

61 See *Burton (Liquidator of Callanish Ltd): Re Audit of His Accounts and Intromissions* [2012] CSOH 167 at para [8] per Lord Hope.

62 [2012] EWHC 1631 (Ch).

63 (1874) LR 9 Ch App 609. For discussion see I. Dawson [1996] JBL 437.

64 See Insolvency Rules 1986 r. 4.179(1). On whether the rule applies in Scotland see *Clark and Whitehouse, Noters* [2012] CSOH 55 at para [56], where the court noted without demur a concession that the rule did not apply in Scotland. Official receivers fall within the rule – *Re Opera Ltd* [1891] 2 Ch 154, *Re Wyvern Developments Ltd* [1974] 1 WLR 1097 per Templeman J at 1105.

matter how appointed[65]). Supervisors of CVAs may possibly fall under this rule, though there is considerable doubt about this matter.[66] Conversely, administrative receivers are not covered by this rule; that is logical. The most disputed issue is whether a liquidator in a creditors' voluntary liquidation is also subject to the duty to act honourably. The authorities here do not speak with one voice, but, on balance, the rule probably does not apply.[67] This would be the logical conclusion and its force is strengthened by the fact that the courts tend to view the rule of honour as an anachronism in modern conditions, with the result that there is no real appetite to extend its scope. This scepticism is well reflected by the comments of Newey J in *Alitalia Linee Aeree Italian SpA*.[68]

Does it really matter whether the *ex parte James* rule is made applicable or not? In most cases, whether the rule of honour applies or not is of marginal significance. This is because in many instances the particular matter at issue will be covered by specific regulation[69] or by common-law restitutionary principles[70] or by professional etiquette. In other cases, it seems that even if the duty to act honourably is applied, it is subordinated to the overriding obligation to maximize returns for creditors, even if this involves the IP acting in an opportunistic fashion.[71] Officers of the court should not be motivated to act on the basis of sympathy where there is no credible legal justification, as Mann J was at pains to point out in *Re Farepak Food and Gifts Ltd*.[72] Utilitarian senti-

65 Insolvency Act 1986 Sched B1 para 5. See also *Re Movitex Ltd* [1992] BCC 101 and *Re Maltby Investments Ltd* [2012] EWHC 4 (Ch).

66 Support for the rule applying can be found by analogy with *King v Anthony* [1999] BPIR 73 (IVA supervisor). But this case is questioned by D. Milman in *Personal Insolvency Law, Regulation and Policy* (2005) at 79. CVA supervisors are office-holders for the limited purposes of s. 233 of the Insolvency Act 1986 but not generally (s. 231). However, that is a separate status distinct from being an officer of the court.

67 See *Re TH Knitwear Ltd* [1988] Ch 275. Compare *Re John Bateson & Co Ltd* [1985] BCLC 259. But the position may be different if the CVL follows on immediately after an administration – *Re Agrimarche Ltd* [2010] EWHC 1655 (Ch), [2011] 1 BCLC 1.

68 [2011] EWHC 15 (Ch), [2011] 1 BCLC 606 at para [47].

69 The Insolvency Regulations 1994 (SI 1994/2507) (as amended) and the Insolvency Practitioner Regulations 2005 (SI 2005/524) (as amended) are immensely detailed.

70 See *Re Japan Leasing Europe plc* [1999] BPIR 911. Ian Dawson has gone so far as to suggest that restitutionary principles have the capability of replacing the *ex parte James* rule – see [1996] JBL 437 at 460.

71 See for instance here authorities such as *Ford v Transtec Automotive (Campsie) Ltd* [2001] BCC 403.

72 [2006] EWHC 3272 (Ch), [2008] BCC 22. For judicial guidance on final distributions in the Farepak case, see the judgment of Warren J reported in [2009] EWHC 2580 (Ch), [2010] BCC 735.

ments dictating efficient realization of assets tend to prevail over ethical qualms about opportunism. In a sense this assertion is reflected by the outcome in the *Wedgwood Museum Trust* case,[73] even though there was no specific reference to the obligation to act honourably. Here it was held by HHJ Purle that the administrators of a charitable company, which included among its assets a valuable Wedgwood pottery collection that had been gifted to it, were entitled to sell that pottery to generate funds to repay creditors. The pottery had not been gifted to the company on trust. Although the collection was of immense importance in terms of our cultural heritage, the administrators had to act in accordance with the law and to exploit the assets to satisfy the legitimate claims of creditors. The debts in this case included significant group obligations in respect of a deficit in pension funds. In later proceedings[74] in this case, however, the administrators suffered a setback in that although they had been correct in seeking directions, they were not allowed to recover their full legal costs as they had, according to the court, unnecessarily engaged leading counsel. The profession is still mulling over the implications of this consequential ruling. Where the duty to act honourably could be relevant is that it could provide some defence to an officer whose actions were being challenged by disgruntled stakeholders by enabling an officer to justify contentious actions on the basis that it was the right thing to do.[75] An obligation thus becomes a shield.

More generally, can office-holders be classed as fiduciaries? The answer to this in all cases (whether or not 'officer of the court' status applies) would appear to be in the affirmative.[76] This conclusion of course would put them on a par with company directors. The particular consequences of this status for insolvency practitioners are that:

---

[73] [2011] EWHC 3782 (Ch). See also *Amble Assets v Longbenton Foods* [2011] EWHC 1943 (Ch), where the court indicated that an administrator could rely on contractual rights even in circumstances where this might be seen as unfair.

[74] *Re Wedgwood Museum Trust* [2012] EWHC 1974 (Ch). In so deciding, HHJ Purle indicated at para [32] that as officers of the court they should exercise economy. He drew support for this strict discipline when incurring liabilities on behalf of the estate from comments of Lord Neuberger MR in *BNY Corporate Trustee v Eurosail* [2011] EWCA Civ 227, [2011] BCC 399 at paras [102]–[105].

[75] See *Re Wyvern Developments Ltd* [1974] 1 WLR 1097 and *Re Collins & Aikman Europe SA* [2006] BCC 861. There are parallels here with the now superseded s. 309 of the Companies Act 1985 – see *Re Welfab Engineers Ltd* [1990] BCC 600.

[76] See *Re Gertzenstein* [1937] 1 Ch 115, *Oldham v Kyrris* [2003] EWCA Civ 165, [2004] BPIR 165, *Re Kimberley Scott Services* [2011] EWHC 1563 (Ch), [2012] BPIR 135.

- they should not permit a conflict of interest to arise[77]
- they should not compromise their independence,[78] for example by agreeing to fetter their powers[79] (which must be used for a proper purpose[80])
- they should not make a private profit from their position; under Insolvency Rule 4.149 any self-dealing with their associates is voidable
- they should not delegate their responsibility without proper checks.[81]

Although a liquidator is a fiduciary, he is not technically a trustee for individual creditors.[82] One reason for this, as outlined by Romer J in *Knowles v Scott*,[83] is that imposing the higher trustee standard might deter individuals from assuming the role of insolvency office-holder. One has reservations about the validity of this line of thinking, which could be applied to many professional positions these days. All professionals are exposed to litigation risk; that is a fact of professional life in the twenty-first century and this risk can be mitigated by indemnity insurance.

Turning to more specific obligations, liquidators have been held at common law under a positive duty to contact *known* creditors. This was made clear in *Pulsford v Devenish*.[84] But the position is now regulated by the provisions in the Insolvency Rules on the submission of proofs. Thus, under Insolvency Rules 1986 rule 4.73, the onus is on the creditor to submit a proof. The cost of submitting a proof is borne by the creditor (IR 4.78). The liquidator enjoys discretion under IR 11.3(3) on whether to accept late proofs. One question is whether the common-law duty to be proactive in searching out known credi-

---

77 For a full discussion see H. Anderson in A. Clarke, *Current Issues in Insolvency Law* (1991) at 12–20. Note also Insolvency Rule 4.149, for instance. It is the possibility of a conflict of interest that has concerned commentators investigating the prepack phenomenon – see P. Walton (2006) 19 Ins Intell 113. The undesirability of allowing conflicts of interest to operate is reflected by IR 2.119 and 4.108, which specify this as a ground for resignation.

78 *Re Roselmar Ltd (No. 2)* (1986) 2 BCC 99,157, *Re Ng* [1997] BCC 507.

79 This obligation explains why they cannot surrender control of the prosecution of a wrongful trading action – *Re Oasis Merchandising Services Ltd* [1998] Ch 170.

80 *Sutton v GE Capital* [2004] 2 BCLC 662.

81 For an unusual case see *Reid and Stephen, Noters* [2010] CSOH 138, where Lord Glennie commented on this issue at para [183].

82 *Leon v York-O-Matic* [1966] 1 WLR 1450 at 1453 per Plowman J. See also *Knowles v Scott* [1891] 1 Ch 717 at 723 per Romer J.

83 [1891] 1 Ch 717 at 722.

84 [1903] 2 Ch 625. See also *Re Armstrong Whitworth Securities* [1947] Ch 673 and *James Smith & Sons (Norwood) Ltd v Goodman* [1936] Ch 216.

tors has been displaced. The position in English Law is unclear,[85] but principles of stewardship might indicate that the paternalistic approach of the common law still has merit in modern conditions. Moreover, this view would appear to be consistent with the obligation imposed by Art 40(1) of the EC Regulation on Insolvency Proceedings (1346/2000).

The common law has also developed other stewardship-related obligations. For instance, the question of whether an office-holder is required to continue the business of the company once taking office has attracted some discussion. What seems clear is that there is no general obligation to continue to operate the business, which can be shut down on the office-holder taking up office if that is seen as the most appropriate course of action. The only requirement here would be that such decision was reached in good faith, as fiduciary status would dictate. For liquidators this decision to terminate the business would be the normal turn of events.[86] A liquidator should only carry on the business if it is necessary to facilitate the winding-up process, but it must be admitted that the courts would be reluctant to gainsay a professional judgement on that issue.[87] Administrators and administrative receivers might be more inclined to continue a business, but, as the Court of Appeal made clear in *Medforth v Blake*,[88] there is no obligation to do so. *Medforth*[89] was a receivership case and the Court of Appeal laid down important principles in this regard. In particular, it stressed that if a decision is taken to continue a business, that business should be operated according to standards of reasonable competence. This was an important upgrading of stewardship responsibilities, which previously had only required that the office-holder act in good faith.[90] Public confidence in the stewardship function surely demands such an approach.[91] Unfortunately, in *Edenwest Ltd v CMS Cameron McKenna*,[92] the High Court seemed

---

85 *Pulsford v Devenish* (supra) has recently been followed by Laffoy J in Ireland in *Re Unidare plc* [2012] IEHC 114.

86 See *Re Wreck Recovery and Salvage Co* (1880) 15 Ch D 353 and the comments of David Richards J in *Heis v MF Global* [2012] EWHC 3068 (Ch). If liquidators do decide to trade on, note the application of Reg 12 of the Insolvency Regulations 1994 (SI 1994/2507).

87 See *Re Great Eastern Electric Co Ltd* [1941] Ch 241.

88 [2000] Ch 86. See S. Frisby (2000) 63 MLR 413.

89 Supra. For a recent discussion of the duty of care issue see Hildyard J in *Edenwest Ltd v CMS Cameron McKenna* [2012] EWHC 1258 (Ch).

90 See the Privy Council advice in *Downsview Nominees v First City Corporation* [1993] AC 295. The timing of this ruling was unfortunate to say the least with the furore raging over the apparently heavy burden of professional fees.

91 See M.S. Wee [2008] 20 SAc LJ 559.

92 [2012] EWHC 1258 (Ch). Another first instance authority, however, *International Leisure Ltd v First National Trustee Co Ltd* [2012] EWHC 1971 (Ch), [2012] BCC 738, on one reading might suggest that *Medforth* (supra) does upgrade

prepared to retain the general approach in *Downsview*[93] by indicating that any duties in this respect are derived from equitable principles. A statutory provision stating quite clearly that receivers should display reasonable care when discharging their realization duties would be welcome.

Looking at matters in the round and with one eye on professional discipline, it can now be asserted with some confidence that insolvency practitioners should display reasonable care when discharging their office or else face the possibility of a claim in negligence.[94] So a negligent sale of assets may expose an insolvency practitioner to a liability to compensate the estate.[95] Curiously, the official receiver appears to enjoy immunity from such discipline.[96] This immunity surely cannot be justified. A duty to take reasonable care must not however be extended into a commitment to guarantee a return to creditors or that the aims of a CVA will be achieved.[97] There are many factors outside the control of insolvency practitioners (such as the state of the property market) that can skew what might appear to be a viable rescue/realization strategy.

One issue that sometimes arises concerns the question of to whom do insolvency practitioners owe duties? The answer to this is not free from confusion and may depend on which type of office-holder we are looking at. Liquidators may owe duties to unsecured creditors collectively, but certainly do not owe duties to individual creditors unless special circumstances giving rise to such duty are present. Administrators would be in the same position.[98] Administrative receivers owe duties to the company over whose assets they have been appointed and also to the debenture holder appointing them. Administrative receivers certainly do not owe legally enforceable duties to unsecured creditors.[99]

Downsview (supra). The Irish courts have struggled with the apparent tension between *Medforth* (supra) and *Downsview* (supra) – see the comments of Clarke J in *Moorview Developments v First Active plc* [2009] IEHC 214.

93 Supra.

94 This is clear for trustees in bankruptcy – see s. 304 of the Insolvency Act 1986 – but strangely less explicit in other instances. Some inkling of a comparable duty for administrators may be gleaned from para 4 of Sched B1. In Ireland receivers must display reasonable care when conducting realizations – Companies Act 1963 s. 311A. A similar provision applies in New Zealand – s. 19 of the Receiverships Act 1993.

95 *McAteer v Lismore* [2012] NICh 7, [2012] BPIR 812.

96 See *Mond v Hyde* [1998] BCC 44.

97 See *Heritage Joinery v Krasner* [1999] BPIR 683, *Pitt v Mond* [2001] BPIR 624.

98 *Oldham v Kyrris* [2003] EWCA Civ 1506, [2004] BPIR 165.

99 *Lathia v Dronsfield Brothers Ltd* [1987] BCLC 321, *International Leisure Ltd v First National Trustee Co Ltd* [2012] EWHC 1971 (Ch) at para [30] per Edward Bartley Jones QC.

The nature of the role played by an office-holder was best explained by Lord Millett in *Official Receiver v Wadge, Rapps and Hunt.*[100] In particular, Lord Millett emphasized that we are not simply talking about a crude process of realization and distribution – the role extends into matters of investigation and protection of the public interest. This is clear from s. 132 of the Insolvency Act 1986, which requires official receivers to investigate the causes of the company's failure. It is thus a multi-dimensional function. This point is often forgotten in the public debate about the professional costs incurred in liquidating a company. Liquidators cannot be expected to finance the discharge of public duties from their own pockets.

4.6 STATUTORY OBLIGATIONS

When we look at the position of insolvency practitioners dealing with distressed companies, it is important to point out that the provisions of the Companies Acts apply, unless specific exemptions are granted.[101]

Perhaps the most important requirement of stewardship is the duty to take possession of and preserve the estate. This is spelled out by legislation. So, for instance, in s. 143(1) of the Insolvency Act 1986 we find liquidators being required to get in, realize and then distribute the assets. Principles of distributive justice have been developed to facilitate this latter task; most notably the *pari passu* rule of rateable distribution when paying dividends to creditors.[102] For CVLs this fundamental rule is embodied in s. 107 of the Act, whereas for reasons that are opaque, the rule is manifested in IR 4.181(1) for compulsory liquidations. We should also note the discrete rules relating to payment of preferential claims (Insolvency Act 1986 ss. 40, 386 and 387) and the operation of the reserved fund for unsecured creditors (s. 176A). Under s. 143(2) the insolvency practitioner will in conducting these tasks be subordinated to the official receiver. The public interest in company liquidation is once again highlighted.

We can dwell on this particular responsibility and investigate what it involves. Clearly, it mandates the seizure of assets that are available for distribution amongst creditors.[103] It must be remembered that English law takes a

100 [2003] UKHL 49, [2004] 1 AC 158.

101 See *Re TXU Europe Group Ltd* [2011] EWHC 2072 (Ch), [2012] BCC 363. For one such exemption see Companies Act 2006 s. 193.

102 On the responsibilities of a liquidator here, see *Lomax Leisure Ltd v Miller* [2007] BPIR 1615.

103 The estate may be subject to prior claims. So for instance there may be exclusions under s. 426 of the Proceeds of Crime Act 2002 for certain corporate assets.

wide view of 'property' and intangible assets are included – see s. 436 of the Insolvency Act 1986 for confirmation of this fact. This has the effect of expanding the stewardship regime. A cause of action is a form of intangible asset. Should an office-holder pursue such a claim in order to realize its potential?[104] Or should a claim be assigned? There is statutory power to do so.[105] This is often one of the most difficult issues to confront an office-holder.[106] Taking legal advice is particularly important in this situation as, provided such advice is followed,[107] it will strengthen the office-holder's position in the event of a challenge. A common conundrum arises where the office-holder, having decided not to litigate, is faced with an offer to purchase the claim. This offer will sometimes come from the company directors or shareholders. If the offer is genuine and is not simply an attempt by potential defendants to stifle a claim against themselves,[108] and suitable indemnities are offered to protect the position of the insolvency practitioner, the sensible course of action is for the office-holder to accept such an offer.[109] Failure to do so could lead to a challenge by the aggrieved would-be purchaser. That said, there may be an obligation to shop around.[110] Office-holders still have residual concerns that by assigning the claim they may end up exposing themselves to a liability in costs as a third party under s. 51 of the Senior Courts Act 1981 if the claim is unsuccessfully pursued, but if there is an outright sale that concern is unlikely to materialize.[111] That said, office-holders are human, and some insolvency

---

Comparable exclusions for LLP assets are prescribed by s. 431. If liquidators go ahead and seize assets in breach of these restrictions, protection may be available under ss. 432 and 433.

[104] On the pursuit of litigation see Insolvency Act 1986 Sched 1 para 5 (administrators), Sched 4 para 4 (liquidators).

[105] Insolvency Act 1986 Sched 4 para 6 (liquidators), Sched 1 para 2 (administrators and administrative receivers). See generally *Rawnsley v Weatherall Green and Smith North Ltd* [2009] EWHC 2482 (Ch), [2010] BCC 406. The power to assign may, however, be restrained by contract – *Quadmost v Reprotech (Pebsham) Ltd* [2001] BPIR 349.

[106] It can be a problem for directors also – *Colin Gwyer Associates Ltd v London Wharf (Limehouse) Ltd* [2003] 2 BCLC 153.

[107] Compare *Re Edennote Ltd* [1996] BCC 718 (advice taken by liquidator) with *Faryab v Smith* [2001] BPIR 246 (advice not sought by trustee in bankruptcy).

[108] This issue was considered by the Court of Appeal in *Whitehouse v Wilson* [2005] EWCA Civ 1688, [2007] BPIR 230, and a range of views was expressed by members of the court as to what was the appropriate public interest in such a situation.

[109] On this issue see *Faryab v Smith* [2001] BPIR 246.

[110] See *Re Edennote Ltd* [1996] BCC 718.

[111] But see the discussion of this difficult matter in *Hunt v Harb* [2011] EWCA Civ 1239, [2012] 1 WLR 317, where the Court of Appeal (in discussing the position of a trustee in bankruptcy) made it clear that there is no absolute immunity from the risk of liability. It would appear that for liquidators the risk is even more minimal.

practitioners will inevitably worry about even remote possibilities. If the office-holder decides to settle the claim, judicial interference is unlikely.[112]

We could also note s. 132 of the Act here; this imposes an obligation on the official receiver to investigate the causes of the corporate failure in cases of compulsory liquidation.

There are other statutory obligations to note. For instance, an official receiver is under a duty to investigate the failure in cases of compulsory liquidation (s. 132 of 1986 Act). Other office-holders may in effect be subject to a de facto obligation to do likewise.[113] There is the duty to file documents.[114] There is an important whistleblowing obligation imposed by s. 7(3) of the Company Directors Disqualification Act 1986[115] in respect of directors who appear to be unfit to manage. This particular obligation, which is executed through the submission of the so-called D Report, is supplemented by SIP 4 and in July 2012 the Insolvency Service issued updated guidance to practitioners on this responsibility.[116]

One further obligation is the duty to keep separate accounts (a classic indicia of stewardship). This is well recognized in the legislative matrix.[117] Liquidators in compulsory liquidations must also make use of the Insolvency Services Account.[118] This ceased to be an obligation for liquidators in CVLs in 2004 and indeed such liquidators are now debarred from using this Account.[119]

The authorities do recognize that the discharge of obligations embodies a cost element. In an era of value for money, any obligation is ripe for review. So in 2009[120] the rules on advertising were deregulated so as to produce a potential cost saving. Discretionary advertising is now the order of the day.

Obligations may be imposed by general laws (such as the duty under s. 188 of the Trade Union and Labour Relations Act 1992 to consult when considering

---

112 See *Re Greenhaven Motors Ltd* [1997] BCC 547.

113 See *Coyne and Hardy v DRC Distributors Ltd* [2008] EWCA Civ 488, [2008] BCC 612.

114 See *Re Arctic Engineering Ltd (No. 2)* [1986] 1 WLR 686. One interesting issue concerns the duty to preserve company records after the insolvency process has completed. See SIP 17. If there is a follow-up insolvency regime, clearly such documents should be handed over – but it is less than clear what is the position on dissolution.

115 Reinforced by SIP 4.

116 See Insolvency Service website item 2 July 2012. On accessing the D Report, see *DETI v Black* [2012] NI Master 1.

117 See Insolvency Regulations 1994 (SI 1994/2507) Regs 5 and 7.

118 See Insolvency Act 1986 s. 403.

119 See Insolvency (Amendment) Regulations 2011 (SI 2011/2203).

120 See Legislative Reform (Insolvency) (Advertising Requirements) Order 2009 (SI 2009/864).

redundancies of workers[121]). Health and safety issues cannot be ignored.[122] The restrictions of competition law will continue to apply once a company enters an insolvency regime.[123] In terms of distributional matters, there is a well-established obligation to ensure that preferential claims are paid out.[124] This obligation has lost much of its significance post-2003 with the abolition of Crown preference, but it has now been supplemented by a duty to ensure that unsecured creditors receive their due out of the prescribed part.[125] It is interesting to compare these obligations with the relative freedom enjoyed by directors as to which (and when) claims of creditors should be paid. Directors (subject to the law of preference as embodied in s. 239 of the Insolvency Act 1986) enjoy greater latitude as to who should be paid. Whilst drawing comparisons we should record there is no provision directly comparable to s. 172 of the Companies Act 2006 rendered applicable to insolvency practitioners. One can see that the shareholder wealth maximization principle is irrelevant as a starting point here, but presumably that could be supplanted by a creditor benefit maximization rule. In this context it is worth recording that in Ireland receivers in effect have a duty to have regard to the interests of employees, who can access certain control procedures if this is not done.[126] This debate over whether a s. 172 duty should be applied to insolvency practitioners may be where rhetoric loses touch with reality. It must always be remembered that IPs have legally enforceable duties to employees and to the environment.

---

121 Insolvency practitioners are in the same position as directors – see *Pambakian v Brentford Nylons Ltd* [1978] ICR 665, *GMB v Rankin* [1992] IRLR 514 and *Re Hartlebury Printers Ltd* [1993] 1 All ER 470. The administrator in the Woolworths administration was found to have breached this duty – see *USDAW v WW Realisations* [2012] EWHC 2 (Misc)(ET). When an insolvency practitioner such as an administrator or administrative receiver takes up post they have 14 days to reflect on whether to adopt contracts of employment – Insolvency Act 1994 ss. 1 and 2.

122 See *Meigh v Wickenden* [1942] 2 KB 160.

123 A point made by I. Rose (2008) 1 CRI 177.

124 *Woods v Winskill* [1913] 2 Ch 303, *Westminster CC v Haste* [1950] Ch 442. In view of suggestions that insolvency practitioners were not observing this obligation, SIP 14 was introduced.

125 See Insolvency Act 1986 s. 176A as supplemented by the Insolvency Act 1986 (Prescribed Part) Order 2003 (SI 2003/2097). Note that an office-holder can seek under s. 176A(5) to have this fund disapplied on grounds of economic cost but such an application must be all or nothing – partial disapplication will not be permitted. A recent consultation exercise carried out in 2011 suggests that this provision and the calculation of the prescribed part is likely to remain unchanged in the foreseeable future.

126 See Irish Companies Act 1990 s. 171. In English law Lightman J went on record in a speech to the ILA to call for the duty then found in s. 309 of the Companies Act 1985 to be applied to insolvency office-holders – see [1996] JBL 113.

Finally, an insolvency practitioner may have responsibilities in respect of his stewardship of company property, which may in turn generate tensions with regard to similar responsibilities to creditors to maximize realizations. A perfect example of this situation is where the company holds a waste management licence imposing onerous commitments on the company to protect the environment. Should such a licence be disclaimed by the insolvency practitioner in order to maximize realizations? Is it justifiable to do this and throw the cost of protecting the environment onto the state? This very scenario arose in *Official Receiver v Environment Agency (Re Mineral Resources and Bluestone Chemicals)*,[127] where the Court of Appeal held that a waste management licence could be disclaimed. This decision will have facilitated the conduct of a winding-up, but it leaves a number of matters unresolved. One such issue concerns the impact of disclaimer upon a trust fund set up to deal with the clean-up regime. We discuss this below at para 4.8.

An insolvency practitioner has a duty to keep proper records during the period of stewardship. There may also be a duty to preserve existing company records. SIP 17 offers relevant guidance here. The question of destruction of company records is covered by Regulations 3A and 16 of the Insolvency Regulations 1994 (SI 1994/2507) in cases of administration and liquidation.

4.7 OPERATIONAL CONSIDERATIONS

One significant difference between the stewardship exercised by directors in the twilight zone and that by an insolvency practitioner once a formal insolvency process has begun concerns the criterion of time. In the former scenario it is not unusual to find directors playing for time for strategic reasons. This might involve attempts to exhaust periods of vulnerability for transactional avoidance[128] or other tactical purposes.[129] By way of contrast, all of the pressure on insolvency practitioners works in the opposite direction. Administrators must act expediently[130] and now have a one-year cut-off period attached to their appointment.[131] No other corporate insolvency practitioner (with the

---

[127] [2001] Ch 475, [2000] BCC 487 – allowing the appeal from *Re Mineral Resources Ltd* [1999] 1 All ER 746.

[128] See Insolvency Act 1986 ss. 238, 239 and 245. The company must be insolvent or rendered insolvent by the transaction at the relevant time (see s. 240).

[129] See *Morphitis v Bernasconi* [2002] EWCA Civ 289, [2003] Ch 552, where the prolongation was due to a desire to avoid the restrictive effect of s. 216 of the Insolvency Act 1986. Legal advice given to the directors undoubtedly strengthened their defence. See Chapter 3 ante.

[130] Insolvency Act 1986 Sched B1 para 4.

[131] Ibid. para 76.

exception perhaps of a CVA supervisor who is committed to the termination date indicated in the agreed CVA terms) is in such a time-sensitive position by virtue of legal obligation,[132] but other pressures may require speedy action. It is unlikely that the provisions of Art 6 of ECHR (now directly applicable through the agency of the Human Rights Act 1998) are engaged to compel insolvency practitioners to resolve the estate with despatch,[133] but the position here is still open to debate.[134]

The need for quick action in maximizing the options for a distressed firm has been judicially sanctioned on a number of occasions.[135] It has led to the emergence of the 'prepack'[136] phenomenon. This practice (which appears to have originated in the USA[137]) involves the directors contacting an IP who before appointment will identify a buyer for the business and then on taking up office will complete the sale transaction in favour of that buyer. This is profoundly controversial because it raises issues both as to the independence of the IP[138] and also possible questions of undervalue sales, particularly where the business is sold without external marketing to an entity controlled by the directors.[139] Fundamental stewardship questions about fettering discretion and obtaining best value are engaged, particularly where the business is sold to the directors. Many prepacks involve this element of phoenixism. In spite of these

---

132 But trustees in bankruptcy have been required to speed up realization processes under s. 283A of the Insolvency Act 1986. For an extreme example of a protracted insolvency process, see the BCCI episode – the liquidation lasted some 21 years (*The Times*, 18 May 2012). A 28-year liquidation featured in *Jackson, Official Liquidator of Weir Construction (Contracts) Ltd* [2012] CSOH 51, but the prolonged nature of the exercise there was explained by the need to neutralize contaminated land before it could be safely disposed of.

133 See the bankruptcy cases of *Holtham v Kelmanson* [2006] EWHC 2588 (Ch), [2006] BPIR 1422, *Foyle v Turner* [2007] BPIR 43.

134 See *GJ v Luxembourg* [2000] BPIR 1021.

135 See *Re T & D Industries plc* [2000] 1 WLR 646, *Re Transbus Ltd* [2004] 2 All ER 911.

136 See S. Frisby [2009] 3 LFMR 242, V. Finch [2006] JBL 568 and [2011] 11 JCLS 1, B. Xie, [2011] JBL 513 and [2012] 21 IIR 85. For critique see C. Lim [2010] 4 LFMR 568. A useful comparative perspective is offered by M. Wellard and P. Walton in [2012] IIR 143.

137 See V. Finch [2006] JBL 568. In some senses prepacks mirror the old technique of hiving down, which was much favoured by receivers, but a hiving down would take place after the commencement of the receivership without the suggestion that it had been prearranged.

138 The fundamental concern is that the administrator is fettering his discretion before taking up appointment. Outside the narrow question of prepacks, this is an issue that can cause concern in the courts – see Norris J in *The New Northumbria Hotel Ltd v Maymask (148) LLP* [2010] EWHC 1273 (Ch) at para [6].

139 See P. Walton (2006) 19 Ins Intell 113.

genuine concerns in a number of early cases, the courts gave this mechanism the green light,[140] though some judges were more cautious.[141]

In view of public concern, SIP 16 was introduced with effect from 1 January 2009.[142] Under SIP 16 the administrator must keep records on why a prepack was deemed appropriate (para 2). It is stressed that the administrator is there to act for the company and not for its directors (para 3). Para 9 is critical in that it specifies no less than 17 items of information that must be given to creditors when they are eventually notified of the prepack. The issue of timing of such notification is addressed by para 11.

The courts have been happy to support prepack sales where SIP 16 has been complied with,[143] though it should be noted that compliance with SIP 16 is not a guarantee of judicial support if the circumstances under which the prepack was entered into merit further investigation.[144] Tacit legislative support for prepacks is evidenced by the introduction of Insolvency Rule 2.67A (see below). But there has been an issue of non-compliance with SIP 16, which has been evidenced in reports to the Insolvency Service.[145] As a consequence, in 2011 the government threatened to introduce delegated legislation to regulate prepacks,[146] but this threat was removed in January 2012 on the basis that the current informal rules appeared to be working.[147] Certainly, compliance rates with SIP 16 are now in excess of 75 per cent. The Insolvency Service has conducted an informal survey suggesting that concerns may be present with regard to 7 per cent of prepacks.[148] That said, many practitioners believe that compliance rates must be further improved if legislative intervention is to be avoided. It may well be that the heat will be taken out of the issue before then in that the use of prepacks on administration has now to deal with the cost implications of the Court of Appeal precedent of *Key2 Law (Surrey) LLP v*

140 See for example *DKLL Solicitors v HMRC* [2007] EWHC 2067 (Ch), [2007] BCC 908, *Re Kayley Vending Ltd* [2011] 1 BCLC 114, *Re Johnson Machine and Tool Co Ltd* [2010] EWHC 582 (Ch), [2010] BCC 382, *Re European Directories DH6* [2010] EWHC 3472 (Ch), [2011] BPIR 408.

141 Exemplified by the general subtext of the judgment of HHJ Purle in *Re Johnson Machine and Tool Co Ltd* (supra) where the prepack was approved but associated expenses disallowed.

142 See 10th IPC Annual Report (2009) for comment on the delay in adopting SIP 16.

143 See *Re Halliwells LLP* [2010] EWHC 2036 (Ch), [2011] BCC 57.

144 See *Re UK Steelfixers Ltd* [2012] EWHC 2409 (Ch), [2012] BCC 751.

145 See editorial in [2009] 258 SMCLN 1.

146 Public disquiet played a role here – so we have an instance of external monitoring by the media.

147 See Ministerial Statement 25 January 2012.

148 See *Insolvency Service Annual Report and Accounts 2011/12* (HC 358) at 10.

De'Antiquis,[149] where it was confirmed that the Transfer of Undertakings (Protection of Employment) Regulations 2006[150] (TUPE) will apply to prepack sales on administration. From the viewpoint of a potential purchaser of a distressed business, this is an unwelcome surprise. One possible outcome that has been discussed by practitioners might be the constructive use of liquidation as a prepack vehicle in order to avoid this particular difficulty. Liquidation is specifically excluded from TUPE. Another alternative that is being talked about is the so-called 'stalking horse agreement'[151] (another US practice) under which a sale is agreed on a conditional basis. Insolvency practice is thus seen to be constantly evolving in reaction to a changing regulatory environment.

An everyday aspect of the operation of the insolvency regime will be the making of new contracts. Although a basic issue, there has been a fair degree of uncertainty associated with it, as the Cork Committee noted.[152] Normally an insolvency practitioner will be acting as an agent of the company in making new contracts. But that status does not necessarily exclude personal liability. So, for instance, an administrative receiver will be personally liable on contracts made whilst acting as such. Similar rules would appear to apply to administrators, but in both cases this liability would be covered by an indemnity. For liquidators there is no presumption of personal liability, as was made clear in *Stewart v Engel*.[153] If an indemnity is not available to cover contractual liability, presumably this item would fall under the expenses heading (see Insolvency Act 1986 Sched B1 para 69). Issues can often arise as to the capacity in which the insolvency practitioner is acting. So in *Wright Hassall LLP v Morris*[154] the Court of Appeal found that an administrator had assumed personal responsibility for legal fees notwithstanding the fact that the CFA agreement had been signed 'as administrator'.

4.8 EXTRAORDINARY POWERS

It goes without saying that an office-holder will be invested with all of the powers previously available to directors. But, in addition, office-holders are given special powers/rights to facilitate the discharge of their responsibilities.

---

149 [2011] EWCA Civ 1567, [2012] BCC 375.

150 SI 2006/246.

151 See the piece by M. Moses and I.G. Williams in [2012] (Autumn) Recov at 34.

152 Cmnd 8558 para 469.

153 [2000] BPIR 383. See also *Stead Hazel & Co v Cooper* [1933] 1 KB 840.

154 [2012] EWCA Civ 1472, [2012] BPIR 1310.

The most distinctive of these is the power of disclaimer of onerous commitments. But this is only conferred explicitly[155] on liquidators operating in English law (see ss. 178 et seq of the Insolvency Act 1986). Scottish liquidators do not enjoy a statutory power of disclaimer.[156] We have already noted that a liquidator inherits the existing ongoing contractual commitments of the company (see para 4.2 above). Disclaimer however permits a liquidator to terminate an ongoing onerous contract and thereby to deprive the other contracting party of future benefits thereunder. In return, the counterparty is given rights against the estate as an unsecured creditor (which may, of course, be virtually worthless). The procedure of disclaimer has been deregulated over passage of time. A court order is no longer required since 1985 and further bureaucracy has been cut by the Legislative Reform (Insolvency) (Miscellaneous Provisions) Order 2010 (SI 2010/18). The courts for the most part have been supportive of this power to disclaim. So in *Re Celtic Extraction*[157] they held that a waste management licence could be disclaimed notwithstanding the potential risk to the environment resulting from disclaimer. On the other hand, in *Re SSSL Realisations (2002) Ltd*,[158] the Court of Appeal decreed that a contract was not onerous simply because it was unprofitable.

Office-holders have wide powers of investigation. In particular there is the much feared public examination procedure which is available on compulsory liquidation under the terms of s. 133 of the Act. The Cork Committee was keen to revive this procedure, which had fallen into disuse (see paras 654 and 1752). There are more widely available powers for office-holders – see in particular ss. 235 and 236 of the Insolvency Act 1986. These powers (explained further in SIP 2) enable office-holders to interrogate company officers and to require the handing over of documentation. Fellow office-holders may also be at the wrong end of the exercise of such powers, though the court expressed the hope

---

155 For an unusual case where administrators were given this power by decision of the courts – *Re P&C and R & T (Stockport) Ltd* [1991] BCC 98. The Scots courts were able to come to a similar result in *Clark and Whitehouse, Noters* [2012] CSOH 55 by citing the need for administrators to act in the interests of all creditors. This power of disclaimer is not unique to English law – liquidators in Ireland and Australia enjoy a similar licence to offload onerous commitments – see Companies Act 1963 s. 290 and Australian Corporations Law 2001 s. 568. The same is true of New Zealand, where the disclaimer power was extended in 2006 – Companies Act 1993 s. 269.

156 See *Clark and Whitehouse, Noters* [2012] CSOH 55.

157 [2001] Ch 475 (*Official Receiver v Environmental Agency*). Lightman J in a speech to the ILA was critical of this ruling – see (2001) 14 Ins Intell 57 and 69. On the impact of disclaimer on trust funds designed to deal with the environmental cost issue see *Environment Agency v Hillridge* [2003] EWHC 3023 (Ch), [2004] 2 BCLC 358.

158 [2006] Ch 610.

in *Re Trading Partners Ltd*[159] that compulsion would not be required and a spirit of comity would prevail. The fact that these documents might be held by third parties is not a barrier in itself.[160] The courts again have been quite supportive of these powers.[161] In Australia recently they have been held to be constitutional even when used by a receiver appointed out of court.[162] These powers of investigation are not generally available to all insolvency office-holders – for example, supervisors of a CVA cannot exploit them as they are not within the linking provision found in s. 234. Although they represent a power, a failure to use these powers may reflect badly upon an insolvency practitioner.[163]

Office-holders may also be allocated special litigation rights which are not available either to a company or its creditors. For example, the right to bring wrongful trading proceedings against directors. This right (found in s. 214 of the Insolvency Act 1986) is currently limited to liquidators. It is one thing to enjoy the power to bring proceedings, but it is an entirely different matter when one considers the practical issue of funding.[164] Such a claim cannot be assigned nor can finance be received in circumstances where control of the proceedings is surrendered to the financier.[165] This reflects the fiduciary nature of the power and represents an application of the maxim '*delegatus non potest delegare*'. The best inducement that the liquidator can offer is to point out that a major unsecured creditor offering finance will benefit from a successful claim by virtue of any dividend.[166] Another strategy is to use the threat of a wrongful trading claim (which inevitably has stigma attached to it from the viewpoint of the target director) to induce a director to settle out of court.[167]

---

159 [2002] BPIR 606.

160 See *Re British and Commonwealth Holdings plc (Nos 1 and 2)* [1992] 3 WLR 853.

161 See *Shierson v Rastogi* [2002] EWCA Civ 1624, [2002] BCC 1005.

162 *Saraceni v Jones* [2012] WASCA 59.

163 See the observations of the court in *Coyne and Hardy v DRC Distribution Ltd* [2008] EWCA Civ 488, [2008] BCC 612.

164 For an up-to-date summary of the position see K. Crinson and S. Morphet (2011) 24 Ins Intell 108.

165 See *Re Oasis Merchandising Services Ltd* [1998] Ch 170. Compare the position in New Zealand as reflected by s. 260A of the Companies Act 1993 as amended by s. 21 of the Companies Amendment Act 2006.

166 There are recorded instances of creditors funding wrongful trading claims – see *Re Produce Marketing Consortium Ltd (No. 2)* (1989) 5 BCC 569 and *Singla v Stockler* [2012] EWHC 1176 (Ch), [2012] BPIR 1061 at para [3] per Briggs J.

167 See *Re Langreen Ltd* (21 October 2011, unreported) where the practice (which one suspects is not uncommon) came in for some mild criticism from Registrar Derrett at para [41].

Looking more generally at recovery litigation, it is possible to use conditional fee agreements and ATE insurance deals to secure external funding to pursue recovery claims. A threat to this in the form of civil justice reform was headed off[168] when the profession secured exemptions from the provisions of ss. 44 and 46 of the Legal Aid, Sentencing and Punishment of Offenders Act 2012. Sections 44 and 46 curb the recovery of CFA success fees and ATE insurance premiums in certain species of litigation. These exemptions, detailed in a Written Ministerial Statement from Jonathan Djanogly of the Ministry of Justice delivered on 24 May 2012, are scheduled to last until April 2015.

Under paras 70 and 71 of Sched B1, an administrator can interfere with property held subject to security. This was considered by Richard Snowden QC in the High Court in *Re Capitol Films Ltd.*[169]

Another interesting power concerns the right to intermeddle with goods held by the company subject to title retention.[170] Such goods can be sold without fear of liability in conversion, provided the supplier owner is properly compensated. Only administrators have this power[171] as it is not given to office-holders generally. The justification for this is that it may promote corporate rescue – but that is open to question in an era where many administrations are little more than disguised liquidations. A rethink is required and the possibility of making the power more widely available would be timely to reconsider.

We should also note that an office-holder is in a special position with regard to the supply of utilities. An office-holder can now by virtue of s. 233 of the 1986 Act require a supplier to maintain supplies without first settling existing arrears.[172] In effect, and this was recommended by the Cork Committee (para 1462), the office-holder is treated as a new customer, completely unconnected with the company. This represents a change to the pre-1986 position where the insolvency practitioner could be forced to pay the arrears.[173] However, it seems that the law does not prevent the supplier from substantially increasing its prices for fresh supplies. This is a cause of concern within the turnaround industry.[174] There have been calls by R3 for the new Enterprise and

168 For background see the editorial comment in [2011] 296 SMCLN 1. The reform derived from the report of Lord Justice Jackson on *Review of Civil Litigation Costs: Final Report* (2010).

169 [2010] EWHC 3223 (Ch), [2011] BPIR 334. For discussion of the costs aspects of this, see S.L.C. McLennan (2012) 25 Ins Intell 123.

170 *Aluminium Industrie Vaassen v Romalpa Aluminium Ltd* [1976] 1 WLR 676.

171 Insolvency Act 1986 Sched B1 para 72.

172 See Companies Act 1993 s. 275 for a similar provision in New Zealand.

173 *Re Wellworth Cash and Carry Ltd* (1986) 2 BCC 99,265.

174 See for example the Memorandum submitted to Parliament by R3 on 29 June 2012 in the context of the Enterprise and Regulatory Reform Bill at para 29.

Regulatory Reform Bill to extend s. 233 to deal with this issue. At the time of manuscript submission no such provision had been included in the Bill.

A final dramatic power of certain office-holders is the power to seek the dissolution of the company. Directors, of course, enjoy a similar power for solvent concerns.[175] Dissolution mechanisms are provided for at the end of some insolvency processes.[176] We are talking here about liquidators and administrators. Of particular note is the power given to official receivers under s. 202 of the Insolvency Act 1986 to seek the early dissolution of a hopelessly insolvent company without undertaking a full winding-up procedure. This is a useful tool and its availability should be extended to its full potential – administrators were given a similar power by para 84 of Sched B1 of the Insolvency Act 1986. Such a facility is not necessary in cases of CVA or administrative receivership.

4.9 STATUTORY AND OTHER FORMS OF PROTECTION FOR INSOLVENCY PRACTITIONERS

We have already seen that insolvency practitioners are not trustees and therefore it seems that they cannot seek the protection of s. 30 of the Trustee Act 1925.[177] But that does not mean they are naked and totally exposed.

First, they can rely on a right of indemnity from their appointor. Such an entitlement may be derived from legislation (see Insolvency Act 1986 s. 34) or via the explicit terms of their appointment.

There are also special provisions in the Insolvency Act 1986 designed to offer succour to insolvency practitioners. For example, under s. 232 of the Act the acts of an office-holder remain valid notwithstanding any defects in appointment. There is a comparable provision in para 104 of Sched B1 for administrators, but the court has held[178] that it is subject to the *Morris v Kanssen*[179] limitation in that it only protects against trivial errors and not fundamental flaws in the appointment. Presumably a similar argument would hold good for s. 232. Also s. 234 enables an office-holder to recover company property currently being held by a third party. There is no guarantee that the court will assist in such an application – thus in *Re La Senza*[180] a s. 234 appli-

175 Companies Act 2006 s. 1003.

176 See for example Insolvency Act 1986 ss. 201–5 and Sched B1 para 84.

177 *Re Windsor Steam Co Ltd* [1929] 1 Ch 151.

178 See *Re Care Matters Ltd* [2011] EWHC 2543 (Ch), [2011] BCC 957 per Norris J at para [8].

179 [1946] AC 459.

180 [2012] EWHC 1190 (Ch).

cation was refused by Sir Andrew Morritt C because it would undermine a haulier's lien in respect of the company's goods. That lien had to be redeemed and the haulage charges met before the goods could be recovered by the administrators. The continued exercise of the lien was permitted notwithstanding the operation of the moratorium in administration.

In *OBG Ltd v Allen*[181] the House of Lords had to consider the potential liability of an administrative receiver for economic torts where there had been an irregular appointment. The House of Lords came up with a conclusion that in effect offered immunity to the insolvency practitioner. This was achieved by refusing to extend the principle of strict liability for conversion to situations involving intangible assets. Lord Hoffmann speaking *obiter* felt that this conclusion was entirely consistent with the terms of s. 232 of the Insolvency Act 1986.

Finally, we should note s. 246 of the Act, which enables office-holders to resist the assertion of liens over company documents. This is important as an office-holder may need such documents in order to understand the task ahead.

Arguably, office-holders can rely on s. 1157 of the Companies Act 2006 on the basis that they are company officers. This point was confirmed by Harman J in *Re Home Treat Ltd.*[182] But this view is not without some doubt. In *Rawnsley v Weatherall Green & Smith North Ltd*[183] HHJ Behrens, without citing any authorities, thought it was seriously arguable that office-holders could not seek solace in that statutory provision. Whether it matters is a more pertinent question, as office-holders have available to them a range of alternative protective mechanisms.

4.10 JOINT, CONCURRENT AND CONSECUTIVE STEWARDSHIP

The debate so far has proceeded on the assumption that the insolvency practitioner will be working in solo. That is misleading. In most large insolvencies there will be joint appointments made. Such a possibility is expressly envisaged for liquidators and administrative receivers by s. 231 of the Insolvency Act 1986. Section 7(6) also anticipates multiple CVA supervisors. This phenomenon undermines the idea of personal responsibility by recognizing

---

181 [2007] UKHL 21, [2008] 1 AC 1. See also the similar issues in *Mir Steel UK Ltd v Morris* [2012] EWCA Civ 1397 dismissing the appeal from *Lictor Anstalt v Mir Steel* [2011] EWHC 3310 (Ch).

182 [1991] BCC 165. Harman J relied on the old authority of *Re X Co Ltd* [1907] 2 Ch 92.

183 [2009] EWHC 2482 (Ch), [2010] BCC 406 at para [66].

that teamwork is involved. It also throws up a number of interesting issues that have some importance in practice. So, for instance, paras 100–103 of Sched B1 deal with joint and concurrent administrators. Although the legislation tries to anticipate issues, not all questions have been resolved. So, questions have been raised as to whether liquidators can act jointly and severally with regard to CVLs initiated in the wake of a para 83 administration exit.

It may also be overlooked that multiple insolvency practitioners (or single individuals wearing different hats) may be involved with a company at any one time. So it is quite likely that an administrator may be acting as a CVA supervisor. A company may be undergoing receivership and liquidation at the same time, in which case the liquidator must step aside and allow the receiver to realize the security. We thus have a different form of stewardship.

A single company may be the subject of consecutive insolvency processes. So a company that has undergone administration or receivership may need to be liquidated. In administration the CVL exit under para 83 of Sched B1 is particularly prevalent. In this context the liquidator should pay close scrutiny to the stewardship of his fellow professional. This control mechanism may be diluted by the fact that it is often the same IP who succeeds to the office of liquidator on a CVL exit.

4.11 ASSISTED STEWARDSHIP

It would be a mistake to assume that once an insolvency practitioner accepts office, he or she is left without assistance in the task ahead. Insolvency practitioners, like many other stewards, will invariably have recourse to legal advice and in following that advice they will enjoy a degree of protection. Moreover, in all cases the court can offer succour. However, it is becoming clear that the courts are keeping a careful look out for what they consider to be the wasteful engagement of lawyers.[184]

If the insolvency practitioner is characterized as an officer of the court,[185] the protection of the doctrine of contempt of court becomes available.[186] Interference with the discharge of office by an officer of the court is a risky activity that could ultimately lead to imprisonment for contempt of court. As officers of the court they can always approach the court for the award of additional powers if these are necessary to achieve their remit. HHJ Norris indi-

184 See the comments of Lord Neuberger MR in *BNY v Eurosail* [2011] EWCA Civ 227, [2011] BCC 399 at [102]–[105]. Note also HHJ Purle's comments in *Re Wedgwood Museum Trust* [2012] EWHC 1974 (Ch) at para [32].

185 See the discussion above at para 4.5.

186 On this see the discussion in *Thomas v Jakes* [2012] EWHC 525 (Ch).

cated in *Re MG Rover Espana SA*[187] that the court would be sympathetic to such an application.

More usefully, an office-holder, whether appointed by the court or not, can apply to the court for directions where the legal position on some particular matter is unclear.[188] Such directions, which bear comparison to *Beddoe* applications[189] in trust law, can provide real practical assistance and reassurance. An office-holder who acts in accordance with judicial directions is fireproof. A few contemporary examples of the directions' jurisdiction may offer useful insights. In *Re Equilift Ltd*,[190] HHJ Purle was asked to assist a liquidator who was concerned that certain funds may be held on trust and not available for general distribution. The guidance given was based upon counsel's opinion on the trust status of claims. A procedure was proposed for dealing with disputed claims coupled with a clear steer that if the liquidator followed such procedure the court would be sympathetic to any request for a pardon based upon s. 61 of the Trustee Act 1925.

The issue in *Re WW Realisation 1 Ltd*[191] was whether the administrators of a large retail concern could impose a cut-off date for the receipt of claims by landlords and local authorities claiming that sums due to them might be an administration expense. The administrators had done everything to alert these groups as to the need to make such a claim, but the response had been patchy. David Richards J allowed an official cut-off date for claims to be submitted to be fixed at 28 days after the final letter was sent out to interested parties and directed that after that date the administrators could make distributions to the secured creditors on the basis of claims actually submitted.

It is not only through the mechanism of giving directions that the court can assist the stewardship role. Witness the decision of Newey J in *Re York Gas Ltd*.[192] The problem here was a potential conflict of interest facing an administrator. The proposed solution was to appoint an additional administrator to mitigate any conflict.

Stewardship can also be assisted through the mechanism of a creditors' committee. Such committees have featured in liquidation law for some time.

---

187 [2005] BPIR 1162 at para [18].

188 See Insolvency Act 1986 s. 7(4) (supervisors), s. 35 (administrative receivers), s. 112 (liquidators in a voluntary liquidation), Sched B1 para 63 (administrators).

189 So named after *Re Beddoe* [1893] 1 Ch 547. There is also another link with the law on fiduciaries in that the confidentiality procedure adopted in *Re Moritz (Deceased)* [1960] Ch 251 may also be available to insolvency practitioners – see *Craig v Humberclyde Industrial Finance* [1999] BPIR 53.

190 [2009] EWHC 3104 (Ch), [2010] BCC 860.

191 [2010] EWHC 3604 (Ch), [2011] BCC 383.

192 [2010] EWHC 2275 (Ch), [2011] BCC 447.

They were introduced into administrations and administrative receiverships in 1986 largely as cosmetic reforms. Unfortunately, the consensus seems to be that such committees do not perform effectively.[193] The OFT pointed out in its Market Study of June 2010 that in 80 per cent of cases the proposals of the administrators are not questioned.

4.12 STEWARDSHIP AND CROSS-BORDER INSOLVENCY

The difficult task facing an insolvency practitioner is greatly magnified if the company has assets overseas, an increasingly common phenomenon these days. Issues of cross-border insolvency then arise. There have been positive moves here to ensure cooperation if the main insolvency proceedings are started in this jurisdiction.[194] So, for example, under the EC Regulation on Insolvency Proceedings 1346/2000 (ECRIP), an office-holder in another Member State working through secondary or territorial insolvency proceedings must cooperate with the IP running the main proceedings.[195] A comparable provision is to be found in Art 26 of Sched 1 of the Cross Border Insolvency Regulations 2006 (SI 2006/1030). Conversely, an English office-holder may on occasions find himself subordinated to an overseas main proceedings insolvency regime. This can happen both under ECRIP or via other legal cooperative mechanisms.[196] Increasingly, the common law[197] had developed principles of international comity to extend such cooperation to cases not falling within ECRIP or the Cross Border Insolvency Regulations 2006, which sought to implement the UNCITRAL Model Cross Border Insolvency Law. This was a valuable development because the statutory mechanisms have limited utility. However, the common law appears to have expended its energy with the restrictive decision of the Supreme Court in *Rubin v Eurofinance*[198] and this has disturbed insolvency practitioners who

---

[193] See M. Mumford and A. Katz, *Making Creditor Protection Effective* (2010) and their comments with regard to Recommendation 23.

[194] But jurisdiction problems can arise where insolvency proceedings are opened in one Member State in ignorance of what is happening to the company in another Member State – see *Re Eurodis Electron plc* [2011] EWHC 1025 (Ch), [2012] BCC 57.

[195] ECRIP 1346/2000 Art 31.

[196] Possibly under s. 426 of the Insolvency Act 1986 – see *McGrath v Riddell* [2008] UKHL 21, [2008] BCC 349.

[197] See *Cambridge Gas Transport Corp* v *Official Committee of Unsecured Creditors of Navigator Holdings plc* [2006] UKPC 26.

[198] [2012] UKSC 46, [2012] 3 WLR 1019. This was an appeal joined with the appeal in *Re New Cap Reinsurance Corp*.

fear the cost implications of a decline in judicial comity in situations where explicit statutory mechanisms do not come into play.

The courts have been prepared to give guidance to insolvency practitioners in this situation. They have allowed them to make payments that were not strictly required by English law and have permitted them to transfer funds to a foreign liquidation in the interests of expediency in appropriate circumstances.

Thus in *Re Collins & Aikman Europe SA*,[199] the court (Lindsay J) allowed the administrators to make payments in to creditors in various Member States in fulfilment of certain promises made. Although this was strictly beyond the general distribution regime, it was felt to be necessary to avoid the complications of secondary proceedings being instituted in those other Member States. Again in *Re MG Rover Espana SA*,[200] HHJ Norris authorized the administrators to make payments to employees employed in another Member State to facilitate the administration. He also appended a statement in his order explaining for foreign stakeholders the nature of the UK administration procedure. These creative decisions should be treated with some circumspection as they sit uneasily alongside the comments of Newey J in *Alitalia Linee Aeree Italian SpA*.[201]

By way of clarification it should be remembered that the English courts can assist a foreign insolvency practitioner under the aforementioned measures.[202] Before leaving this issue we should also note two other EU measures. First of all, there is the EC Judgments Regulation (44/2011), which deals with the allocation of jurisdiction in civil cases generally. Although there is in Art 1(2)(a) a carve-out specified for insolvency proceedings specified (hence the need for ECRIP), this has been interpreted[203] in restrictive fashion with the result that not all civil proceedings instituted by an insolvency practitioner will fall under ECRIP – many will be covered by the Judgments Regulation.[204] This is a particular problem in the context of avoidance claims where issues arise as to the juristic basis of the claim – does it arise under general law or solely under insolvency law?[205] We should also note that service of proceedings is not a

199 [2006] BCC 861.

200 [2005] BPIR 1162.

201 [2011] EWHC 15 (Ch), [2011] 1 BCLC 606.

202 *Re Chesterfield United Inc* [2012] EWHC 244 (Ch).

203 *Gourdain v Nadler (C 133/78)* [1979] 3 CMLR 180.

204 If the liquidator assigns a claim the pursuit of that claim by the assignee apparently falls under the Judgments Regulation – see *F. Tex (C 230/10)* [unreported]. But compare *Polymer Vision R & D Ltd v van Dooren* [2011] EWHC 2951 (Comm), where the claim against the insolvency practitioner was held to fall under ECRIP.

205 See *Seagon v Deko Marty Belgium NV C 339/07* [2009] 1 WLR 2168 and *Byers v Yacht Bull Corp* [2010] EWHC 133 (Ch), [2010] BCC 368.

matter for ECRIP but rather is dealt with by the EC Service Regulation (1393/2007).[206]

4.13 STATUTORY ACCOUNTABILITY PROCEDURES

In addition to creating specific obligations, the notion of insolvency stewardship has been reinforced by statute in a number of respects.

First, as we noted above, office-holders are in theory answerable to a creditors' committee. Such committees are in most instances not mandatory.[207] So under s. 49 of the Insolvency Act 1986 the creditors may establish such a committee on administrative receivership. Para 57 of Sched B1 permits the creditors to establish a committee in cases of administration. Where such a committee is established, the exercise of certain powers will require the assent of any such committee, or, failing that, the court.[208] In particular administrators must obtain creditor approval for their plans and if such approval is not forthcoming they should by virtue of para 55 of Sched B1 of the Insolvency Act 1986 go back to the court for directions.[209] Also the pursuit of recovery/avoidance actions by liquidators now in the wake of the Enterprise Act 2002 require assent in order to be properly constituted, though there is a possibility of retrospective sanction.[210] Generally doubts remain as to the effectiveness of creditors' committees in English law.[211]

The misfeasance procedure in s. 212 of the Insolvency Act 1986 can be used against liquidators and administrative receivers for any breach of duty to the company, including negligence.[212] Witness *Re Centralcrest Ltd*,[213] where a major creditor used the procedure to call an errant liquidator to account for continuing to trade on the business and increasing the deficiency for creditors

206 See *Re Baillies Ltd* [2012] EWHC 285 (Ch), [2012] BCC 554.

207 See Insolvency Act 1986 s. 141. But note under para 56 of Sched B1 that a creditors meeting can be imposed on an administrator if 10 per cent of creditors require it.

208 Ibid. Sched 4 para 3A (introduced by s. 253 of the Enterprise Act 2002). This consent requirement is particularly important if an office-holder is considering recovery proceedings under ss. 213, 214 or avoidance proceedings under ss. 238 or 239.

209 *Lavin v Swindell* [2012] EWHC 2398 (Ch).

210 For discussion see the comments of Peter Smith J in *Gresham International Ltd v Moonie* [2009] EWHC 1093 (Ch), [2010] BPIR 134.

211 See S. Wheeler (1994) 21 JLS 350, R. Bork [2012] 21 IIR 127.

212 The old authority of *Re B Johnson Builders Ltd* [1955] Ch 634 is no longer good law in view of the revised wording of s. 212. The Jenkins Committee (Cmnd 1749) (1962) recommended this change in para 503.

213 [2000] BCC 727. See also *Re Home and Colonial Ltd* [1929] WN 223, *Argylls Ltd v Coxeter* (1913) 29 TLR 355.

in the process. The equivalent provision for administrators is found in para 75 of Sched B1 of the Insolvency Act 1986. That said, the courts are reluctant to make a finding of misfeasance because once again that would involve them double-guessing the exercise of professional judgement, a matter they do not feel equipped for. It should be noted that in response to a claim of breach of duty an office-holder may in theory have recourse to judicial protection in the form of a pardon given under s. 1157 of the Companies Act 2006.[214] This is rarely required because the courts are more reluctant to criticize IPs than directors.

It is often not appreciated that liquidators may themselves fall foul of the disqualification regime contained in the Company Directors Disqualification Act 1986. Although ss. 6 and 8 cannot be invoked against liquidators, the language of s. 4 is sufficiently wide to admit of this possibility. A recent and rare illustration of this is to be found in *Wood v Mistry*,[215] where successor liquidators were able to secure from Newey J a 12-year disqualification against a former insolvency practitioner who had committed various breaches of duty whilst acting as a liquidator.

The court has general powers to determine disputed points in a liquidation. So in *Re Movitex Ltd*,[216] the Court of Appeal ordered liquidators to disclose documents pertaining to their decision to commence litigation against individuals, litigation which proved both abortive and expensive.

Insolvency practitioners may themselves be at the wrong end of an application to the court under s. 236 by another office-holder seeking information about the earlier conduct of the insolvency. For instance, in *Re Delberry Ltd*,[217] a liquidator was enabled to obtain information from administrative receivers about a possible 'prepack' sale of the company's assets which was implemented during the course of the receivership. The courts have indicated that it is unfortunate to find one IP having to go to court to use s. 236 – this issue of access to information should be resolved as a matter of professional courtesy.

Access to information held by liquidators may be achieved by creditors or contributories via the facility in s. 155 of the Insolvency Act 1986. For instance in *Sunwing Vacations Inc v E-Clear (UK) plc*[218] a party to arbitration proceedings secured a court order obtaining access. The liquidators remained neutral on such application.

214 See *Re Home Treat Ltd* [1991] BCC 165.

215 [2012] EWHC 1899 (Ch).

216 [1992] 1 WLR 303.

217 [2008] EWHC 925 (Ch), [2008] BCC 653. See also *Re Trading Partners Ltd* [2002] 1 BCLC 655.

218 [2011] EWHC 1544 (Ch), [2011] BPIR 1524.

A formal system of regulation now exists in the form of recourse to the courts by creditors who wish to challenge the actions of liquidators. Before the Insolvency Act 1986 such matters were dealt with on an ad hoc basis using principles developed in bankruptcy law. In a compulsory liquidation s. 168(5) of the Act permits an aggrieved party to complain to the court. A challenge to the exercise of powers may also be launched under s. 167(3). Reported case law reveals a mixed picture of success and failure for challenges. So in *Re Edennote Ltd*[219] the challenge failed. Similarly the courts refused to interfere with the actions of the insolvency practitioner in *Leon v York-O-Matic Ltd.*[220] The most recent authority here is *Coote v Rubin*,[221] where the court supported the desire of the liquidator to compromise a claim. By way of comparison in *Faryab v Smith*,[222] the court overturned a decision of a trustee in bankruptcy.

Similar mechanisms exist for administrators. So under para 74 of Sched B1 of the Insolvency Act 1986, an application may be made to the court complaining of unfair harm. The experience with this provision (and its predecessor) is not likely to encourage such complaints.[223]

One of the basic issues here is that most judges tend to apply a *Wednesbury*-style test[224] when reviewing the actions (or omissions) of office-holders, and will only intervene if the behaviour is such as would not be contemplated by any reasonable IP. This orthodox attitude has required a rethink in view of the ruling of Arnold J in *Bramston v Haut.*[225] Here the court referred to developments in public law as indicating that a more interventionist approach could be justified. On appeal, the Court of Appeal[226] took a different view and stated

---

219 [1996] 2 BCLC 389, [1996] BCC 718. See also *Re Greenhaven Motors Ltd* [1999] BCC 463 and *Hamilton v Official Receiver* [1998] BPIR 602.

220 [1966] 1 WLR 1450 – Plowman J refused to interfere with the sale of assets by a liquidator in a compulsory liquidation. Note also *Harold Pitman Ltd v Top Business Solutions* [1984] BCLC 593.

221 [2011] BCC 596.

222 [2001] BPIR 246.

223 See *Re Lehman Bros (International) Europe* [2009] EWHC 2869 (Ch), [2009] BCC 632 (also reported as *Four Private Investment Funds v Lomas* [2009] 1 BCLC 161) and *Re Zegna III Holdings Inc* [2009] EWHC 2994 (Ch), [2010] BPIR 277. Under the old administration order regime found in s. 27 of the Insolvency Act 1986 an application was rejected in *Re Charnley Davies Ltd* [1990] BCC 605. Recently in Scotland the courts have suggested that a more interventionist line may be appropriate in some instances – *Clark and Whitehouse, Noters* [2012] CSOH 55.

224 *Associated Provincial Picture Houses v Wednesbury Corporation* [1948] 1 KB 223.

225 [2012] EWHC 1279 (Ch), [2012] BPIR 672. But see *Linfoot v Adamson* [2012] EWHC Misc 16 (CC) per HHJ Behrens at paras [56]–[58] and *Ricoh Europe Holdings BV v Spratt* [2012] EWHC 579 (Ch) at para [48] per HHJ Pelling QC for more orthodox approaches to this question.

226 [2012] EWCA Civ 1637.

that intervention should only be undertaken in those rare cases where it could be said that the office-holder was acting in a perverse manner.

Where a company is undergoing a CVA, an aggrieved party can under s. 7(3) apply to the court to challenge the supervisor. No particular ground is specified here. In the case of a supervisor of a CVA, one other form of challenge is to dispute the validity of the arrangement itself on the specific grounds that a material irregularity had occurred or that it operates in an unfairly prejudicial manner. Such challenges (made under s. 6) must be mounted within 28 days and they usually fail.[227] There are *two* reasons for this. First, the court will always be impressed by the voting mathematics and will reason that the majority do not act perversely. Second, for each ground of challenge *both* limbs of the vitiating factor will need to be established. Thus in cases of procedural irregularity the criterion of materiality looms large. Equally any prejudice that is established must be unfair. In judging unfairness the courts will adopt a commercial perspective.

There has been some success in recent years with CVAs that are clearly designed to deprive creditors of valuable rights without adequate compensation. So we have seen judicial rejection of 'guarantee stripping' arrangements in the retail sector. Under such arrangements solvent guarantors of rent obligations are released from their commitments. This is particularly objectionable where the guarantor is the solvent parent company of an insolvent tenant. So in *Prudential v PRG Powerhouse*,[228] the challenge by the landlords was upheld by Lewison J. The message was reiterated with some force in *Mourant v Sixty Ltd*,[229] where the court struck down the CVA and Henderson J also drew the attention of the appropriate professional regulators to the circumstances of the case.

Finally, though this is largely a theoretical possibility, it would appear that the DBIS could by using the residual provisions in the Companies Act 1985 investigate the stewardship of an insolvent company whilst its affairs are being handled by an insolvency practitioner.[230] Such an outcome is unlikely simply because of the inherent delay involved in DBIS investigations.

---

227 For typical examples of unsuccessful applications, see *Swindon Town Properties v Swindon Town FC* [2003] BPIR 253, *SISU Capital Fund v Tucker* [2006] BPIR 154, *HMRC v Portsmouth FC* [2010] EWHC 2013 (Ch), [2011] BCC 149.

228 [2007] BCC 500.

229 [2010] BCC 882, [2010] EWHC 1890 (Ch). The judge thought it curious that the office-holders did not attend the hearing to put their side of the story through adversarial argument – see para [90] of the judgment.

230 This would follow from *R v Board of Trade ex parte St Martins Preserving Co Ltd* [1965] 1 QB 603.

4.14 REMOVAL APPLICATIONS

We have seen that directors can be removed from office by their shareholders. In the case of insolvency office-holders, removal can only occur if the court sanctions it; this is true even in the case of administrative receivers, as is clear from Insolvency Act 1986 s. 45(1). This is an extreme form of control, though the number of cases where aggrieved stakeholders seek to invoke the removal jurisdiction appear to be growing.

Discrete removal provisions are made for liquidators and administrators. In the former case ss. 171 and 172 are the operative provisions depending on whether the company is undergoing CVL or compulsory liquidation.[231] In both instances the removal may be effected by court order or by creditors. In the case of administrators the removal mechanism is found in para 88 of Sched B1 of the Insolvency Act 1986. The courts also have the power to remove administrative receivers under s. 45 of the 1986 Act, but strangely they have no power to appoint a replacement.[232] In the case of CVAs the supplemental powers of the court under s. 7(3) of the 1986 Act could be deployed to effect a replacement.

Looking at removal applications in the round, certain common principles emerge. First, the jurisdiction is to be used sparingly.[233] The courts recognize that holding office as an insolvency practitioner is a difficult responsibility and is bound to create friction with certain stakeholders. There is a marked reluctance to gainsay professional judgement. Finally, there is resistance to adding to the costs of administering the insolvent estate by having the trauma of a change of stewardship under which the new insolvency practitioner will be forced to retrace the steps of his predecessor.[234] In essence, what is required is that there is due cause to effect a removal.[235] It should also be pointed out that an appellate court will be loathe to upset any decision on removal made by a first instance judge.[236]

---

231 Note also Insolvency Act 1986 s. 108(2) for all voluntary liquidations.

232 A point made forcefully in *Re A & C Supplies Ltd* [1998] BPIR 303.

233 Removal was refused in *Re Abbey Forwarding Ltd* [2010] EWHC 1644 (Ch), [2010] BPIR 1053 and *Re Kimberley Scott Services Ltd* [2011] EWHC 1563 (Ch), [2012] BPIR 135.

234 See for example *AMP Music Box Enterprises v Hoffman* [2002] EWHC 1899 (Ch), [2002] BCC 996.

235 See *Hobbs v Gibson* [2010] EWHC 3676 (Ch). Note also *Re Keypack Homes (No. 1)* [1987] 3 BCC 588 and *AMP Music Box Enterprises v Hoffman* [2002] EWHC 1899 (Ch), [2002] BCC 996.

236 This is apparent from the Privy Council advice in *Parmalat Capital Finance Ltd v Food Holdings Ltd* [2008] UKPC 23.

Against these formidable pressures there is a clear recognition that an office-holder may be replaced even though no complaints of any substance have been established against that office-holder.[237] What matters is whether the office-holder has retained the confidence of key stakeholders so as to ensure the proper administration of the insolvency process. The overriding concerns are the apparent integrity and effectiveness of the ongoing insolvency process.

An instructive modern authority is *Finnerty v Clark*.[238] Here administrators had been removed by a registrar on the grounds that they had failed to institute proceedings under s. 244 of the Insolvency Act 1986 against a secured creditor in spite of receiving a promise of indemnity against adverse costs from the applicants, who had an interest in such proceedings being taken. The registrar ordered removal and replacement notwithstanding the fact that the incumbent administrators were acting in good faith. This removal was (unusually) overturned by The Chancellor, Sir Andrew Morritt, on appeal. The decision of The Chancellor was then upheld by the Court of Appeal. The view taken by the courts was that the decision not to embark on the s. 244 litigation, which was taken after legal advice, fell within the margin of appreciation of office-holders. The court did, however, suggest that the matter might be the subject of reconsideration by the administrators. A similar reluctance to adopt the draconian step of removal was apparent both in the approach of Norris J in *Re Kimberley Scott Services Ltd*[239] and of Proudman in *Doffman and Isaacs v Wood and Hellard*.[240]

Where an insolvency practitioner has been removed it would not be uncommon to find the office-holder being required personally to pay the costs of the removal application.[241]

4.15 REWARDING STEWARDSHIP: REGULATING FEES AND DISBURSEMENTS

This is an issue that is raised in all cases of stewardship because issues of efficiency and potential exploitation can arise. In essence we have the scenario of

---

237 This point was stressed in *Re Buildlead Ltd (No. 2)* [2004] EWHC 2443 (Ch), [2005] BCC 138. Compare *Clydesdale Finance Services v Smailes* [2009] EWHC 1745 (Ch), [2009] BCC 810, where removal was decreed in circumstances where the court felt that criticism of the insolvency practitioners was justified.

238 [2011] EWCA Civ 858, [2011] BCC 702 (CA); confirming [2010] EWHC 2538 (Ch), [2011] BCC 64 (The Chancellor, Sir Andrew Morritt).

239 [2011] EWHC 1653 (Ch), [2012] BPIR 165.

240 [2011] EWHC 4008 (Ch), [2012] BPIR 972.

241 On this possibility see the discussion in *Coyne and Hardy v DRC Distribution Ltd* [2008] EWCA Civ 488, [2008] BCC 612.

'spending other people's money'.[242] So under s. 31 of the Trustee Act 2000 provision is made for these matters, but usually there the estate will be solvent; matters become more acute when we are dealing with an insolvent estate. There is certainly nothing new about challenges being made to the costs of an insolvency procedure,[243] but this has been a vexed issue since the public outcry over the Maxwell affair.[244] This led to the introduction[245] of Statement of Insolvency Practice 9. Although this self-regulatory measure helped to allay public concern, it was felt necessary to reinforce the message by strengthening the initiative. This was done by the 2004 Practice Statement[246] issued by Chief Registrar Baister on 15 July 2004. The central message conveyed by this Practice Statement was that where an office-holder was appointed by the court, there was an expectation that principles of transparency and value for money should govern claims for remuneration and expenses rather than relying on a crude time-based criterion.[247] These are not wildly different from those applied by the Irish courts.[248] The same may be said in theory about the US bankruptcy courts but the suggestions[249] from US researchers are that such criteria are not being applied with similar vigour across the Atlantic.

Most of the reported instances involving the Practice Statement[250] involve bankruptcy cases, but there is no doubt that principles can be extracted from this context that are applicable in the corporate insolvency context. One case involving corporate insolvency is *Re Super Aguri Ltd.*[251] In this instance

---

[242] See the illuminating US piece on this syndrome by C.A. Baker in (1996) 38 Ariz L Rev 35.

[243] See *Re Potters Oils Ltd (No.2)* [1986] 1 WLR 201, where a challenge by a liquidator made under s. 36 of the Insolvency Act 1986 as to the cost of a receivership met with failure.

[244] On this affair see the article by Ferris J in [1999] Ins Law 48. Ferris J himself chaired a committee looking at this issue – see K. Theobald (1998) 14 IL & P 300. For the Maxwell litigation see *MGN v Maxwell* [1998] BCC 324. Ironically at the end of the day the Chief Taxing Master approved 99 per cent of the claim for fees and expenses in Maxwell – see *MGN v Maxwell* [1999] BCC 684.

[245] SIP 9 was introduced (or, more correctly, reformulated) in December 2002.

[246] [2004] BPIR 953. For further enlightenment see S. Baister (2006) 22 IL & P 50. In this Practice Statement Chief Registrar Baister built upon principles he developed in *Re Cabletel Installation Ltd* [2005] BPIR 28. The Practice Statement received strong support from the Court of Appeal in *Brook v Reed* [2011] EWCA Civ 331, [2011] BCC 424.

[247] Indeed, time-based reward was criticized by PO Lawrence J in the old authority of *Re Carton Ltd* (1923) 39 TLR 194 at 197.

[248] See *Re Haydon Private Clients Ltd* [2012] IEHC 505.

[249] See L. Lo Pucki and J.W. Doherty, *Professional Fees in Corporate Bankruptcies* (2011).

[250] Supra.

[251] [2011] BCC 452, [2011] BPIR 256.

Registrar Jacques upheld the claim submitted by the administrators. This was seen as a complex administration fully justifying the professional costs.

The 2004 Practice Statement has now been included in Part V of the general Practice Direction: Insolvency Proceedings,[252] which took effect in February 2012. There appear to be no significant differences with the 2004 version and the case law decided thereunder will remain persuasive. To be precise, the criteria are that any remuneration claim be justified with the claimant not being given the benefit of the doubt. Value for money is the order of the day and this is achieved by introducing the requirement that any effort be proportionate to the likely benefits that will accrue to the estate.

The 2004 Practice Statement was not the only reform to note in this context. In complex cases there is now clear authority that the court can draw upon the services of an independent expert assessor.[253] Turning to legislation, the Insolvency (Amendment) Rules 2005 (SI 2005/527) introduced further pro-transparency measures. Regulation 36A was introduced into the Insolvency Regulations 1994 (SI 1994/2507). This had the effect of entitling creditors, directors and contributories to ask for a written statement of the time spent and at what cost. This statement must be supplied within 28 days. For example, under the reformulated Insolvency Rule 4.131 a creditor can challenge remuneration. Under the Insolvency Practitioner Regulations 2005 (SI 2005/524) new provisions were made in Regs 9 and 15 with regard to the keeping of time records. All of these measures work together in promoting better stewardship.

4.16 CONTROLLING EXPENSES BY ALLOCATING SPECIAL PRIORITY RIGHTS

So far we have been looking at quantum. But in the context of an insolvent estate an equally significant issue is the relevant *priority* of insolvency expenses.

As far as liquidations are concerned, the priority of the liquidator's claim for remuneration and expenses is governed by Insolvency Rule 4.218(3). In terms of priority there are some 14 items listed *above* it in the ranking. The House of Lords made it clear in *Re Toshoku Finance UK plc*[254] that there is no scope for judicial tinkering with this statutory order of priority. For the most part the courts have followed this injunction.

252 [2012] BPIR 409.
253 *Re Independent Insurance Co (No. 1)* [2002] 2 BCLC 709.
254 [2002] UKHL 6, [2002] 1 WLR 67.

In administrations the key provisions on remuneration and expenses are located in para 99 of Sched B1 and Insolvency Rule 2.67. Under para 99 the outgoing administrator enjoys a charge over the company's assets and in *Re MK Airlines Ltd* [255] The Chancellor Sir Andrew Morritt opined that this charge could be enforced by the appointment of a receiver. Note that this claim is also subordinated to a large number of other prior items. Any unforeseen increase in the former items will clearly affect the willingness of an office-holder to assume the responsibility. This is one reason why decisions which appear to expand the scope of administration expenses are capable of provoking a fierce response from the insolvency professions. There is also concern about potential damage to the business rescue strategy. One such case that has attracted the ire of the profession is *Goldacre Offices Ltd v Nortel Networks (UK) Ltd*,[256] where the obligation to pay rent on premises occupied during the administration was held to be an expense. Subsequent decisions have complicated the position, producing elements of absurdity.[257] Again in *Bloom v Pensions Regulator*,[258] a liability to meet pension commitments received similar prioritized treatment. We await the ruling of the Supreme Court on this latter authority.

If one looks at the cases on expenses, one can see the courts applying principles of fair play to the stewardship role performed by office-holders. This is most readily apparent in the so-called *Lundy Granite*[259] principle, which decrees that if an insolvency practitioner uses the property of another during the course of the insolvency, that usage should be recognized by treating the rent as a liquidation expense. This principle was applied to provisional liquidations by Nicholas Strauss QC (sitting in the High Court) in *Re MK Airlines Property Ltd.*[260]

The whole issue of insolvency expenses was the subject of major scrutiny by Morgan J in *Neumans LLP v Andronikou.*[261] Here we had a comprehensive analysis of the differences between administration and liquidation expenses

---

255 [2012] EWHC 1018 (Ch).

256 [2009] EWHC 3389 (Ch), [2010] Ch 455 – followed in Scotland in *Cheshire West and Chester BC, Petitioners* [2010] CSOH 115, [2011] BCC 174 and in England in *Leisure Norwich II Ltd v Luminar Lava Ignite Ltd* [2012] EWHC 951 (Ch), [2012] BCC 497.

257 Commented on by Morgan J in an *ex cathedra* paper delivered to the ILA in Bristol on 9 October 2012 – see ILA website bulletin 12 October 2012 for further details.

258 [2011] EWCA Civ 1124, [2012] BCC 83. The Pensions Regulator on 26 July 2012 issued guidance on its policy in the wake of this decision.

259 *Re Lundy Granite Co* (1871-72) LR 6 Ch App 462.

260 [2012] All ER (D) 142 (May).

261 [2012] EWHC 3088 (Ch). See also *Re Bickland* [2012] EWHC 706 (Ch).

with some discussion of CVA expenses and the potential impact of s. 51 of the Senior Courts Act 1981 thrown in. The key issue in the case was the claim of solicitors acting for the company, which had undergone a succession of insolvency procedures, to recover their costs. Morgan J was able to offer some limited relief at the end of the day but the case stands out for illustrating the complexity of the current law.

Insolvency Rule 2.67A was introduced in 2010[262] to facilitate prepacks. This permits pre-administration expenses incurred in connection with a prepack to be included as administration expenses.

Whilst dealing with this issue of priority, it would be convenient to address the question of trust assets. It is not uncommon for an office-holder managing an insolvent estate to find that the estate is in possession of assets that belong beneficially to a third party. This might arise for instance where a liquidator takes over in the wake of a failed CVA.[263] Although the office-holder will not formally take over the trusteeship from the company, it seems clear that the responsibilities of the office-holder towards the estate extend to such trust assets. In other words, there is a duty to identify and preserve the trust. This may involve incurring expenditure. In such a scenario there is a clear line of authority best illustrated by the decision of Edward Nugee QC in *Re Berkeley Applegate Ltd (No. 2)*,[264] to the effect that the identification/preservation costs can be charged to the trust and not to the insolvent estate. The interest of the insolvency practitioner in recovering trust-related costs has been characterized as akin to a proprietary interest.[265] This is an appropriate position to adopt.

The claim of an insolvency practitioner for remuneration will be an unsecured claim, albeit prioritized via IR 4.218(3)(o) for liquidators and IR 2.67(1)(d) for administrators. But we should note the use of the lien to support such claim.

4.17 ENDING THE INSOLVENCY PROCEDURE

There are two issues to address here. First, what are the options available for an insolvency practitioner when it comes to bringing the insolvency procedure

262 Introduced via Insolvency (Amendment) Rules 2010 (SI 2010/686).

263 See *Re NT Gallagher & Sons Ltd* [2002] EWCA Civ 404, [2002] 1 WLR 2380.

264 [1989] Ch 32. Compare *Re Eastern Capital Futures Ltd* (1989) 5 BCC 223, *Re Rusjon Ltd* [2007] EWHC 2943, [2008] 2 BCLC 234. The principle would appear to apply in Ireland except to the extent that it is excluded by specific legislation – see *Re Custom House Capital Ltd* [2012] IEHC 382.

265 *Green v Bramston* [2010] EWHC 3106 (Ch), [2011] BPIR 44 – see para [42] of the judgment of HHJ Cooke.

to an end? The answer to that will depend upon which type of corporate insolvency procedure we are investigating.

In the case of receivership, assuming that the company is insolvent, the company will be placed in liquidation. Administrative receivers enjoy no power to seek the dissolution of the company.

For a winding-up, the options are essentially to seek dissolution through the standard route, which by virtue of s. 201 triggers automatic dissolution after the elapse of three months from the submission of final accounts in a CVL or by the official receiver using the expedited procedure in cases where there is nothing to realize (see Insolvency Act 1986 s. 202).

Under the pre-2003 model of administration there were serious difficulties in dealing with administration exit. Considerable creativity on the part of the courts was required to produce a cost-effective exit route.[266] Under the new post-Enterprise Act model, a range of options has been exhaustively delineated. But that does not mean that uncertainties have been eliminated. So in *Re Globespan Airways Ltd*,[267] a timing issue arose. Form 2.34B had been delivered to the Companies Registry to signal that the exit from administration was to be via CVL. Briggs J held that on the basis of para 83(6) of Sched B1 the administration ended at this date when the form was delivered and not at the later date when the notice was actually registered by the Registrar. Companies House disputed this interpretation and on appeal the Court of Appeal held[268] that the administration ends when the Registrar actually registers the notice. To facilitate this interpretation and to combat any practical difficulties by having this later conversion date, the administration is automatically extended to cover this hiatus.

A CVA will come to an end automatically when the specified time period has expired. A CVA supervisor may also act before then if it is clear that the arrangement is going nowhere.[269] Indeed there may be a duty to do so under the terms of the CVA.

The second question is of personal concern to the insolvency practitioner. That is the matter of release. This is a common question in most cases of stewardship. It enables the steward to draw a line under his/her management of the estate without constantly looking back over his shoulder. The relevant provisions here for liquidations are ss. 173 and 174 of the Insolvency Act 1986 for voluntary and compulsory liquidations respectively and para 98 of Sched B1 for administrations.

---

266 See for example *Re Norditrack Ltd* [2000] BCC 441.

267 [2012] EWHC 359 (Ch), [2012] BCC 479.

268 [2012] EWCA Civ 1159.

269 Witness the exemplary actions of the supervisor in *Vadher v Weisgard* [1998] BPIR 295.

4.18 INSOLVENCY PRACTITIONERS OPERATING IN A SHRINKING WORLD

In the same way that we noted in Chapter 3 that directors operate in a globalized economy, so inevitably do insolvency practitioners. More and more do we find UK insolvency practitioners having to conduct their operations against the backdrop of a transnational context. We considered a number of aspects of this changing situation in para 4.12 above, particularly in relation to the exercise of powers of UK insolvency practitioners.

One less high-profile issue should now be discussed. This involves the free movement of professional insolvency services within the EU. We observed above that UK insolvency practitioners have to be licensed. We also noted the relatively small number of local IPs available for servicing the market for insolvency services in the UK. Does this discrepancy present a market opportunity likely to be exploited by overseas practitioners?

There are EC measures to take account of here. First, we have the EU Directive on the Recognition of Professional Qualifications 2005/36. This was implemented in English law by the European Communities (Recognition of Professional Qualifications) Regulations 2007.[270]

More generally there is the EU Services Directive (2006/123), which seeks to further free movement of services as mandated by Art 56 of the TFEU. Looking at Annex I of this Directive, it is clear that insolvency services are covered within its ambit.

4.19 REFORM?

The Office of Fair Trading Market Study[271] conducted in June 2010, which noted both the existence of and positive impact of control by secured creditors over the activities of IPs, will be now studied in some detail. This study concluded that there was a need for greater regulation of insolvency practitioners in situations where a secured creditor was likely to make a full recovery. In such cases it was argued that the secured creditor had no incentive to oversee the actions of the insolvency practitioner. Only in those cases where the secured creditor itself was facing a haircut was there real control on the insolvency practitioner. This was a contentious view to adopt. As a result of this thesis the OFT recommended a number of changes designed to tighten up IP regulation. These included the introduction of an independent complaints-

---

270 SI 2007/2781.

271 For comment see A. Hudson [2010] (Autumn) Recov 27.

handling regime. It was hardly surprising that this approach did not go down well with the profession and its rearguard action was supported to some extent by the Insolvency Service in a document[272] issued in December 2011. The Insolvency Service is not opposed in principle to independent complaints-handling, but it does recognize that there are a number of practical difficulties that should be resolved first.

As we go to press we await the outcome of the so-called Red Tape Challenge, which took place in August/September 2012. This is a government initiative to promote deregulation where regulation is unnecessary. The outcomes of this exercise were not known at the manuscript completion date.

We return to some of these questions of reform in Chapter 6.

---

[272] See *Insolvency Service Consultation on Reforms to the Regulation of Insolvency Practitioners* (2011).

5. Comparative and EU perspectives on the governance of distressed firms

5.1 A CAVEAT

We have made a number of comparative points in passing in the commentary above. This chapter will now seek to offer more systematic comparative insights into the central stewardship issues covered in Chapters 3 and 4, as applicable both to company directors and insolvency office-holders operating in other jurisdictions. As a result of offering such alternative insights, policy-makers in the UK may acquire ideas for legal reform. The Cork Committee made some limited use of comparative analysis in its 1982 report[1] and more recently policymakers have looked at, but not been totally convinced by, measures available under US bankruptcy law to fund corporate rescue. However, whilst lauding this tendency to adopt a broad perspective, we should first issue a note of caution with regard to the general suitability of such legal transplants.[2] Comparative study is, without doubt, valuable in offering insights into how different jurisdictions tackle what may appear to be common problems. But it must not be assumed that solutions adopted successfully in one jurisdiction will necessarily be equally effective in a different legal system. Legal transplants as instruments of reform must therefore always be viewed with some circumspection. Subtle cultural and 'institutional' differences may change the dynamics of effective reform.[3] The 'law in the books' does not always translate perfectly into the law as it operates in practice. That reality is now generally accepted by most scholars of corporate law. With that important caveat in mind, we should at least examine the possibilities of learning lessons from the stewardship experience of broadly comparable jurisdictions in dealing

---

1 See Cmnd 8558, Chapters 14, 15, 21, 27 and 28. That said, the number of jurisdictions chosen for comparative purposes was modest.

2 For the classic analysis of the problems associated with legal transplants see A. Watson, *Legal Transplants: An Approach to Comparative Law* (1974). Note also P. Legrand [1997] 4 Maas Jo of Euro and Compar Law 111 and M. Dean (2011) 31 Leg Studs 570 at 570–72. For a summary of the issues see D. Milman, *National Corporate Law in a Globalised Market* (2009) at 24–6.

3 See K. Pistor, M. Raiser and S. Gelfer [2000] 8 Econ of Trans 235.

with distressed firms. Our focus will be to try to identify novel aspects of governance worth considering for adoption in English law. In other words, there will be some 'cherry-picking', but, in so searching for novelty, we should not close our eyes to obvious commonality.

One can detect convergence[4] in terms of general principles of corporate governance for the simple reason that the basic principles on which limited liability ventures should operate now attract a fair degree of consensus. The limited liability company, whether widely held or close in nature, is ubiquitous and so increasingly is the limited liability partnership.[5] Differences, however, do begin to appear once we drill down into specific points of substantive law relating to the regulation of such common entities.

5.2 ATTITUDES IN COMMON-LAW JURISDICTIONS TOWARDS THE TWILIGHT ZONE STEWARDSHIP DILEMMA

The problem of prescribing and regulating appropriate managerial strategy in the twilight zone is well known across all common-law jurisdictions that have adopted the limited liability company.[6] Notions such as agency, trusts and fiduciaries also have travelled around the globe as a result of the influence of English law. A short survey will confirm that analysis.

5.2.1 Australia

In Australia, the challenges of stewardship, both before and after the initiation of formal insolvency proceedings, are broadly similar to those encountered in the UK. Indeed, it should be recalled that the common-law idea of a duty owed by directors to creditors (which is discussed in Chapter 3) emerged from that jurisdictional source in the late 1970s. It is therefore ironic to note the ruling in *Spies v The Queen*[7] where the idea of a *fiduciary* duty owed to creditors by

---

4 See Chapter 1 in A. Dignam and M. Galanis, *The Globalisation of Corporate Governance* (2009). See also J. Zhao [2011] 62 NILQ 361.

5 The LLP originated in the USA in response to ruinous litigation against the audit profession. It spread to Jersey and then Great Britain – see P. Morris and J. Stevenson (1997) 60 MLR 538. It was introduced in Northern Ireland via the LLP Act (Northern Ireland) 2002. Singapore adopted the idea in the LLP Act 2005 (5/2005). India followed this well-trodden path in 2008.

6 INSOL uses the twilight zone terminology – see for example its *Directors in the Twilight Zone* report (now in its 3rd edition, 2011).

7 [2000] HCA 43. For comment see A. Hargovan [2003] 21 C & S LJ 390.

directors was dismissed by the High Court of Australia. A similar rejection of the conceptual basis of this duty has occurred in Canada (see below), but where this leaves us is open to debate, as the existence of a duty to creditors seems to be accepted, even if its proper juristic basis is questioned. Increasingly it has evolved into statutory expression.

That said, there are differences in emphasis between the UK and Australian jurisdictions. Not least is the prohibition on the appointment of corporate directors that one finds in Australia. The minimum age for directors is also sensibly pitched at the higher level of the age of 18. Taken together, these provisions reflect an attitude of requiring greater personal responsibility for those who assume the stewardship of a limited company.

On the other hand, Australia now has a statutory 'business judgement rule'. This is to be found in s. 180(2) of the Corporations Law, a provision that apparently was introduced in 1999 to assuage managerial concerns about their increased exposure to litigation risk. That exposure to risk was exemplified by the decision in *Daniels v AWA*,[8] where the use of objective standards to judge directorial decision-making was very much to the fore. The supporters of this change say that it very much lessens the burdens on the executive class. Directors thus have a defence where they act in good faith in a matter in which they do not have a conflict of interest, have been properly informed and have acted rationally[9] in the best interests of the company. But it has its limitations – it does not apply where it is alleged that insolvent trading (see below) has taken place. Not all commentators are convinced either of the merits of the business judgement rule, or indeed whether it will have any practical effect.[10]

For companies that end up in a state of insolvency, a central provision is section 588G of the Corporations Law, which deals with insolvent trading. This resembles the English law of wrongful trading, though in one significant respect it is more helpful to directors. This is because it establishes in s. 588H *four* clear statutory defences.[11] These include absence from office due to illness, a reasonable belief that the company was solvent, reasonable reliance upon a competent delegate and reasonable steps taken to stop the debt being incurred in the first place. Objectivity is very much to the fore here. Note that there is no business judgement rule applied here (at present) and enforcement is enhanced by the availability of flexible litigation funding techniques.

---

[8] (1995) 13 ACLC 614.

[9] On rationality see *ASIC v Rich* [2009] NSWSC 1229. See generally M. Legg and D. Jordan [2010] 269 SMCLN 1.

[10] See for example P. Redmond 'Safe Harbours or Sleepy Hollows: Does Australia Need a Statutory Business Judgement Rule?' Chapter 11 in I. Ramsay (ed.), *Corporate Governance and the Duties of Company Directors* (1997).

[11] There is also a possibility that general relief under s. 1318 might also be available – see *Hall v Poolman* [2007] 215 FLR 243.

There is in Australia now a legal obligation imposed on directors with respect to the entitlements of employees (see the 'GEERS' scheme, which was introduced in 2001).[12] This takes the form of a prohibition not to undertake arrangements that would have the effect of denying employees their entitlements. It is enforced through a civil penalty regime.

The group situation is specifically addressed in Australia. So, directors of subsidiary companies can under s. 187 of the Corporations Law act in pursuance of the interests of the group provided their company is not insolvent. Equally, a parent company can in defined circumstances be made to contribute to the debts of an insolvent subsidiary (see s. 588V).

Further change in the rules dealing with directors operating in the twilight zone is on the horizon. There has been particular concern expressed about the syndrome under which directors walk away from distressed companies without formally liquidating them with the result that employee protective rights are not brought into play. In particular, special legislative provisions including those under the Corporations Amendment (Phoenixing and Other Measures) Act 2012 (Cth) have been introduced to combat the phoenix syndrome. These reforms, which appear to be based upon the UK model, have attracted some concern in managerial circles, but complementary reforms have been introduced via tax legislation[13] to impose personal liability on those company directors who abandon companies with tax arrears without ensuring that they are properly liquidated.

5.2.2 Canada

Directors in Canada are also expected to display a standard of reasonable care whilst managing the business. This is apparent from s. 122 of the Canadian Business Corporations Act, a model statute which may then be adopted by the various Canadian Provinces.

In Canada, in spite of concerns that directors are too readily exposed to litigation risk, there is no formal business judgement rule. Certainly, it finds no expression in the Canadian Business Corporations Act (CBCA). However, in *Peoples Department Stores v Wise*,[14] the Canadian Supreme Court in dismissing the idea that directors of distressed businesses owe a *fiduciary* duty to

---

[12] General Employee Entitlements and Redundancy Scheme. For a comprehensive review of this scheme and related issues see C.F. Symes, *Statutory Priorities in Corporate Insolvency Law* (2008) Chapter 5, especially at p. 146.

[13] See Tax Law Amendment (2012 Measures No. 2) Act 2012 (Cth).

[14] [2004] SCC 68 – discussed by J. Sarra in [2006] 15 IIR 1, W.A. Gray (2005) 41 Can Bus Jo 184 and A. Keay (2005) 18 Ins Intell 65. For comment on the earlier stages of this test litigation, see W.A. Gray [2003] 39 Can Bus Jo 242.

creditors may have introduced a business judgement rule by the back door. In order to understand this decision in context, it is pertinent to remind readers that in Canada the main statutory grievance procedure available to shareholders (and comparable with s. 994 CA 2006 in the UK) can also in certain circumstances be accessed by creditors. It was the existence of this statutory remedy (see CBCA s. 241) that influenced this surprising outcome in the Canadian Supreme Court.

There are no specific legislative rules prohibiting reckless/wrongful trading in Canada and this has prompted speculation as to the potential of a US-style deepening insolvency doctrine (see below) coming into play.[15]

5.2.3 India

Indian corporate law is on the point of undergoing major reform. This was long overdue as the basic legislation, the Companies Act 1956 (although subsequently amended on an ad hoc basis), was enacted shortly after independence. Clearly the 1956 legislation was based upon the English model and there are clear parallels in its treatment of directors to the position in English law. So there is civil and criminal liability for fraudulent trading[16] under s. 542 of the 1956 Act and a misfeasance procedure in s. 543. But there has always been greater state control over companies and prohibitions on corporate directors and directors holding multiple offices.

Looking at the new Companies Bill which was published in 2011, certain points emerge. The new legislation will replace the 1956 Act and represents a mixture of consolidation and reform. For example, there is likely to be a requirement that companies promote social responsibility by setting aside 2 per cent of net profits for such purposes. The basic provisions relating to directors of insolvent companies are more predictable, with the ban on fraudulent trading being continued, but no suggestion that a concept of wrongful trading will be introduced. There will be a succinct statement of directors' duties.

5.2.4 Ireland

The Irish approach towards regulating directors of distressed companies mirrors English law in many respects. The basic duties that one finds in English law, whether generated by common law or statute, are replicated. For example, the common-law duty to husband assets for the benefit of creditors was recognized by the Irish courts in *Re Frederick Inns Ltd.*[17]

---

15 See J. Girgis [2008] 53 McGill LJ 167.
16 See S. Preetha [2011] 4 NUJS Law Rev 231.
17 [1994] 1 ILRM 387.

The enforcement of such managerial duties by insolvency practitioners is very similar to the position in English law. The concept of fraudulent trading is recognized by s. 297 of the Companies Act 1963. But instead of using the English terminology of wrongful trading, the Irish have chosen the label 'reckless trading' (see s. 297A of the Companies Act 1963).[18] The idea of reckless trading appears to have been influenced by the model operating in South African law and New Zealand also employs this concept (see below). Disqualification of directors is also possible in Ireland under s. 160 of the Companies Act 1990, though it is a sanction that has seen limited usage in practice. This is because, unlike in English law, insufficient thought was given to the practicalities of enforcement when the concept was first introduced. Improved reporting mechanisms were introduced in the case of CVLs by s. 56 of the Corporate Law Enforcement Act 2001. The disqualification regime was reviewed by the High Court in Ireland in *Re PSK Construction*.[19] Here directors had continued to trade on without making adequate provision for tax liabilities. In the case of one director this was found to constitute reckless trading and also to merit a disqualification. For the other director, although a reckless trading finding could not be sustained, a disqualification (albeit for a lesser period) was deemed appropriate. Disqualification under Irish law is a serious step requiring conduct that goes beyond mere incompetence and involves conduct that is more deviant than that which might merit a restriction order. What is required is proof of a lack of commercial probity. The Supreme Court considered the disqualification regime in *Director of Corporate Enforcement v Byrne*[20] and overturned a disqualification order which could not be justified on the basis of the findings made against the particular director.

One important differentiating mechanism found in Ireland is the restriction order regime established by s. 150 of the Companies Act 1990.[21] The Cork Committee (1982, Cmnd 8558), when reviewing English law, liked this sort of intermediate model, but it was not formally adopted in English law.[22] Certainly restriction is a less serious sanction than disqualification. This Irish

---

[18] For the leading case on reckless trading see *Re Hefferon Kearns Ltd (No. 2)* [1993] 3 IR 191, where the claim alleging reckless trading failed before Lynch J as the directors could show some steps were taken to minimize loss to creditors and the court was reluctant to use hindsight to condemn them. Note also *Re PSK Construction Ltd* [2009] IEHC 538.

[19] [2009] IEHC 538.

[20] See [2009] IESC 57.

[21] For an overview see N. Fitzgerald (2004) 20 IL & P 108.

[22] Arguably the obtaining of leave under s. 17 of the Company Directors Disqualification Act 1986, where conditions are attached to such leave, might operate to the same effect in English law.

provision will require those directors who become subject to restrictions to comply with certain conditions (such as requiring a minimum capital or an independent director to be appointed) before being permitted to become a company director in the future. The restrictions continue for five years.

Looking at the growing case law on s. 150, certain points stand out. First, the Irish courts have indicated[23] that this procedure is not unconstitutional. This is an important constitutional hurdle that must be surmounted. As to potential targets for restriction, in *Re Worldport Ltd*[24] the court held that although a company can be a shadow director under Irish company law, this is not possible for the purposes of any restrictions imposed under s. 150 as this provision is concerned with *de jure* directors. What sort of conduct might attract a restriction order? Well failure to cooperate with an incumbent insolvency practitioner might suffice, as happened in *La Moselle Clothing Ltd v Soualhi.*[25] The Supreme Court in *Re Squash (Ireland) Ltd*[26] supported this general approach towards restriction orders. Other typical forms of conduct meriting restriction include reckless trading and failure to set aside sufficient funds to meet tax liabilities. However, when considering whether to impose a restriction order the court will be reluctant to judge directors on the basis of hindsight. This important insight was stressed by Finlay Geoghegan J in *Re Derbar Developments Ltd*,[27] where the court refused to grant a restriction order. By way of comparison, in *Re Mitek Holdings*[28] the Supreme Court upheld a five-year restriction order in the case of a director who had failed to act responsibly and had not looked after the interests of his own company in order to protect the group interest.

The sanctions specified in ss. 150 and 160 of the 1990 Act sound impressive; but official statistics suggest that usage is somewhat limited, with restriction orders being used more than disqualifications. This may reflect the more serious nature of disqualification. In *Director of Corporate Enforcement v Byrne*,[29] the Supreme Court took the opportunity to compare and contrast the restrictions order regime with the disqualification mechanism. The crucial points of differentiation are that a more serious form of misconduct is required to justify a disqualification than is required in order to form the basis of a restriction order.

---

23 In *Re Verit Hotel* [1997] 1 ILRM 110.

24 [2009] 1 IR 398. On shadow directors generally see *Re Hocroft Developments* [2009] IEHC 580.

25 [1998] 2 ILRM 345.

26 [2001] IESC 200, [2001] 3 IR 35.

27 [2012] IEHC 144 at para [10].

28 [2010] IESC 31.

29 [2009] IESC 57.

5.2.5 Malaysia[30]

Corporate and corporate insolvency law in Malaysia cannot disguise the dominant influence of English law. Thus under the Malaysian Companies Act 1965 the basic rules governing the responsibilities of company directors are very similar to those operating in the UK. One difference of note, however, is the ban on corporate directors as reflected in s. 122(2) of the Companies Act 1965.

However, with the growing influence of Australian corporate law ideas, it is no surprise to see that Malaysia now has a version of the business judgement rule. This was introduced in 2009 and is located in s. 132(1B) of the Companies Act 1965. By way of contrast, wrongful trading is treated as a crime under s. 303 of the Companies Act 1965.

5.2.6 New Zealand

Again, there are similar features in the New Zealand model of corporate law. The New Zealand method of regulation of directorial conduct is quite sophisticated, yet laid out in extremely lucid fashion in the Companies Act 1993.[31] So, for instance, the duty of reasonable care is highlighted by s. 137. Provision is made for reckless trading liability in s. 135 and one-off transactions that can harm creditors are caught by s. 136. Somewhat surprisingly, bearing in mind the growing US influence, there is no formal business judgement rule in operation. Directors can delegate, but remain liable for the actions of those to whom they delegate.

A company cannot be appointed as a *de jure* director, but can find itself characterized as a director by virtue of conduct akin to that of a shadow director.

Amendments to the 1993 Act made in 2006 seek to curb phoenixism by a provision that bears great similarity to the UK Insolvency Act 1986 s. 216.[32] Greater use is made of criminal liability to punish miscreant directors, as is apparent from s. 380.

The possibility of recovery actions against directors is enhanced by a number of technical changes brought about by the 2006 Act. So, for instance, claims vested exclusively in liquidators can be assigned as part of an exploitation strategy (see Companies Act 1993 s. 260A).

---

[30] For discussion see R. Tomasic (ed.), *Insolvency in East Asia* (2006) Chapter 10.

[31] See S. Watson [1998] JBL 495.

[32] See Companies Amendment Act 2006 s. 35 inserting ss. 386A–E into Companies Act 1993. For general discussion see T. Keeper [2008] NZ Bus Law Quart 21.

5.2.7 Singapore[33]

Again this jurisdiction is heavily influenced by English law and the rules applicable to directors have much in common save that corporate directors are prohibited from assuming office (see s. 145(2) of the Companies Act).

Singapore did break with English law tradition by introducing an automatic disqualification for company directors where there had been two failures recorded over a five-year period. This draconian step[34] was introduced in 1984 but was abandoned three years later and the system of disqualifications in s. 149 of the Companies Act bears similarity to the UK position.

Singapore has resisted the temptation to introduce the business judgement rule. This strict view of directors is reinforced by the fact that wrongful trading can attract criminal sanctions under s. 339(3) of the Companies Act.

5.2.8 South Africa

The law on corporations in South Africa was rewritten by the South African Companies Act 2008, the provisions of which required some tidying up in 2010 and 2011.[35] This 2008 Act replaced the 1973 general legislation on companies and also amended the 1984 statute on close corporations. Indeed, it will no longer be possible to incorporate new close corporations.

The standard of care imposed on company directors is very much objective in nature according to s. 76(3) of the 2008 Act. There are some interesting provisions made with regard to the well-established reckless trading mechanism. Companies are obliged by s. 22 not to trade recklessly. Section 77 of the 2008 Act now covers this matter. The state now also has the power under the 2008 Act to direct the company to desist from such activity. Failure to comply can result in the company's business being closed down. As far as the individual directors are concerned, reckless trading may be an offence under s. 214 and the risk of civil liability is raised by s. 77. Note also that directors are obliged pursuant to s. 129(7) to notify creditors in distress if they decide not to take advantage of the rescue options made available to them (see below).

The 2008 legislation introduced, via s. 76(4), a local variant of the business judgement rule into South Africa.[36] So under s. 76(4) of the 2008 Act a director is protected if he acts bona fide for the benefit of the company, avoids a

33 An overview is to be found in R. Tomasic (ed.), *Insolvency in East Asia* (2006) Chapter 12.

34 For discussion see C.T.S. Kian (1988) 4 IL & P 44.

35 I am indebted to Professor J. Henning for pointing this out in his talk at the Institute of Advanced Legal Studies on 26 March 2012.

36 For comparative analysis see J.J. du Plessis (2011) 32 Co Law 347 and 377.

conflict of interest, takes reasonable steps to be informed and objectively takes a reasonable business decision.

5.3 US APPROACHES TO STEWARDSHIP BY EXECUTIVES OF DISTRESSED FIRMS

Although there are common-law elements at work in corporate insolvency law in the various states in the USA – elements that would be familiar to an English lawyer – there are significant cultural differences towards risk-taking in management.

In particular, we will consider the significance of the 'business judgement rule'[37] in the US and regulatory mechanisms designed to guide the conduct of directors of corporate firms. This rule, which is developed through the courts rather than being embodied in the Model Business Corporations Act, states that a director acting in good faith who takes the precaution of being properly informed and who has no self-interest in the matter cannot be sued for a rational business judgement that turns out to cause loss to the company. The rule, which has subtle variations from state to state, is essentially procedural in nature, conferring protection as it does on directors who undertake business decisions after complying with certain preconditions. It raises a rebuttable presumption offering a shield against liability. It has been characterized as a rule of evidence rather than substantive law. The business judgement rule emerged in the decades post-1945. Perhaps the most controversial authority on the business judgement rule is *Smith v Van Gorkom.*[38] Here the Supreme Court in Delaware held that the defence of business judgement cannot be deployed in circumstances where the actions of the directors could be characterized as grossly negligent. There was a requirement that directors properly inform themselves before taking managerial decisions. This particular ruling, which was seen as harsh in some quarters, surprised the executive community and the effects of the decision were quickly (and predictably) mitigated by corrective legislation in Delaware.[39]

---

[37] For discussion of this concept see S.M. Bainbridge [2004] 57 Vand L Rev 83, where there is a good critique of the important authority of *Cede v Technicolor Inc* 634 A 2d 345 (1994). Note also the pieces by M.B. Hemraj in [2004] 15 ICCLR 192 and (2003) 24 Co Law 218.

[38] 488 A. 2d 858 Del (1985).

[39] See Delaware Corporations Act s. 102(b)(7) – companies incorporated in Delaware can include provisions in their constitutions exculpating directors for a lack of care. For discussion see C.W. Furlow [2009] Utah L Rev 1061 at 1064.

A leading exposition now is to be found in *Re Walt Disney Co Derivative Litigation.*[40] Here the Delaware Supreme Court reaffirmed its support for the overall principle.

As with any case law development, there are bound to be uncertainties associated with the scope of the principle. For example, to what extent does it operate where the corporation is in distress? The case law tends to feature its defensive usage in derivative claims brought by stockholders of solvent concerns. Moreover, can it be of benefit to company officers who are not directors? This issue has apparently arisen recently in California and generally has attracted academic concern.

In the USA there is no explicit legal obligation imposed upon directors to cease trading when the business becomes insolvent and, indeed, the business judgement rule might arguably protect against liability in such circumstances. That said, there is the emerging concept of 'deepening insolvency',[41] which suggests that directors may be under a duty to take proactive action (for example by accessing Chapter 11, which is available to companies which have not yet technically become insolvent) to prevent the company from getting deeper in the mire and thereby causing loss to creditors and stockholders. The degree to which this doctrine is generally accepted by the US courts is again in dispute.

The business judgement rule has, as we have seen above, spread to a number of jurisdictions that look to US corporate law for inspiration.[42] There are elements of commonality in these local adaptations, but it is a matter of debate as to whether it can be said to be the same rule.[43]

5.4 THE CONTINENTAL EUROPEAN PERSPECTIVE ON DIRECTORS AND STEWARDSHIP

As far as national continental systems of corporate law are concerned, a different set of parameters apply. In technical parlance we find a preference for insider governance models, as opposed to the external forces so typical of the Anglo-American approach.

---

40 906 A 2d 27 (Del Sup Ct, 2006).

41 See O.E.F. Lobo (ed.), *World Insolvency Systems* (2009) at 798–800. See also W.A. Brandt and C.E. Vance (2006) 19 Ins Intell 156 and M. Schillig (2009) 30 Co Law 298.

42 Australia introduced it in 1999. New Zealand has so far resisted its introduction, as has China. In Japan the courts have developed a local business judgement rule.

43 See J.J. du Plessis (2011) 32 Co Law 347 and 377.

One reason for this is the adoption of a two-tier model of board structures, with the main management board being rendered subject to the scrutiny of a supervisory board. Much has been written about this internal governance model[44] and a wide range of opinions have been expressed as to its pros and cons. As we have indicated above, the main management board works under the purview of the supervisory board. The supervisory board consists of representatives of various stakeholder groups and has the power to appoint the management board members, though it cannot interfere with day-to-day management nor remove management board members without good cause. Proponents of this model argue that this enables the stakeholder interest to be properly protected. Indeed, generally in jurisdictions such as Germany, there is a tradition of viewing companies as social institutions rather than as tools simply to maximize shareholder wealth.

Sticking with Germany for the moment, it is worth recording that under s. 93(1) of their public company (AG) law, a business judgement rule is applied to protect directors.[45] Case law developments have indicated that there may be potential for out-of-pocket creditors to sue the controllers of a firm qua shareholders rather than in their capacity as directors.[46]

Arguably, the stewardship 'duty' to stakeholders featured in the UK's s. 172 of the Companies Act 2006 has been inspired by this continental perspective as it seeks to treat companies as more socially responsible institutions. Certainly, across the EU there is a stronger desire to protect the interests of employees where a company is distressed, as is evidenced in particular by the French system.

Across the EU it is often the case that directors are expected to take proactive steps once the company enters the area of financial difficulty. The EU requirement to call a shareholder meeting in the event of a serious loss of capital, which is found in Art 17 of the Second Company Law Harmonisation Directive (77/91) and which is now transposed into English law by s. 656 of the Companies Act 2006, is very much a minimum standard.[47]

Counterparts to the UK wrongful trading provision can also be detected in substance (though not in name) in many EU jurisdictions.[48] In *Re Office Metro Ltd*,[49] the English court pointed to the possibility of wrongful trading type

---

44 See Chapter 7 in A. Dignam and M. Galanis, *The Globalisation of Corporate Governance* (2009).

45 For discussion see T. Naruisch and F. Liepe [2007] JBL 225.

46 For discussion of this possibility see C.Z. Qu [2011] JBL 330.

47 See the discussion of the position in Luxembourg as explained by M. Gerber and D. Cantele in (2007) 18 ICCLR 409.

48 See P. Omar [2003] 6 Ins Law 239.

49 [2012] EWHC 1191 (Ch), [2012] BPIR 1049.

proceedings being available in Luxembourg as one justification for its refusal to open secondary proceedings in English law under the EC Regulation on Insolvency Proceedings (1346/2000).

5.5 STEWARDSHIP BY OFFICE-HOLDER POST-COMMENCEMENT OF INSOLVENCY PROCEEDINGS

Common-law systems mirror the position in English law. Office-holders such as liquidators and receivers are widely recognized. There are also local variants on both the administrator and the CVA supervisor models.

In **Australia** we have the traditional tools of liquidation and receivership, which proceed in much the same way as their English counterparts. Since 1961 there was a rescue procedure called 'official management in operation', but this simply did not work. Accordingly, in the wake of the Harmer Report,[50] we saw the introduction by the Corporate Law Reform Act 1992 of the new model of voluntary administration. The distinctive features of this dominant regime, which is located in Part 5.3A of the Corporations Act (ss. 435A et seq), are that it can be accessed with minimal court involvement simply as a result of a board resolution. There is, however, no debtor in possession as such, as there is a stewardship role played out by an insolvency practitioner. The aim of voluntary administration is to secure a deed of company arrangement with creditors, though in many instances this does not happen. This reform has now settled down, but there has in recent months been heated discussion[51] as to whether Australia should take the next step to introduce specific measures to introduce a prepack procedure to further facilitate business rescue. The business turnaround lobby would support such a move, but there is opposition, particularly in the light of concerns over the operations of phoenix companies.

The **Indian** system bears a fair degree of similarity to English law, particularly with regard to the role of liquidators, though it should be noted that there is a state investment fund (the Rehabilitation and Insolvency Fund) used to promote corporate rescue.[52] This fund will continue if the 2011 Bill is enacted.

The picture in **Ireland** bears great similarities to that found in English law. There are, however, unique provisions related to stewardship that are worth

---

[50] *General Insolvency Inquiry* (1988) (Australian Law Reform Commission Report No. 45).

[51] See M. Wellard [2011] Aus Ins Jo 12. Note also the useful comparative article by M. Wellard and P. Walton [2012] IIR 143.

[52] See Companies Act 1956 s. 441C.

highlighting. In Ireland receivers are, by virtue of s. 316A(1) of the Companies Act 1963, under a statutory duty to take reasonable care when conducting realizations. Employees can under s. 316 enforce this duty. Employees can even seek the disqualification of a company director. They also in effect owe enforceable duties to have regard to the interests of employees because mechanisms exist to enable employees to call office-holders to check.[53]

Perhaps the most distinctive feature of the Irish insolvency regime is the court examiner model,[54] which was introduced in haste via the Companies (Amendment) Act 1990. There is no direct parallel in English law, though the examinership regime has traces of administration, CVA and provisional liquidation all embedded within it. There is also an air of Chapter 11 of the US Bankruptcy Code beneath the surface. An examiner can be appointed to assist in the rescue of a distressed company. In some senses it represents a variant on the debtor in possession model. Normally it will be the company that seeks the appointment of an examiner as this will ensure a three-month period of protection. Once appointed, an examiner will work with the directors to prepare a rescue plan, though the examiner can assume the powers of the directors if appropriate. When examinership was first introduced it attracted much opposition from banks, who viewed it as a threat to security enforcement. The law was then reformed by the Companies Amendment No. 2 Act 1999 to address some of the concerns raised by banks and to require that there be a reasonable prospect of survival. Looking at case law on examinership, one or two authorities deserve highlighting as they well reflect the fine dividing line here. So in *Re Gallium Ltd*[55] the Supreme Court upheld the appointment of the examiner as they were convinced by the independent evidence as to the prospects of success. The need for the court to be fully apprised of all relevant facts when the petition is first made to it comes across from the comments of the Supreme Court in *Re Vantive Holdings Ltd*,[56] where the court felt that the petitioner had not discharged the onus of proof. The court will not consider a new petition that merely seeks to clarify omissions in the first petition. One senses that as a result of these reforms there is less tension associated with examinership these days, but also less extensive usage. In the post-global financial crisis scenario, the problem of trying to fund any rescue has become more difficult, but there may be pressure upon the courts to minimize economic disruption by striving to give companies a second chance.

---

53 See Companies Act 1990 s. 171 (seeking directions) and s. 160(4) (requesting disqualification).

54 For an up-to-date overview see I. Lynch-Fannon and G.F. Murphy, *Corporate Insolvency and Rescue* (2nd ed., 2012) Chapters 12 and 13.

55 [2009] IESC 8.

56 [2009] IESC 69.

As far as insolvency procedures are concerned, the position in **New Zealand** is governed by the Receiverships Act 1993 and the Companies Act 1993. This regime has recently undergone significant change.[57] So under the Companies Amendment Act 2006 we see some dramatic reforms in this area and upgrades to what was a fairly antiquated insolvency model. It introduces via a new Chapter 15A into the Companies Act 1993 a new corporate rescue option modelled upon the Australian voluntary administration regime. The powers of liquidators in respect of disclaimer and assignment of causes of action have been widened.[58] At the same time New Zealand has signed up to the UNCITRAL Model Law on Cross Border Insolvency through its Insolvency (Cross Border) Act 2006.

Singapore reflects a position similar to that found in the UK. A regime called judicial management[59] turns out on closer examination to bear more than a passing resemblance to the UK administration model.

South Africa has warmly embraced the idea of business rescue. Indeed, with its judicial management model (introduced in 1926), it can claim to have been a pioneer in that enterprise-friendly policy.[60] Notwithstanding this, judicial management ultimately failed to deliver an effective modern rescue regime. Under the Companies Act 2008, the business rescue mechanisms have been strengthened by abolishing judicial management and replacing it in Chapter 6 of the Act with new modern procedures enabling a rescue process to be initiated out of court with the benefit of a moratorium and then managed by an independent practitioner.[61] As these reforms only took effect just over a year ago, it is too early to pronounce with confidence on their effectiveness.

Looking at the **USA**, once insolvency appears likely, the focus of discussion switches to the governance aspects of the Chapter 11 bankruptcy procedure under the US Bankruptcy Code.[62] The literature here is voluminous. If we concentrate on our search for distinctive features, we note that Chapter 11 is the classic illustration of debtor in possession at work and is also available for firms that are not technically insolvent. When a company enters Chapter 11, it gets immediate protection from creditors through an automatic stay

57 See D. Brown and T.G.W. Telfer, *Personal and Corporate Insolvency Legislation* (2007).

58 See ss. 21 and 22 of the 2006 Act, which have amended ss. 269 and 260A respectively of the Companies Act 1993 in these matters.

59 For discussion and consideration of reform options see G. McCormack [2008] 20 SAc LJ 396.

60 See H. Rajak and J. Henning (2000) 116 SALJ 262.

61 For analysis see J. Rushworth [2010] Act Jur 375 and R. Bradstreet [2011] SALJ 352.

62 For an excellent comparative overview see G. McCormack, *Corporate Rescue Law: An Anglo American Perspective* (2008).

mechanism. A trustee is appointed to develop a rescue plan, though in most cases the trustee is not involved in daily management unless there are doubts about the present incumbents. There is some uncertainty as to whether the trustee is equally subject to the business judgement rule.[63] Another distinctive feature of Chapter 11 is the 'cramdown' element under which dissenting classes of creditors can be forced to cooperate with the rescue. Mechanisms exist for the super priority of rescue funding.

Chapter 11 has some impressive features but its critics suggest that it is an expensive process. One unfortunate problem with the Chapter 11 procedure is that it does seem possible that those advising companies to use this procedure can direct them to a favourable state jurisdiction. 'Favourable' in this context might simply mean a jurisdiction that is favourable to the interests of those same professional advisers by offering a light touch when reviewing professional fees. It has been argued by Lo Pucki and Doherty that this freedom to choose jurisdictions under which to initiate the Chapter 11 procedure should be constrained by Congress.[64]

On the positive side, the policymakers have reacted to the cost issue and in reforms introduced in 1994 and 2005 have made available a Chapter 11-lite procedure for SMEs. This is commendable.

5.6 EUROPEAN HARMONIZATION: THE IMPACT UPON THE GOVERNANCE OF DISTRESSED FIRMS

For the most part there is no harmonization at EU level of substantive corporate insolvency law. This blindspot, which is due to the property law elements of the insolvency regime, has caused difficulties, not least with regard to the growing tendency of foreign distressed forms by using the EC Regulation on Insolvency Proceedings (1346/2000) to seek to relocate their centre of main interests into this country shortly before opening formal insolvency proceedings.[65] Apart from infuriating local creditors, this phenomenon featuring mobile distressed debtors shows a lack of a level playing field. This Regulation is under review at present, though fundamental reform seems unlikely, except in the sense that steps will be taken to promote business rescue.[66]

---

63 See the helpful discussion by C. Xiao-Chuan Weng (2010) 34 Fordham Int Law Jo 124.

64 See L. Lo Pucki and J.W. Doherty, *Professional Fees in Corporate Bankruptcies* (2011) at 272.

65 This phenomenon has been noted in Chapter 1 above.

66 This seems apparent from the European Commission Press Release (IP/12/1354) of 12 December 2012.

One consequence of these market forces and also the desire to protect the national economy has been the rush to develop new corporate rescue models. Spain has recently done this to prevent its companies seeking to exploit the English scheme of arrangement model.[67] Germany has introduced new corporate rescue procedures in 2012.[68] Under the so-called 'ESUG' model, a debtor in possession option is introduced.

One exception to this lack of uniformity at EU level lies in the area of employee protection. The rules relating to state guarantee funds[69] (which seek to protect claims to arrears of wages on the insolvency of an employer) and the protection of employees' rights on any transfer of undertakings[70] are harmonized. The latter rules, which have provided a continuing source of vexation for insolvency practitioners wishing to restructure distressed businesses, have recently been applied in the prepack scenario (see Chapter 4 above). Suggestions that the problems had been fixed by an amendment[71] to EU legislation may therefore have been premature.[72]

There are also a number of insolvency-related issues tied up with the question of state aid.[73] Through state aid the issue of state involvement in distressed companies can take on a new dimension. For example, for a Member State to permit an insolvent company to continue to trade with the aid of state financial guarantees, or even through the agency of concessionary legislation directed towards the mitigation of potential liability of directors who trade on, might be viewed as a form of illegal state aid contrary to Art 107 TFEU. State aid is not restricted to the simple direct provision of economic assistance. That said, in order for this conclusion to be arrived at there must be some evidence of a drain on state resources (for example

---

[67] For comment see L. Elms and T. Camacho [2012] 5 CRI 180.

[68] For an excellent account see R. Bork, *Rescuing Companies in England and Germany* (2012). See also the piece by R. Bork in (2012) 25 Ins Intell 22 and the follow-up piece by I. Fletcher (ibid.) at 24.

[69] See Insolvency Directive 2008/94.

[70] Under the EC Acquired Rights Directive (2001/23).

[71] See Transfer of Undertakings (Protection of Employment) Regulations 2006 (SI 2006/246), especially Regs 8 and 9. For discussion see M. Sargeant [2006] JBL 549.

[72] Witness cases such as *Key2Law (Surrey) LLP v D'Antiquis* [2011] EWCA Civ 1567, [2012] BCC 375.

[73] On state aids in general, see TFEU Art 107 and the piece by P. Godfrey in (2003) 19 IL & P 166. The topic is well covered by textbook literature – see S.M. Colino, *Competition Law in the EU and UK* (7th ed., 2011) Chapter 27. See also P. Scott., C. Thomas and R. Goodman (2008) 1 CRI 154. A valuable empirical study was produced for the Commission in 2009 – see *Should Aid Be Granted to Firms in Difficulty?* (2009).

through the surrender of tax debts[74]) and also the aid must be granted on a selective basis. The case law of the European Court of Justice[75] draws fine distinctions here and one suspects a further development will be required. The giving of a guarantee might constitute a state aid but the provision of a letter of comfort would not.[76] While there may be a defence of legitimate expectation, what is clear is that an order that state aid be returned cannot be resisted on the grounds that to repay the support would render the business insolvent.[77] This apparently heartless approach smacks of ideas of creative destruction being used to protect the integrity of the market as a whole. The EU state aid model is not, however, completely inflexible or insensitive to the needs of distressed companies. Thus there are formal procedures under which Member States may afford support in the form of rescue aid or restructuring aid, but only on condition that the European authorities are properly notified and their approval is secured.

Looking to the future, there may be moves to harmonize. For example, research is currently under way looking at the law on directors' duties[78] in order to get a clearer picture of how that position differs (or converges) across Member States. This must surely indicate that a harmonization proposal is on the horizon.

5.7 OVERVIEW

This brief survey of how stewardship issues are dealt with in the context of distressed and insolvent firms leads to one clear conclusion. All jurisdictions are now in the game of promoting business rescue and all are looking at ways to provide effective constraints to combat managerial misbehaviour. The differences lie in the balance between these often competing goals. There is nothing wrong with a diversity of approach here, as this may properly reflect

---

74 See *Ladbroke Racing v Commission (Case T-67/94)* [2008] ECR II-1.

75 *Ecotrade Srl v AFS (C 200/97)* [1998] ECR I-7907, *Spain v Commission (C480/98)* [2000] ECR I-8717.

76 See *France Telcom (C81/10)* unreported.

77 Practical impossibility of recovery (for example the fact that the recipient company has been wound up and dissolved) is an acceptable defence. It may be that it was the order to the Greek government to recover unlawful state aid is what pushed Olympic Airlines over the edge – see *Re Olympic Airlines SA* [2012] EWHC 1413 (Ch), [2012] BPIR 1163 at para [1]. Any claim by a state against the assets of the insolvent company will, however, be unsecured and not preferential.

78 The European Commission launched a study of this issue in 2011. A report is expected shortly.

local economic policy and perceived priorities. One might detect greater controls on access to limited liability in other jurisdictions (by controlling who may become a director), but there is great similarity on directors' duties and how they are formulated. Business rescue is a global phenomenon with many common models operating in different jurisdictions.

6. Reflections and reform

6.1 STEWARDSHIP COMPARISONS

The essential nature of the stewardship role performed by directors and insolvency practitioners with regard to distressed companies has a number of similarities. Both are fiduciaries and agents; neither are trustees (save in exceptional circumstances[1]). There is an expectation that standards of reasonable care will be maintained. One of the most common facets of their respective stewardship obligations is the growing recognition of the importance of keeping themselves well informed of essential facts.

But there are significant differences to note. For instance, when constructing an appropriate set of rules, we must bear in mind that a director may also be a stakeholder in some different capacity – for example, as a shareholder,[2] an employee[3] or even as a creditor.[4] These different (and potentially conflicting) roles can complicate matters when analysing stewardship issues. Above all, we should never underestimate the emotional ties that a director may have for a business. This is particularly true in the context of small private companies where there may be a family tradition engaged. Employees and other stakeholders (even creditors) may have been known personally to a director as individuals for years. The nature of the insolvency practitioner's interest in the distressed business is fundamentally different. Yes, an insolvency practitioner will have a financial interest in maximizing realizations to ensure that there are sufficient funds available to meet his claim for fees and expenses. There is nothing untoward in that sentiment.[5] Professional standing, especially a repu-

[1] For the circumstances where directors may become trustees, see the comments of Kay J in *Re Faure Electrical Accumulator Co Ltd* (1889) 40 Ch D 141. A CVA supervisor does become a trustee of funds collected – *Re NT Gallagher & Sons Ltd* [2002] EWCA Civ 404, [2002] 1 WLR 2380, *Re Zebra Industrial Projects Ltd* [2004] EWHC 549 (Ch) [2005] BPIR 1022, and *Wood v Heart Hospital* [2009] BPIR 1538.

[2] This is particularly relevant in the private company context.

[3] See M. Butler and D. Milman (2012) 33 Co Law 165.

[4] For example, where a director has loaned money to the company.

[5] This point was reinforced in the personal insolvency context in *Official Receiver v Negus* [2011] EWHC 3719 (Ch), [2012] BPIR 382.

tation for success in maximizing returns for creditors from a distressed debtor, also matters. Equally, there may be an issue of professional pride in a job well done, particularly where some form of rescue has been achieved. But, at the end of the day, an insolvency practitioner inevitably will not have the strong personal feelings for the business that a director may have. This reality must be borne in mind when evaluating the law and considering the potential for reform.

Insolvency practitioners will have to evaluate issues of viability before taking office. This is particularly true of voluntary arrangements and this requirement was formalized by s. 2 of the Insolvency Act 2000. This need to be circumspect is reinforced by SIP 3 (see Appendix II). In cases of administration there has always been a threshold which the proposed appointee must address.[6] Under the new Schedule B1 procedure there is a requirement to indicate the objective of the administration – see Sched B1 para 3. This requirement for the exercise of caution in the task ahead is in stark contrast with the freedom offered to would-be directors. The nature of the management role differs. Insolvency practitioners are very much tied to a prearranged plan. So an administrator must under para 68 of Sched B1 manage in accordance with the approved proposals. If the plan is voted down by creditors (which, in itself, is a rare occurrence), the administrator should then revert to the court for fresh guidance.[7]

There is another difference. Directors are subject to minimal entry requirements in order to access limited liability.[8] Insolvency practitioners are now tightly controlled in terms of access to the profession and their entitlement to hold office. Directors may operate more in a team-based model, whereas insolvency practitioners are appointed by name to an office and may have a more individualized approach to stewardship, though that individuality may be constrained both by the culture within their firm and by industry standards. Directors are answerable (to the point of removal) to their shareholders whilst the company remains solvent; insolvency practitioners will often report to a creditors' committee, but the actual effectiveness of such committees remains in doubt.[9] Certainly, creditors do not on the whole enjoy a power of removal without recourse to the court and the courts generally are reluctant to order removal, as we saw in Chapter 4. Insolvency practitioners therefore enjoy a

---

6 For old-style administration see *Re Colt Telecom Ltd (No. 2)* [2002] EWHC 2815 (Ch), [2003] BPIR 324, where the infamous 'rule 2.2 report' (so named after the relevant provision in the Insolvency Rules operating in that period) was the focus of attention.

7 *Lavin v Swindells* [2012] EWHC 2398 (Ch).

8 As to minimum age see Companies Act 2006 s. 157.

9 See S. Wheeler (1994) 21 Jo of Law and Soc 350, R. Bork [2012] 21 IIR 127.

greater sense of security of tenure. This underpins their stewardship and facilitates the taking of bold decisions. Directors (particularly of private companies) face less scrutiny and regulation of their remuneration than that experienced by insolvency practitioners.

Stewardship may admittedly be the subject of judicial intervention in both cases – most famously in the case of the targeting of directors through an unfair prejudice petition brought under s. 994 of the Companies Act 2006. For insolvency practitioners intervention may be in the form of exposure to various legal complaints mechanisms under the Insolvency Act 1986 (see Chapter 4 above). But on closer examination, the underlying purpose of these forms of intervention differs. In the former case, the shareholder petitioner is usually looking to exit the company at fair value, whereas in the latter instance the purpose of the applicant (who may be a contributory or creditor) is to overturn the exercise by an insolvency practitioner of professional discretion in a specific instance for tactical gain.

Finally, on occasions insolvency practitioners have to assume a quasi-judicial function (e.g. when evaluating claims by creditors for the purposes of proof and voting or when an administrator has to decide whether to grant leave to permit hostile action to be taken against the company). One rarely finds this role being played out by directors, save in the context of approving share transfers.[10]

Other distinctions can be found in the fact that the office-holder can manage the company under a limited moratorium and in the existence of formal procedures requiring them to terminate stewardship (for administrators see Insolvency Act 1986 Sched B1 para 79(2) and (3)).

This chapter will speculate on how future developments might emerge and offer up proactive recommendations for reform. These suggestions follow.

6.2 BANNING CORPORATE DIRECTORS

We looked at this issue in Chapter 1. The Companies Act 2006 has through s. 155 moved in a constructive direction by imposing a requirement that all companies should have at least one natural person acting as a director, but it may well be time to go for an outright prohibition on companies taking on the directorial office. This would place UK corporate law in step with many other major corporate law jurisdictions.[11] It certainly would boost public percep-

[10] This role has been firmed up by the Companies Act 2006 s. 771(2) in that reasons for a refusal to accept transfer must now be given.

[11] See, for example, the jurisdictions listed in para 1.4 above. See also Chapter 5. But note that within Europe there are other jurisdictions, such as France, that permit corporate directors.

tions of proper stewardship. However, if such a reform were made, there would have to be appropriate transitional arrangements to avoid short-term chaos in addressing this process of change. The new bar might, for example, only apply to the holding of directorships in newly incorporated companies.

6.3 BETTER GUIDANCE FOR DIRECTORS OF DISTRESSED COMPANIES

There is already some information on offer for the public for those who wish to consult it. For example, the DBIS and the Insolvency Service produce useful guidance notes.[12]

Organizations such as the Confederation of British Industry and the Institute of Directors also offer valuable insights.[13] But should we go further? The new provisions in the Companies Act 2006 undoubtedly seek to enlighten directors as to their responsibilities in general, but perhaps we now need a specific focus on what is good stewardship for those who are managing distressed businesses. Such a well-intentioned move might be frustrated by the refusal of some directors, particularly of small firms, to take any notice of the guidance already available. As being informed is becoming an important feature of stewardship, that refusal to engage should be a relevant consideration when considering sanctions against directors of failed companies.

One of the recommendations of the Sharman Report[14] is that there should be more research on the performance of corporate governance rules in cases of insolvency and 'near misses'. Such research may well lead to improved guidance for directors operating in the twilight zone.

There have been suggestions that we should introduce a US-style business judgement rule as a safe harbour for directors making difficult decisions in times of corporate financial stress. This idea has been floated on a number of previous occasions in this country. The Law Commission considered it in 1999 but rejected its introduction.[15] The Company Law Review[16] also rejected any

---

[12] For example see *A Guide for Directors* (Insolvency Service) (June 2011) (URN 11/1016), *Re-use of a Company Name After Liquidation* (Insolvency Service) (March 2012) (URN 12/640).

[13] See the *Director* magazine produced by the IoD and the CBI's *Business Voice*.

[14] *Going Concern and Liquidity Risks: Lessons for Companies and Auditors* (June 2012).

[15] See Law Commission, *Regulating Conflicts of Interest and Formulating a Statement of Duties* (Report No. 261) (1999).

[16] See *Developing the Framework* (2000) at para 3.69. Accordingly this issue of introducing the business judgement rule did not feature in the final report.

legislative reform to this effect, preferring instead to see a natural evolution through the processes of case law. Quite frankly, it is not seen to be necessary to introduce such a rule on a formal basis. The courts[17] are quite aware of the dangers of using hindsight to judge commercial decisions in times of stress and it is far better to leave this matter in their capable hands.

One reform worth revisiting is the introduction of an anticipatory declaration facility to offer authoritative guidance to directors on whether they should continue to trade. Such a facility, protected by an in-camera hearing, was recommended by the Cork Committee.[18] There is a parallel in applications under s. 127 of the Insolvency Act 1986 and under s. 1157 of the Companies Act 2006. In fairness these are rarely used, but their availability one day may prove worthwhile.

6.4 A RETHINK ON SANCTIONS FOR DIRECTORS

The possibilities for changing current legislative provisions designed to penalize directors who fail to live up to required standards whilst managing distressed companies should be considered. Have we got the balance right? Are the current methods of sanctioning directors cost-effective, an increasingly important factor these days? Would it make sense to have an *automatic* period of disqualification for all directors of companies that fail? In spite of the fact that automatic disqualification is applied to undischarged bankrupts and the like, the usual answer to this latter question must be 'no'[19] as this would be unfair in many instances and susceptible to challenge under the European Convention on Human Rights on the grounds of being disproportionate. Access to limited liability is now seen as a fundamental right and it should not be denied without justification. When this idea of an automatic ban was last mooted in the 1970s it was not promoted by the Cork Committee,[20] which in Chapter 45 favoured more discriminating tools to deal with the problem. With the current crisis in capitalism and with the fundamentals of corporate governance being re-evaluated it may be an opportunity to rethink the position. It might be cheaper to apply an automatic ban and then to throw the cost of accessing limited liability upon the entrepreneur. There is a possibility that such an automatic ban might be introduced for directors of failed banks.[21]

---

17 See for example *Re Hawkes Hill Publications Ltd* [2007] BCC 937.

18 Cmnd 8558 para 1798.

19 See A. Hicks [1988] JBL 27 at 48.

20 See Cmnd 8558, Chapter 45.

21 See Treasury Consultation Document 3 July 2012, *Sanctions for Directors of Failed Banks*.

If that happens, it could trigger a more general response by corporate law policymakers.

One solution would be to introduce a presumption that a director of an insolvent company would automatically be subject to a two-year cooling-off period unless that director could persuade the court that there was no need for such a hiatus. Such a reversal of the burden of proof has much to commend it, though a quick method of adjudicating appeals should be considered.

The possibility of extending the s. 10 disqualification power under the Company Directors Disqualification Act 1986 to cases where a breach of s. 216 has been established is also worth looking at.[22]

As to other sanctions, it may be that English law should look again at the options available. This general issue was considered in the Company Law Review[23] a decade ago, but a comparison with other jurisdictions reveals a picture of greater diversity.

English law does make limited use of the criminal law to punish directors who fail to live up to their stewardship expectations. So the general law of theft as laid down in s. 1 of the Theft Act 1968 might be deployed against them. We have noted the offence of fraudulent trading, now found in s. 993 of the Companies Act 2006. There are also offences embodied in the Insolvency Act 1986, such as s. 206 (fraud in anticipation of winding-up) and s. 217 (breach of the restrictions imposed in s. 216). Disqualified directors who ignore their disqualification commit an offence under s. 13 of the Company Directors Disqualification Act 1986.

We need to look at who has the right to exploit civil recovery claims against directors. There seems to be no logic in denying an administrator a right to bring a wrongful trading action, or indeed to prevent a creditor from so doing. Reform on both points should be considered.[24] If we are to remain reliant upon disciplining directors through recovery actions, it is opportune to look again at how such actions might be financed.[25] The current rules operating in this arena in the UK are very restrictive and do not compare well with the position found in similar jurisdictions (such as Australia and New Zealand). The campaign to tackle CFAs and ATE insurance agreements in litigation that harmed the public purse certainly posed a threat that the profession became quickly aware of. Its representatives fought an effective rearguard action to forestall such a move.

---

22 As suggested by S. Griffin in J. de Lacy (ed.), *The Reform of UK Company Law* (2002) at 227.

23 For *Final Report* see URN 01/942.

24 See M. Mumford and A. Katz, *Making Creditor Protection Effective* (2010), Recommendations 21 and 22.

25 This was certainly the view of M. Mumford and A. Katz (supra) (2010), Recommendation 15.

The protection offered in the Legal Aid, Sentencing and Punishment of Offenders Act 2012 is welcome, though it is only in place for a short period up to April 2015.

We should also consider whether there might be an increased role for the private sector here. In an era when the Insolvency Service has faced significant economies, should we not look at ways of transferring the burden of policing errant directors onto the private sector? This could be done by opening recovery procedures to private sector actors in return for a share of profits. This idea might offend some traditionalists who object to the legal system being used in this mercenary way, but if it delivers better returns for creditors and deters managerial misbehaviour, surely it is worth looking at.

A final reform worthy of consideration concerns the ability of directors to tap into the state redundancy fund to claim arrears of wages when their firm becomes insolvent. They are able to do this because of their legal standing as employees, a status which is somewhat fictional in an owner-managed business.[26] At a time when every line of public expenditure is being reviewed, this item should be looked at carefully. The existence of this state subsidy may have the effect of encouraging directors to trade on at a time when intervention should be the order of the day. But it must be remembered that there may be EU complications to overcome for any such reform to take place.

6.5 RESTRICTING ACCESS TO LIMITED LIABILITY

One suspects that one of the fundamental problems underlying stewardship failings with regard to the management of companies is that too many ill-suited individuals set up businesses and become directors whilst enjoying the protection of limited liability. Society has to decide whether it wishes to restrict this freedom. It may do so by imposing entry qualifications or by requiring a minimum share capital. Both ideas go against the underlying laissez-faire philosophy in the UK, but that does not mean that they should be ignored.[27] As to the former possibility, would it be outlandish to suggest that at least one person on a board of directors should have some formal management qualification? We are not talking about having an MBA, but evidence of participation in a short management course surely should not be too much to ask. A recent R3 survey suggests that there is support for improved financial

---

[26] But nevertheless the courts have supported orthodoxy and have reaffirmed this status – *Secretary of State for BERR v Neufeld* [2009] EWCA Civ 280, [2009] BCC 687.

[27] Such ideas have been floated by Philip King but with the conclusion that they are unlikely to attract official backing – see [2012] Recovery (Spring) 46.

training for managers. If business is seen as so important for the health of the country, perhaps more should be done to educate young people in the realities and ethics of business as part of their core curriculum. The minimum share capital idea, having been dismissed a decade ago, should be revisited. Critics would say that to introduce this new barrier would deter enterprise – but we must always bear in mind the possibility of using the partnership model for new entrants to business. Something should be done to ensure that new limited liability ventures operate on a firmer foundation to prevent the high infant mortality rate. Minimum share capital offers little real protection to creditors but it might well cause some would-be entrepreneurs to pause for thought and to consider the implications of their commercial decisions. Another idea that has been mooted[28] (and indeed is in operation in some respects) is the idea of a deposit for future tax liabilities of the company.

6.6 AN ENLARGED ROLE FOR THE STATE IN CORPORATE GOVERNANCE?

In the current economic climate any suggestion of additional state input might appear incongruous, if only on grounds of the initial cost. But input that is productive for the state in the long term should not be ruled out. The current system imposes significant costs upon the state. The state is a substantial stakeholder in all UK companies, primarily through its position as a major tax creditor, but also because of its role as the ultimate guarantor of a proportion of arrears of wages owed by insolvent employers. Indeed, in the wake of the global economic crisis it has been compelled to become a shareholder in a number of financial institutions, with that shareholding being managed by UK Financial Investments Ltd,[29] a body set up in November 2008 in the immediate aftermath of the global financial crash. Should that role as a shareholder be expanded with regard to all public companies in the interests of promoting better corporate governance? Critics of such a suggestion would point to the initial outlay for the exchequer and the fact that government agencies do not have a good record of promoting effective corporate governance. On the other hand, the state loses millions of pounds each year through companies which

---

28 See S. Fennell [2012] (Autumn) Recov 32.

29 See its Annual Report for 2010/11 (July 2011, HC 1396). There is a touch of déjà vu here, as the nationalization of the coal mines and the railways in the early twentieth century was triggered by the financial predicament of those private companies running those key components of the UK economy. These are not isolated examples – see generally in Chapters 3 and 8 in J. Foreman-Peck and R. Millward, *Public and Private Ownership of British Industry 1820–1990* (1994).

fail – anything that could reduce that loss would be a positive move. Those who resist state investment ignore the fact that a large percentage of the shares held in UK listed companies (more than 40 per cent) are now held by foreign investors and increasingly by foreign sovereign wealth funds. If these investors see UK companies as a good bet, why do we as an intelligent nation shy away from the idea of state investment? Is it because this raises the spectre of socialism and engenders fears of a return to old-style nationalization?

Were we to go down this road, the investment would have to be timely and justified on commercial grounds. Any attempt to use state investment simply to prop up a distressed firm, whether that assistance be in the form of equity subscription or debt concession, would be likely to fall foul of the reasonable market economic investor test under EU state aid law.[30] In the changing political climate post-global economic crisis, this idea deserves a balanced airing.

If the state were to play a greater role in companies, this would raise the spectre of public law ideas being imported into commercial law. Many would see this as a negative step as it could disrupt commercial decision-making.[31] Others would embrace the idea as being long overdue and an antidote to the failings of the current system.[32]

6.7 QUALIFICATION AND REGULATION OF INSOLVENCY PRACTITIONERS

This issue has attracted attention both in the UK and Australia[33] in the past two years.

Enabling firms, as opposed to individuals, to be appointed as office-holders would be a sensible move. This would reflect the reality on the ground and there is no suggestion that a corporate body is being used for any sort of tactical purpose. As firms of insolvency practitioners now operate using the LLP model with the benefit of separate personality, the arguments about the consequences of unincorporated associations holding office are no longer apposite. An astute observer might detect an inconsistency between this proposal and our previous recommendation in para 6.2 on banning corporate directors. It is

---

30 See *Tubacex (C342/96)* [1999] ECR I-02459 for the market investor test. We discuss state aid in Chapter 5 above.

31 Witness the recent Irish case of *Treasury Holdings v NAMA* [2012] IEHC 297.

32 See K. Greenfield, *The Failure of Corporate Law: Fundamental Flaws and Progressive Possibilities* (2007).

33 See Australian Senate Inquiry, *The Regulation, Registration and Remuneration of Insolvency Practitioners in Australia: The Case for a New Framework* (2010).

submitted that this differential approach can be justified as the downside risks are completely different. Moreover, if we are prepared to allow a corporate body to be a trustee,[34] it is difficult to see why corporate bodies should be prevented from holding insolvency office. There is a counter-argument that cannot be dismissed lightly – the current system in the UK works on the premise of an individual holding office. The old conservative adage 'if it's not broke don't fix it' still justifiably commands respect.

6.8 COMPLAINTS PROCEDURES

Setting up a single Insolvency Ombudsman regime to deal with complaints against IPs would be a smart move that would enhance public confidence. The Cork Committee urged this reform (see para 1772). The Office of Fair Trading also recommended it in its 2010 study. The current system in which each of the recognized professional bodies maintains its own complaints structure is balkanized. That does not mean that it is failing, but greater public confidence would be generated by having a uniform complaints-handling system.[35] This might even help the development of good practice. This idea has been resisted by the insolvency profession[36] but in the long term it may well serve their interests to go along with it.

6.9 STANDARDIZED POWERS FOR INSOLVENCY PRACTITIONERS

Insolvency practitioners have wide powers but these are not uniform. Should the power of disclaimer of onerous assets be made more widely available? The short answer to this should be 'yes'. Certainly, it is difficult to see why it should be denied to administrators now that their role in many senses mirrors that of liquidators. Administrators cannot bring misfeasance claims[37] nor can they pursue wrongful trading actions. Do these lacunae make any sense in the modern corporate insolvency framework? Again the answer will be in the negative and it is interesting to note that the Cork Committee came out in

---

34 See Trustee Act 1925 s. 68.

35 Such a model has been introduced for solicitors via Part 6 of the Legal Services Act 2007.

36 See December 2011 Insolvency Service, *Consultation on Reforms to the Regulation of Insolvency Practitioners*.

37 *Irwin v Lynch* [2010] EWCA Civ 1153, [2011] 1 WLR 1364, [2011] BPIR 158.

favour of a more extensive range of applicants for a wrongful trading claim (see Cmnd 8558 para 1792) and also supported greater harmonization of powers and duties (ibid, para 788f). When the primary legislation is reviewed, one hopes that the policymakers will not lose sight of these recommendations as both would enhance stewardship. Although the drafting of Schedule B1 has attracted criticism, the clear way in which the powers and duties of administrators are laid out is commendable and may serve as a future model.

6.10 TIME LIMITS FOR ALL INSOLVENCY PROCEEDINGS?

The experiment with a one-year cut-off for administrations appears to have worked. Is it time to extend that policy to liquidations, receiverships and CVAs? There is certainly an argument for this period being made applicable to liquidations, but other considerations come into play for receiverships and CVAs. In the case of receivership this is a contractual remedy and to retrospectively change its characteristics might be open to legal challenge on the grounds of undue interference with property rights contrary to Art 1 of the First Protocol. Against this, it may be argued that post-2003 many administrations involving para 14 appointments possess this same feature and therefore there is no justification for differentiation. CVAs involve consensual agreements between unsecured creditors and any time limit may be justified on that basis.

6.11 RETHINKING THE PRIORITY OF EXPENSES

This is an area of considerable uncertainty that causes much vexation for insolvency practitioners. This is particularly true as there are significant differences on what may be regarded as expenses between the administration and liquidation regimes, as Morgan J was at pains to stress in *Neumans LLP v Andronikou*,[38] a case which perfectly illustrates the Byzantine complexity of this area of the law. The decision of the Supreme Court in *Bloom v Pensions Regulator*[39] (which is expected to be handed down in the first half of 2013) is awaited with interest in this connection and may, depending on the outcome, provide the springboard for change. Modifying the rules governing the treat-

---

38 [2012] EWHC 3088 (Ch).

39 [2013] UKSC (forthcoming) – this is the appeal from [2011] EWCA Civ 1124, [2012] BCC 83.

ment of expenses incurred by insolvency practitioners whilst conducting the insolvency process should be on any reform agenda. We have made considerable progress here with the advent of the idea of value for money and transparency in connection with the stewardship of insolvency practitioners.

6.12 PROMOTING DIVERSITY

Scholars with interests in gender studies often point out that the relatively poor performance of UK business might be linked to the lack of boardroom diversity. We saw in Chapter 2 above that this is a difficult hypothesis to establish, but there is no denying that a gender gap exists. Can anything be done to close this gap? Having a legally enforceable quota system would be fraught with difficulty, but the state ultimately has the right to regulate limited liability. Would some gentler strategy, such as a voluntary code of practice for listed companies, be a positive step? If this step is taken, the issue of gender diversity amongst insolvency practitioners could also come into sharp relief. Progress has been made in recent years in this respect, but the issue must be kept at the forefront of the minds of the leaders of the profession.

6.13 MISCELLANEOUS REFORMS

There are a number of possibilities to note under this residual heading.

The policy of transactional avoidance on insolvency, which has as a collateral goal the promotion of ethical stewardship, is hampered by the operation on the rules of preference in English law. In particular, under s. 239 of the Insolvency Act 1986, it must be shown that the company (aka the directors) was influenced by a desire to prefer when entering the transaction. The ruling of Millett J in *Re MC Bacon Ltd*[40] confirms this requirement. This has enabled banks to use last-minute fixed charges[41] to bolster their priority position without fear of challenge. This is turn may undermine any role they should play as responsible monitors of a distressed firm. This would not be permitted in many common-law jurisdictions where the focus would be on the *effect* of the grant of security and not the motivation behind it.[42] Our nearest neighbour,

40 [1990] BCC 78.

41 This practice is countered in the case of floating charges by s. 245 of the Insolvency Act 1986.

42 See the ILA-funded study by D. Milman and R. Parry, *A Study of the Operation of Transactional Avoidance Mechanisms in Corporate Insolvency Practice* (1997).

Scotland, does not require any intention to prefer, as is clear from the wording of s. 243 of the Insolvency Act 1986.

Looking at the duties of insolvency practitioners, it must be apparent to all that they have grown up in ad hoc fashion. Is it time to modernize? A standardization based upon Sched B1 might be worth considering. Although this Schedule has come in for a fair degree of criticism for its drafting, in substance it provides a useful matrix when viewed in the light of subsequent judicial interpretation. This idea of consolidation has been pursued with regard to directors' duties by the Companies Act 2006. Imposing a duty of reasonable care on LLP members by explicit statutory provision would help standards of stewardship in that increasingly important organizational constituency. Rather the position has been left to common law, as the comparable provision for company directors (s. 174 of the Companies Act 2006) was not rendered applicable.[43]

Entry into formal insolvency regimes in English law involves a formal admission of insolvency. Is this helpful? Should the entry criteria be relaxed to allow distressed companies that are not technically insolvent access to formal restructuring procedures? The position with regard to the Chapter 11 procedure in the US is much more flexible in this respect.

6.14 THE PROBLEM OF 'RETROSPECTIVE' JUDICIAL RULINGS

One problem that bedevils both corporate managers and insolvency practitioners is our system of judicial decision-making and the fact that it operates retrospectively for its view on industry practices. The courts decide for example in a particular case that an insolvency practitioner has misunderstood the law and that finding then can impact on decisions taken years previously by other practitioners. Sometimes retrospective legislation (such as the Insolvency Act 1994[44]) or some type of extra statutory concession[45] is then

---

43 See the discussion in G. Morse (ed.), *Palmer's Limited Liability Partnership Law* (2nd ed., 2011) at A6-07.

44 Designed to combat the Court of Appeal ruling in *Re Paramount Airways Ltd* [1994] BCC 172 on liabilities resulting from the adoption of contracts of employment. Ironically, this ruling was substantially mitigated on appeal – see *Powdrill v Watson* [1995] BCC 319. The industry practice that was overturned in *Paramount* was based upon a favourable reading of an unreported decision of Harman J in *Re Specialised Mouldings Ltd* (13 February 1987).

45 Witness the Crown Statements issued in the wake of *Leyland DAF* [2004] UKHL 9, [2004] 2 AC 298 and *National Westminster Bank v Spectrum Plus Ltd* [2005] UKHL 41, [2005] BCC 694. These are reproduced as Appendices IX and X in Vol 2 of

issued to offer relief. But this ignores the fundamental problem. A system of prospective overruling in commercial litigation has much to commend it, though few judges have been prepared to sponsor such reform.

6.15 FINAL THOUGHTS: REFLECTING UPON STEWARDSHIP TRENDS

If we reflect upon developments in stewardship as practised by directors and insolvency practitioners over the past 30 years, certain trends stand out. First, access to the role of steward has become more restricted, particularly in the case of those who assume insolvency office. Second, the duties imposed upon those who have the stewardship of limited companies in their hands have been upgraded, largely as a result of the recommendations of the Cork Committee. Inertia and a lack of curiosity are now liable to attract criticism and possibly sanction. The growing tendency of the courts to use 'trustee' rhetoric to describe the role of directors and insolvency office-holders is significant. In view of these developments, the importance of taking legal and professional advice has grown in significance. The democratic controls upon company stewards have moved in a positive direction, particularly with regards to insolvency practitioners,[46] but there is still an underlying philosophy of non-intervention whilst the stewardship is ongoing. The governance system has responded well to the challenges posed by the arrival of the prepack phenomenon. As far as the element of rewarding stewards is concerned, the message is again positive. There are growing controls on directors' remuneration (witness the putative measures for listed companies in the Enterprise and Regulatory Reform Bill 2012) and the position with regard to insolvency practitioners has moved forward apace in the past decade.

On the negative side, there is more to be done on controlling access to limited liability in the first place and only limited progress has been made in terms of the gender profile of those entrusted with the stewardship of limited companies. There are concerns that attempts to curb public expenditure may curb the active pursuit of policies (such as disqualification) which are designed to protect the public. This needs to be carefully watched and there is real concern[47] that the numbers of directors being disqualified is beginning to

the 14th edition of Sealy and Milman *Annotated Guide to Insolvency Legislation* (2011).

46 Witness for example Enterprise Act 2002 s. 253, which requires office-holders to secure creditor permission before instituting recovery claims.

47 As evidenced by the submission of a Memorandum dated 29 June 2012 by R3 to Parliament in the context of the Enterprise and Regulatory Reform Bill 2012. See paras 30–35 of the Memorandum.

drop. Is this a sign of improved commercial morality or a slacking-off in enforcement due to public expenditure cuts? If the public purse cannot be used to protect the public, is there an argument for freeing up the role that may be played by private litigation finance?

There is always an argument for maintaining the status quo in any system of regulation, if only because stability can produce reduced transaction costs. The problem we have in this field is that post-2008 there is a growing crisis of confidence in the way that limited companies and similar firms operate and in the way that their stakeholders are dealt with when such entities fail. Many of these criticisms rest on the continued sustainability of the whole idea of limited liability. That idea is not yet past its 'sell-by date', though policymakers should be concerned to review its operation on a regular basis and to consider any measures that may promote better stewardship of firms that benefit from limited liability. It is clear that the more pressing stewardship concerns arise at the front end of the limited liability 'game' and not when companies pass into the hands of insolvency practitioners. The public may not always be aware of this in the fog of criticism that often surrounds insolvency practitioners, but it is a fact. We hope that a number of the aforementioned suggestions will merit some consideration in policymaking circles and will continue the trend towards enhanced stewardship.

Bibliography

BOOKS

Argenti, J., *Corporate Collapse* (1976) (McGraw-Hill).

Berle, A. and Means, G., *The Modern Corporation and Private Property* (1932) (Macmillan).

Bork, R., *Rescuing Companies in England and Germany* (2012) (Oxford University Press).

Brown, D. and Telfer, T.G.W., *Personal and Corporate Insolvency Legislation* (2007) (LexisNexis NZ).

Charkham, M., *Keeping Better Company* (2nd ed.) (2005) (Oxford University Press).

Cheffins, B. (ed.), *The History of Modern US Corporate Governance* (2011) (Edward Elgar).

Coffee, J., *Gatekeepers: The Professions and Corporate Governance* (2006) (Oxford University Press).

Colino, S.M., *Competition Law in the EU and the UK* (7th ed.) (2011) (Oxford University Press).

De Lacy, J. (ed.), *The Reform of UK Company Law* (2002) (Cavendish).

Dignam, A. and Galanis, M., *The Globalisation of Corporate Governance* (2009) (Ashgate).

Eells, R.S.F., *The Meaning of Modern Business: An Introduction to the Philosophy of Large Corporate Enterprise* (1960) (Columbia University Press).

Farrar, J., *Corporate Governance: Theories, Principles and Practice* (3rd ed.) (2008) (Oxford University Press).

Finch, V., *Corporate Insolvency Law: Perspectives and Principles* (2nd ed.) (2009) (Cambridge University Press).

Fletcher, I., *Law of Insolvency* (4th ed.) (2011) (Sweet and Maxwell).

Foreman-Peck, J. and Millward, R., *Public and Private Ownership of British Industry 1820–1990* (1994) (Clarendon Press).

Gardner, S., *An Introduction to the Law of Trusts* (3rd ed.) (2011) (Oxford University Press).

Goode, R., *Principles of Corporate Insolvency Law* (4th ed.) (2011) (Sweet and Maxwell).

Gray, J. and Akseli, O. (eds), *Financial Regulation in Crisis? The Role of Law and the Failure of Northern Rock* (2011) (Edward Elgar).
Greenfield, K., *The Failure of Corporate Law: Fundamental Flaws and Progressive Possibilities* (2007) (University of Chicago Press).
Gugler, K. (ed.), *Corporate Governance and Economic Performance* (2001) (Oxford University Press).
Hollington, R., *Shareholder Rights* (6th ed.) (2010) (Sweet and Maxwell).
Hudson, A., *Equity and Trusts* (7th ed.) (2012) (Routledge).
Hutton, W., *The Stakeholding Society* (1999) (Polity Press).
Keay, A., *McPherson's Law of Company Liquidation* (2001) (Sweet & Maxwell).
Keay, A., *Company Directors* (2009) (Jordans).
Keay, A., *The Corporate Objective* (2011) (Edward Elgar).
Lester, V.M., *Victorian Insolvency* (1995) (Clarendon Press)
Lobo, O.E.F., *World Insolvency Systems* (2009) (Carswell).
Lo Pucki, L.M. and Doherty, J.W., *Professional Fees in Corporate Bankruptcies* (2011) (Oxford Scholarship Online).
Lowry, J. and Reisberg, A., *Pettet's Company Law: Company Law and Corporate Finance* (4th ed.) (2012) (Pearson).
Lynch-Fannon, I., *Working Within Two Kinds of Capitalism* (2003) (Hart Publishing).
Lynch-Fannon, I. and Murphy, G.N., *Corporate Insolvency and Rescue* (2nd ed.) (2012) (Bloomsbury Professional).
MacLeod, S., *Global Governance and The Quest for Justice. Volume 2: Corporate Governance* (2006) (Hart Publishing).
MacNeil, I.G., *An Introduction to the Law on Financial Investment* (2nd ed.) (2012) (Hart Publishing).
Mallin, C., *Corporate Governance* (3rd ed.) (2010) (Oxford University Press).
McCahery, J.A. and Vermuelen, E.P.M., *Corporate Governance of Non-Listed Companies* (2010) (Oxford University Press).
McCormack, G., *Corporate Rescue Law: An Anglo American Perspective* (2008) (Edward Elgar).
Milman, D., *Personal Insolvency Law, Regulation and Policy* (2005) (Ashgate).
Milman, D., *National Corporate Law in a Globalised Market* (2009) (Edward Elgar).
Moffatt, G., *Trusts Law* (5th ed.) (2009) (Cambridge University Press).
Mokal, R., *Corporate Insolvency Law: Theory and Application* (2005) (Oxford University Press).
Morse, G. (ed.), *Palmers Limited Liability Partnership Law* (2nd ed.) (2011) (Sweet and Maxwell).
Ormerod, P., *Why Most Things Fail: Evolution, Extinction and Economics* (2005) (Faber and Faber).

Parkinson, J., *Corporate Power and Responsibility* (1994) (Oxford University Press).
Proctor, G. and Miles, L., *Corporate Governance* (2002) (Cavendish).
Roe, M., *Political Determinants in Corporate Governance* (2003) (Oxford University Press).
Schumpeter, J., *The Theory of Economic Development: An Inquiry into Profits, Capital, Credit, Interest and the Business Cycle* (1934) (Harvard University Press).
Schumpeter, J., *Capitalism, Socialism and Democracy* (1942) (Harper).
Sealy, L.S. and Milman, D., *Annotated Guide to Insolvency Legislation 2012* (15th ed.) (2012) (Sweet and Maxwell).
Slatter, S. and Lovett, D., *Corporate Turnaround: Managing Companies in Distress* (1999) (Penguin).
Sorensen, A. (ed.), *Directors Liabilities in Case of Insolvency* (1999) (Kluwer Law International).
Symes, C.F., *Statutory Priorities in Corporate Insolvency Law* (2008) (Ashgate).
Tomasic, R. (ed.), *Insolvency in East Asia* (2006) (Ashgate).
Watson, A., *Legal Transplants: An Approach to Comparative Law* (1974) (Scottish Academic Press).
Wearing, R., *Cases in Corporate Governance* (2005) (Sage).
Williams, R., *Disqualification Undertakings* (2011) (Jordans).

CONTRIBUTIONS TO COLLECTED WORKS

Anderson, H., 'Insolvency Practitioners: Professional Independence and Conflict of Interest', in Clarke, A., *Current Issues in Insolvency Law* (1991) (Stevens) pp. 1–25.
Griffin, S., 'The Disqualification of Company Directors in the Management of Insolvent Companies', Chapter 9 in de Lacy, J., *The Reform of UK Company Law* (2002) (Cavendish).
Milman, D., 'From Servant to Stakeholder: The Employee Interest in Company Law', Chapter 8 in Feldman, D. and Meisel, F., *Corporate and Commercial Law: Modern Developments* (1995) (Lloyds of London Press) pp. 147–72.
Milman, D., 'Promoting Distributional Justice on Corporate Insolvency in the 21st Century', in van Boom, W. and Steele, J., *Mass Justice: Challenges of Representation and Distribution* (2011) (Edward Elgar).
Parkinson, J., 'Corporate Governance and the Regulation of Business Behaviour', in Macleod, S. (ed.), *Global Governance and the Quest for Justice: Vol 2 Corporate Governance* (2006) (Hart Publishing).

Redmond, P., 'Safe Harbour or Sleepy Hollow: Does Australia Need a Statutory Business Judgement Rule?' in Ramsay, I. (ed.), *Corporate Governance and the Duties of Company Directors* (1997) (University of Melbourne Centre for Corporate Law and Securities Regulation).

RESEARCH REPORTS

Bloom, N., Genakos, C., Sadun, R. and van Reenen, J., *Management Practices across Firms and Countries* (2011) (Centre for Economic Performance) (Discussion Paper 1109).
Flood, J. and Skordaki, E., *Insolvency Practitioners and Big Corporate Insolvencies* (1995) (ACCA Research Report No. 43).
Hicks, A., *Disqualification of Directors: No Hiding Place for the Unfit?* (1998) (ACCA Research Report No. 59).
Milman, D. and Chittenden, F., *Corporate Rescue: CVAs and the Challenge of Small Companies* (1995) (ACCA Research Report No. 44).
Mumford, M.J. and Katz, A., *Making Creditor Protection Effective* (2010) (Centre for Business Performance – ICAEW).
Seneviratne, M. and Walters, A., *Complaints Handling by the Regulators of Insolvency Practitioners: A Comparative Study* (2009) (Nottingham Law School).
Walters, A. and Seneviratne, M., *Complaints Handling in the Insolvency Practitioner Profession* (2008) (Nottingham Law School).
Wheeler, S. and Wilson, G., *Directors' Liabilities in the Context of Corporate Groups* (1998) (ILA Research Report) (GTI Specialist Publishers).
Williams, C. and McGee, A., *A Company Director's Liability for Wrongful Trading* (1992) (ACCA Report No. 30).

JOURNAL ARTICLES

Ahern, D., 'Nominee Directors' Duty to Promote the Success of the Company: Commercial Pragmatism and Legal Orthodoxy' [2011] 127 LQR 118.
Ahern, D., 'Directors' Duties, Dry Ink and the Accessibility Agenda' [2012] 128 LQR 114.
Ali, S.A., 'Re-Defining Stewardship?' [2012] Jo of Fin Crime 207.
Altman, E., 'Financial Ratios, Discriminant Analysis and the Prediction of Corporate Bankruptcy' [1968] 23 Jo of Fin 589.
Anderson, J., 'Mend or Mar? The Continuing Saga of the Defectively Appointed Administrator Continues: Minmar and Its Aftermath' [2011] 304 SMCLN 1.

Anderson, J., 'Minmar 2: Quite Possibly Mar!' [2012] 309 SMCLN 1.
Anderson, J., 'Minmar: Non Curat Lex?' [2012] 320 SMCLN 1.
Arden, M., 'Regulating the Conduct of Directors' [2010] 10 JCLS 1.
Armour, J., 'Share Capital and Creditor Protection: Efficient Rules for a Modern Company Law' [2000] 63 MLR 355.
Armour, J., Hsu, A. and Walters, A., 'Corporate Insolvency in the UK: The Impact of the Enterprise Act 2002' [2008] 5 ECFLR 148.
Atherton, A., 'Cases of Start-up Financing: An Analysis of New Venture Capitalisation Structures and Patterns' [2012] 18 Int Jo of Entrepreneurial Behaviour and Research 28.
Bacon, A.M., 'At Last PVAs – But was it Worth the Wait?' [1994] 10 IL & P 166.
Bainbridge, S.M., 'The Business Judgment Rule as Abstention Doctrine' [2004] 57 Vand L Rev 83.
Baister, S., 'Remuneration, The Insolvency Practitioner and the Courts' [2006] 22 IL & P 50.
Baker, C.A., 'Other People's Money: The Problem of Professional Fees in Bankruptcy' [1996] 38 Ariz L Rev 35.
Barrett, R., 'Directors' Duties to Creditors' [1977] 40 MLR 226.
Bartlett, F., 'Shadow Director – A Spectre that Haunts the High Street Banker' [1994] 10 IL & P 52.
Bebchuk, L. and Roe, M.J., 'A Theory of Path Dependence in Corporate Ownership and Governance' [1999] 52 Stan Law Rev 127.
Belcher, A., 'Predicting Corporate Failure' [1991] 7 IL & P 64.
Belcher, A., 'The Invention, Innovation and Diffusion of Self Regulation in Corporate Governance' [1996] 47 NILQ 322.
Belcher, A., 'Board Diversity: Can Sex Discrimination Law Help?' [2005] 56 NILQ 356.
Belcher, A., 'What Makes a Director Fit? An Analysis of the Workings of Section 17 of the Company Directors Disqualification Act 1986' [2012] 16 Edinburgh Law Review 386.
Betts, R., 'Characteristics of British Company Directors' [1967] 4 Jo of Man Studs 71.
Birds, J., 'Companies Act 2006 – Revolution or Evolution?' [2007] 49 Manag Law 13.
Black, W., 'R3 Research Looks at Director Disqualification and Whether Lessons can be Learned from Corporate Failure' [2010] (Autumn) Recov 38.
Bork, R., 'The Protective Umbrella Procedure – A New German Restructuring Tool' [2012] 25 Ins Intell 22.
Bork, R., 'Creditors' Committees: An Anglo-German Comparative Study' [2012] 21 IIR 127.

Borrie, G., 'The Professions: Expensive Monopolies or Guardians of the Public Interest?' [1984] JBL 111.
Bradley, C., 'Corporate Control – Markets and Rules' [1990] 50 MLR 171.
Bradstreet, J., 'The New Business Rescue: Will Creditors Sink or Swim?' [2011] SALJ 352.
Brandt, W.A. and Vance, C.E., 'Deepening Insolvency and the UK Wrongful Trading Statute: a Comparative Discussion' [2006] 19 Ins Intell 156.
Burrow, A., 'Lenders in the Shade' [2011] (July) Jo of Law Soc Scot 50.
Butler, M. and Milman, D., 'Business Participants and Employee Status: A Review of the Current Position' [2012] 33 Co Law 165.
Campbell, D., 'The End of Posnerian Law and Economics' [2010] 73 MLR 305.
Carney, W.J., 'Section 40.1 of the American Law Institute's Corporate Governance Project: Restatement or Misstatement?' [1988] 66 Wash Univ L Q 239.
Carter, T., 'The Phoenix Syndrome – The Personal Liability of Directors' [2006] 19 Ins Intell 38.
Cerfontaine, A. and Armstrong, M., 'The Rhetoric of Inclusion? Corporate Governance in Insolvency Law' [2000] Ins Law 38.
Cheffins, B., 'The Stewardship Code's Achilles Heel' [2010] 73 MLR 1004.
Clements, R. and Broadbent, G., 'The Insolvency Practitioners Tribunal' [1987] 3 IL & P 34.
Clench, T., 'Applications for Permission to Act under s. 17 of the Company Directors Disqualification Act 1986' [2008] 21 Ins Intell 113.
Clench, T., 'Being Concerned in the Management of a Company – What Does it Mean?' [2012] 25 Ins Intell 28.
Cook, C., 'Wrongful Trading – Is it a Real Threat to Directors or a Paper Tiger?' [1999] Ins Law 99.
Cooke, T.E. and Hicks, A., 'Wrongful Trading-Predicting Insolvency' [1993] JBL 338.
Copp, S.F., 'Section 172 of the Companies Act Fails People and Planet?' [2010] 31 Co Law 406.
Crinson, K. and Morphet, S., 'Funding for Actions Brought by Insolvency Office Holders' [2011] 24 Ins Intell 108.
Davies, P., 'Directors Creditor-Regarding Duties in Respect of Trading Decisions Taken in the Vicinity of Insolvency' [2006] 7 Euro Bus Org L Rev 301.
Davis, J.H., Allen, M.R. and Hayes, H.D., 'Is Blood Thicker Than Water? A Study of Stewardship Perceptions in Family Business' [2010] Ent Theory and Pract 1093.
Dawson, I., 'The Administrator, Morality and the Court' [1996] JBL 437.
Day, J. and Taylor, P., 'Financial Distress in Small Firms' [2001] Ins Law 97.

Dean, M., 'Legal Transplants and Jury Trial in Japan' [2011] 31 Legal Studies 570.
Dignam, A., 'Exporting Corporate Governance: UK Regulatory Systems in a Global Economy' [2000] 21 Co Law 70.
Donaldson, L. and Davis, J.H., 'Stewardship Theory or Agency Theory: CEO Governance and Shareholder Returns' [1991] 16 Aust Jo of Man 49.
Doyle, L., 'Anomalies in the Wrongful Trading Provisions' [1992] 13 Co Law 96.
Du Plessis, J.J., 'Open Sea or Safe Harbour? American, Australian and South African Business Judgment Rules Compared' [2011] 32 Co Law 347 and 377.
Editorial, 'European Commission Proposes European Private Company and Small Business Act' [2008] 235 SMCLN 1.
Editorial, 'European Commission Proposes Small Business Act' [2008] 236 SMCLN 1.
Editorial, 'Insolvency Service Publishes Report on First Six Months of SIP 16 on Prepacks' [2009] 258 SMCLN 1.
Editorial, 'Lord Davies Reports on Women on Boards' [2011] 291 SMCLN 1.
Editorial, 'Will the Jackson Reforms for Civil Litigation Costs Harm Insolvency Case Development?' [2011] 296 SMCLN 1.
Editorial, 'Women on Boards – Movement Forward but No Proper Mandatory Quotas Yet in the EU' [2012] 325 SMCLN 1.
Edmunds, R. and Lowry, J., 'The Continuing Value of Relief for Directors Breach of Duty' [2003] 66 MLR 195.
Ellis, M. and Verrill, J., 'Twilight Trusts' [2007] 20 Ins Intell 151.
Elms, L. and Camacho, T., 'Schemes of Arrangement: To What Extent has the New Spanish Scheme Been Inspired by its English Equivalent?' [2012] 5 CRI 180.
Ewang, F., 'Regulating Share Capital Transactions and Creditor Protection: A Multifaceted Model' [2007] 21 Aust Jo of Corp Studs 1.
Farrar, J.H., 'Fraudulent Trading' [1980] JBL 336.
Fennell, S., 'The Football Creditor Rule and Unsecured Creditors' [2012] (Autumn) Recov 32.
Ferran, E., 'Creditors' Interests and Core Company Law' [1999] 20 Co Law 314.
Ferris, F., 'Insolvency Remuneration – Translating Adjectives into Action' [1999] Ins Law 48.
Finch, V., 'Insolvency Practitioners: Regulation and Reform' [1998] JBL 334.
Finch, V., 'Controlling the Insolvency Professionals' [1999] Ins Law 228.
Finch, V., 'Public Interest Liquidation: PIL or Placebo?' [2002] Ins Law 157.
Finch, V., 'Re-Invigorating Corporate Rescue' [2003] JBL 527.
Finch, V., "Regulating Insolvency Practitioners – Rationalisation on the Agenda' [2005] 18 Ins Intell 17.

Finch, V., 'Doctoring in the Shadows of Insolvency' [2005] JBL 690.
Finch, V., 'Prepackaged Administrations: Bargains in the Shadow of Insolvency or Shadowy Bargains?' [2006] JBL 568.
Finch, V., 'Pre-Packaged Administrations and the Construction of Propriety' [2011] 11 JCLS 1.
Finch, V., 'Corporate Rescue: Who is Interested?' [2012] JBL 190.
Finch, V., 'Corporate Rescue: a Game of Three Halves' [2012] 32 Legal Studies 302.
Finch, V., 'Insolvency Practitioners: Avenues of Accountability' [2012] JBL 645.
Fisher, D., 'The Enlightened Shareholder – Leaving Shareholders in the Dark: Will Section 172(1) of the Companies Act 2006 Make Directors Consider the Impact of Their Decisions on Third Parties?' [2009] 20 ICCLR 10.
Fitzgerald, N., 'Treatment of Directors of Insolvent Companies under Irish Law' [2004] 20 IL & P 108.
Flannigan, R., 'Fiduciary Duties of Shareholders and Directors' [2004] JBL 277.
Frisby, S., 'Making a Silk Purse out of a Sow's Ear' [2000] 63 MLR 413.
Frisby, S., 'The Second Chance Culture and Beyond: Some Observations on the Prepack Contribution' [2009] 3 FMLR 242.
Frisby, S., 'Insolvency Law and Insolvency Practice: Principles and Pragmatism Diverge?' [2011] 64 CLP 349.
Frith, S. and Jones, B., 'The Insolvent Partnerships Order 1994' [1995] 11 IL & P 14.
Furlow, C.W., 'Good Faith, Fiduciary Duties and the Business Judgment Rule in Delaware' [2009] Utah L Rev 1061.
Gerber, M. and Cantele, D., 'Directors Accountability and Insolvency: Luxembourg's Response towards Wrongful Trading and Mismanagement in Insolvency Procedures' [2007] 18 ICCLR 409.
Girgis, J., 'Deepening Insolvency in Canada?' [2008] 53 McGill LJ 167.
Godfrey, P., 'The Turnaround Practitioner – Adviser or Director?' [2002] 18 IL & P 3.
Godfrey, P., 'State Aid in the Context of Insolvency and Restructuring' [2003] 19 IL & P 166.
Godfrey, P., 'Overseas Companies: Championing the Use of the English Scheme of Arrangement for International Restructuring' [2012] (Winter) Recov 8.
Goode, R.M., 'Wrongful Trading and the Balance Sheet Test of Insolvency' [1989] JBL 436.
Gray, W.A., '*Peoples v Wise and Dylex*: Identifying Stakeholder Interests upon or near Corporate Insolvency – Stasis or Pragmatism?' [2003] 39 Can Bus Law Jo 242.

Gray, W.A., 'A Solicitor's Perspective on *Peoples v Wise*' [2005] 41 Can Bus Law Jo 184.
Griffin, S., 'Extinguishing the Flames of the Phoenix Company' [2002] Curr Leg Prob 377.
Griffin, S., 'The Disqualification of Unfit Directors and the Protection of the Public Interest' [2002] 53 NILQ 207.
Griffin, S., 'Corporate Collapse and the Reform of Boardroom Structures – Lessons from America?' [2003] Ins Law 214.
Griffin, S., 'Problems in the Identification of a Company Director' [2003] 54 NILQ 43.
Griffin, S., 'Limited Liability: A Necessary Revolution?' [2004] 25 Co Law 99.
Griffin, S., 'Confusion Surrounding the Characteristics, Identification and Liability of a Shadow Director' [2011] 24 Ins Intell 44.
Hare, D.M. and Milman, D., 'Corporate Insolvency – The Cork Committee Proposals' [1983] 127 Sols Jo 230–335 seriatim.
Hargovan, A., 'Directors' Duties to Creditors after *Spies v The Queen* – Is the Development of an Independent Fiduciary Duty Dead or Alive?' [2003] 21 C & S LJ 390.
Hawke, N., 'Creditors' Interests in Solvent and Insolvent Companies' [1989] JBL 54.
Hemraj, M.B., 'Company Directors: The Defence of Business Judgment Rule' [2003] 24 Co Law 218.
Hemraj, M.B., 'The Business Judgement Rule in Corporate Law' [2004] 15 ICCLR 192.
Hemsworth, M.C., 'Directors' Powers during Administrative Receivership: The Power to Take Legal Proceedings' [1999] Ins Law 92.
Henderson, D., 'Inability to Pay Debts: Where Are We Now?' [2011] 24 Ins Intell 54.
Hicks, A., 'Disqualification of Directors – 40 Years On' [1988] JBL 27.
Hicks, A., 'Corporate Form – Questioning the Unsung Hero' [1997] JBL 306.
Hicks, A., 'Director Disqualification – The National Audit Office Follows Up' [1999] 15 IL & P 112.
Hicks, A., 'Director Disqualification – Can it Deliver?' [2001] JBL 433.
Hobson, M.D., 'The Law of Shadow Directorships' [1998] 10 Bond Law Rev 184.
Holm, S., 'From Steward to Stuart: Some Problems in Deciding for Others' [2011] 62 NILQ 617.
Houghton, S., 'Interview with Philip King' [2012] (Spring) Recov 46.
Hudson, A., 'OFT Study: Focus on the Bigger Picture, Not the Quick Headline' [2010] (Autumn) Recov 27.
Hunter, M., 'The Nature and Functions of a Rescue Culture' [1999] JBL 491.

Idensohn, K., 'The Regulation of Shadow Directors' [2010] 22 SA Merc Law Jo 326.
Jamieson, N. and Hughes, K., 'The Identification of Shadow Directors under English Law: What Guidance Might *Buzzle* Provide?' [2012] BJIBFL 364.
Jensen, M.C. and Meckling, W.H., 'Theory of the Firm: Managerial Behaviour, Agency Costs and Ownership Structures' [1976] 3 Jo of Fin Econ 305.
Jones, B., 'EU Regulation and Directors' Duties' [2004] 17 Ins Intell 81.
Keay, A., 'The Supervision and Control of Liquidators' [2000] Conv 295.
Keay, A., 'Insolvency Law – Public Interest?' [2000] 51 NILQ 509.
Keay, A., 'The Duty of Directors to Take Account of Creditors' Interests: Has it Any Role to Play?' [2002] JBL 379.
Keay, A., 'Another Way of Skinning a Cat: Enforcing Directors' Duties for the Benefit of Creditors' [2004] 17 Ins Intell 1.
Keay, A., 'Formulating a Framework for Directors Duties to Creditors: An Entity Maximisation Approach' [2005] 64 CLJ 614.
Keay, A., 'What Future for Liquidation in Light of the Enterprise Act Reforms?' [2005] JBL 143.
Keay, A., 'Wrongful Trading and the Liability of Company Directors: a Theoretical Perspective' [2005] 25 Legal Studies 431.
Keay, A., 'Directors' Duties – Do Recent Canadian Developments Require a Rethink in the UK on the Issue of Directors' Duties to Consider Creditors' Interests?' [2005] 18 Ins Intell 65.
Keay, A., 'Wrongful Trading and the Point of Liability' [2006] 19 Ins Intell 132.
Keay, A., 'Section 172(1) of the Companies Act 2006: An Interpretation and Assessment' [2007] 28 Co Law 106.
Keay, A., 'Can Derivative Proceedings Be Commenced When a Company is in Liquidation?' [2008] 21 Ins Intell 49.
Keay, A., 'Office-Holders and the Duty of Directors to Promote the Success of the Company' [2010] 23 Ins Intell 129.
Keeper, T., 'The New Order of the Phoenix' [2008] NZ Bus Law Quart 21.
Kian, C.T.S., 'Disqualification of Directors of Insolvent Companies under the New Singapore Law' [1988] 4 IL & P 45.
Kluvers, R. and Tippett, J., 'An Exploration of Stewardship Theory in a Not for Profit Organisation' [2011] 35 Acc Ref 275.
La Porta, R., et al., 'Law and Finance' [1998] 106 Jo of Pol Econ 1113.
La Porta, R., et al., 'Corporate Ownership Around the World' [1999] 54 Jo of Fin 471.
Legg, M. and Jordan, D., 'The Australian Business Judgment Rule after *ASIC v Rich*' [2010] 269 SMCLN 1.
Legrand, P., 'The Impossibility of Legal Transplants' [1997] 4 Maastricht Jo of Euro and Compar Law 111.

Lele, P. and Siems, M., 'Shareholder Protection: A Leximetric Approach' [2007] 7 JCLS 17.
Lightman, G., 'The Challenges Ahead – Address to the Insolvency Lawyers' Association' [1996] JBL 113.
Lightman, G., 'Attitudes and Values: Developments in Insolvency Law' [2001] 14 Ins Intell 57 and 69.
Lim, C., 'Pre-Pack Receiverships: Unravelled' [2010] 4 LFMR 568.
Linklater, L., 'Section 727 Relief from Liability – Redundant or Relevant?' [2002] 3 Sweet and Maxwell's Co L N 1.
Lynch-Fannon, I., 'The Corporate Social Responsibility Movement and Law's Empire: Is there a Conflict?' [2007] 58 NILQ 15.
Mace, A., 'Challenging Administrators – Can They Ever Do Any Wrong?' [2010] 3 Corp Resc and Insolv 141.
MacNeil, I., 'The FSA Board Report on RBS: Enforcement and Law Reform' [2012] 6 Law and Fin Mark Rev 1.
Mamutse, B., 'Compensating Defrauded Shareholders in Insolvency' [2011] 62 NILQ 75.
Manne, H.G., 'Mergers and the Market for Corporate Control' [1965] 73 Jo of Pol Econ 110.
Manning, L., 'President's Column' [2012] (Winter) Recov 5.
McCann, M. and Wheeler, S., 'Gender Diversity in the FTSE 100: The Business Case Claim' [2011] 38 Jo of Law and Soc 542.
McCormack, G., 'Corporate Rescue Law in Singapore and the Appropriateness of Chapter 11 of the US Bankruptcy Code as a Model' [2008] 20 SAc LJ 396.
McLennan, S.L.C., 'Costs Orders Against Insolvency Practitioners on a Personal and Indemnity Basis' [2012] 25 Ins Intell 123.
Millett, P., 'Shadow Directorship: A Real or Imagined Threat to Banks?' [1991] Insolv Pract 14.
Milman, D., 'Receivers as Agents' [1981] 44 MLR 658.
Milman, D., 'Directors and National Insurance Arrears' [1984] 5 Co Law 91.
Milman, D., 'Derivative Actions Against Receivers' [1986] 7 Co Law 115.
Milman, D., 'Personal Liability and Disqualification of Company Directors – Something Old, Something New' [1992] 43 NILQ 1.
Milman, D., 'Curbing the Phoenix Syndrome' [1997] JBL 224.
Milman, D., 'Clawback and LLPs' [2001] Ins Law 178.
Milman, D., 'The Phoenix Syndrome' [2001] Ins Law 199.
Milman, D., 'Casting Light on the Twilight Zone' [2003] Ins Law 147.
Milman, D., 'Strategies for Regulating Managerial Performance in the Twilight Zone – Familiar Dilemmas: New Considerations' [2004] JBL 493.
Milman, D., 'Two Cases of Interest for Directors Operating in the Twilight Zone' [2008] 21 Ins Intell 25.

Milman, D., 'Governance, Stewardship and the Insolvency Practitioner' [2012] 321 SMCLN 1.
Milman, D. and Cook, G., 'Managing Distressed Companies: Adapting to a New Legal Culture' [2002] 28 Managerial Finance 34.
Mokal, R., 'Encumbered Assets and the Statutory Trust' [2008] 21 Ins Intell 129.
Mokal, R., 'At the Intersection of Property and Insolvency: The Insolvent Company's Encumbered Assets' [2008] SAc LJ 495.
Morris, P. and Stevenson, J., 'The Jersey LLP: A New Legal Vehicle for Professional Practice' [1997] 60 MLR 538.
Moses, M. and Williams, I.G., 'Stalking Horse Agreements and Administrations: Part of the Solution?' [2012] (Autumn) Recov 34.
Mulligan, M. and Tribe, J., 'The Remuneration of Office Holders in Corporate Insolvency – Liquidators, Administrators and Administrative Receivers' [2003] Ins Law 101.
Naruisch, T. and Liepe, F., 'Latest Developments in the German Law on Public Companies by the Act on Corporate Integrity and Modernisation of the Right of Resolution-Amendment (UMAG) – Shareholder Activism and Directors' Liability' [2007] JBL 225.
Noonan, C. and Watson, S., 'The Nature of Shadow Directorship: Ad Hoc Statutory Intervention or Core Company Law Principle?' [2006] JBL 763.
Noonan, C. and Watson, S., 'Examining Company Directors through the Lens of De Facto Directorship' [2008] JBL 587.
Ogowewo, T., 'A Perfect Case for the Application of s. 423 Insolvency Act: *Yukong Line of Korea v Rendsburg Investment Corp of Liberia (No. 2)*' [1999] Ins Law 106.
Okoye, N., 'The BIS Review and Section 172 of the Companies Act 2006: What Manner of Clarity is Needed?' [2012] 33 Co Law 15.
Omar, P., 'European Initiative on Wrongful Trading' [2003] Ins Law 239.
O'Neill, A., 'Part 40 of the UK Companies Act 2006: Disqualification Orders Go Global' [2007] 18 ICCLR 166.
Pasban, M.R., 'A Review of Directors' Liabilities of an Insolvent Company in the US and England' [2001] JBL 33.
Payne, F., 'Insolvency of LLPs' [2005] 18 IL & P 104.
Pettet, B., 'Limited Liability: A Principle for the 21st Century' [1995] CLP 124.
Pistor, K., Raiser, M. and Gelfer, S., 'Law and Finance in Transitional Economies' [2000] 8 Econs of Trans 325.
Preetha, S., 'The Fraudulent Trading Offence: Need for a Relook' [2011] 4 NUJS Law Rev 231.
Prentice, D., 'Creditors' Interests and Directors' Duties' [1990] 10 OJLS 265.
Pritchard, T., 'Trust Assets: Trading in the Twilight Zone' [2007] 23 IL & P 112.

Qu, C.Z., 'Recent German Developments in Company Controllers' Liability in Rescue Situations: A Comparative Evaluation' [2011] JBL 330.

Rajak, H. and Henning, J., 'Business Rescue for South Africa' [2000] 116 SALJ 262.

Reisberg, A., 'Corporate Law in the UK After Recent Reforms: The Good, the Bad and the Ugly' [2010] CLP 315.

Reisberg, A., 'The Notion of Stewardship from a Company Law Perspective' [2011] Jo of Fin Crime 126.

Ridgway, P., 'Personal Liability Notices' [2012] 25 Ins Intell 106.

Roach, L., 'The UK Stewardship Code' [2011] 11 JCLS 463.

Rose, I., 'Competition Law and the Insolvency Practitioner' [2008] 1 CRI 177.

Rotem, Y., 'Company Duplication – Plain Fraud or A Poor Man's Bankruptcy? A Case Study in the Financial Distress of Small Business' [2011] 20 IIR 131.

Rushworth, J., 'A Critical Analysis of the Business Rescue Regime in the Companies Act 71 of 2008' [2010] Act Jur 375.

Sappideen, R., 'Fiduciary Obligations to Corporate Creditors' [1991] JBL 365.

Sargeant, M., 'TUPE – The Final Round' [2006] JBL 549.

Sarra, J., 'Canada's Supreme Court Rules No Fiduciary Obligation towards Creditors on Insolvency – *People's Department Stores v Wise*' [2006] 15 IIR 1.

Scherer, E. and Schimmelpenninck, R.J., 'Equitable Subordination of Shareholder Loans: Going Dutch or the American Way?' [2004] 20 IL & P 54.

Schillig, M., 'Deepening Insolvency: Liability for Wrongful Trading in the United States?' [2009] 30 Co Law 298.

Schulte, R., 'Enforcing Wrongful Trading as a Standard of Conduct for Directors and as a Remedy for Creditors in the Special Case of Corporate Insolvency' [1999] 20 Co Law 80.

Scott, P., Thomas, C. and Goodman, R., 'Insolvency and State Aid' [2008] 1 CRI 154.

Sealy, L.S., 'The Director as Trustee' [1967] CLJ 83.

Sealy, L.S., 'Insolvency Law Embraces Technological Developments' [2010] 274 SMCLN 1.

Simmons, M., 'Wrongful Trading' [2001] 14 Ins Intell 12.

Stolowy, N., 'Transparency and Prevention for Corporate Bankruptcy' [2009] JBL 525.

Tay, D., 'Environmental Liability and the Insolvency Professional' [1994] 3 IIR 61.

Taylor, A., 'Failure to Pay National Insurance Contributions' [2009] 22 Ins Intell 79.

Theobald, K., 'The Ferris Report: Insolvency Practitioner Fees and Remuneration' [1998] 14 IL & P 300.

Todd, G. and Dood, S., 'Insolvency Practitioners Have to be Bonded – Is it as Simple as it Seems?' [2006] 19 Ins Intell 129.
Tomasic, R., 'Shareholder Litigation and the Financial Crisis: The Northern Rock Shareholder Appeal Considered' [2009] 262 SMCLN 1.
Tribe, J., 'CVAs and Rescue: A New Hope and a Tudor Orthodoxy' [2009] JBL 454.
Tribe, J. and Hunt, S., 'Insolvency Bonds: History, Policy and Substance' [2012] 25 Ins Intell 37.
Trower, W., 'Complaining about the Conduct of Insolvency Practitioners' [2009] (November) 3–4 South Digest 24.
Walters, A., 'Wrongful Trading: Two Recent Cases' [2001] Ins Law 211.
Walters, A., 'Directors' Responsibilities to Creditors after Farepak' [2013] 34 Co Law 1.
Walton, P., 'Pre-Packaged Administrations: Trick or Treat?' [2006] 19 Ins Intell 113.
Walton, P., 'Pre-Packaged Administration Begins to Take Shape' [2010] 81 Amic Cur 4.
Walton, P., 'When is a Pre-Packaged Administration Appropriate? A Theoretical Consideration' [2011] 20 Nottm Law Jo 1.
Ward, J., 'Australian Government Moves to Overturn Effects of the Sons of Gwalia Decision and Other Proposed Corporate Law Amendments' [2010] 23 Ins Intell 88.
Watson, A., 'Legal Transplants and Law Reform' [1996] 92 LQR 79.
Watson, S., 'Directors' Duties in New Zealand' [1998] JBL 495.
Wee, M.S., 'Duties of a Mortgagee and a Receiver: Where Singapore Should and Should Not Follow English Law' [2008] 20 SAc LJ 559.
Wellard, M., 'UK Prepack Reforms: Pause for Thought in Australia?' [2011] 23 Aust Insolv Jo 12.
Wellard, M. and Walton, P., 'A Comparative Analysis of Anglo-Australian Prepacks: Can the Means be Made to Justify the Ends?' [2012] 21 IIR 143.
Weng, C. Xiao-chuan, 'Assessing the Application of the Business Judgment Rule and the Defensive Business Judgment Rule in the Chinese Judiciary: A Perspective on Takeover Dispute Adjudication' [2010] 34 Fordham Int Law Jo 124.
Werdnick, R., 'Wrongful Trading Provision – Is it Efficient?' [2012] 25 Ins Intell 81.
Werner, C., 'Phoenixing: Avoiding the Ashes' [2009] 22 Ins Intell 105.
Wheeler, S., 'Empty Rhetoric and Empty Promises: The Creditors' Meeting' [1994] 21 Jo of Law and Soc 350.
Wheeler, S., 'Director Disqualification: Insolvency Practitioners and the Decision Making Process' [1995] 15 Leg Studs 283.
Williams, R., 'Disqualification of Directors: A Remedy Worse than the Disease' [2007] 7 JCLS 213.

Wilson, G., 'Delinquent Directors' [1996] 47 NILQ 344.
Worthington, S., 'Corporate Governance: Remedying and Ratifying Directors' Breaches' [2000] 116 LQR 638.
Worthington, S., 'Reforming Directors' Duties' [2001] 64 MLR 439.
Wortley, B.A., 'The Interpretation of the New Fraudulent Trading Section in the Companies Act 1929' [1934] 50 LQR 405.
Xie, B., 'Regulating Pre Packaged Administrations – An Incomplete Agenda' [2011] JBL 513.
Xie, B., 'Role of Insolvency Practitioners in the UK Prepack Administrations: Challenges and Control' [2012] 21 IIR 85.
Yap, J.L., 'De Facto Directors and Corporate Directorships' [2012] JBL 279.
Zhao, J., 'The Emerging Third Way in the Corporate Objective Debate in Company Law' [2011] 62 NILQ 361.
Zhao, J., 'The Harmonious Society, CSR and Legal Responses in Ethical Norms in Chinese Company Law' [2012] 12 JCLS 163.
Zhao, J. and Tribe, J., 'CSR in an Insolvency Environment: Directors' Continuing Obligations in English Law' [2010] 21 ICCLR 305.

OFFICIAL REPORTS

Australian Senate Report, *The Regulation, Registration and Remuneration of Insolvency Practitioners in Australia: The Case for a New Framework* (2010) (Cth of Australia).
Cadbury Report, *The Financial Aspects of Corporate Governance* (1992) (Gee).
Charity Commission, *Managing Financial Difficulties and Insolvency in Charities* (2000).
Cohen Committee, *Report of the Committee on Company Law Amendment* (1945) (Cmnd 6659).
Companies House, *Statistical Tables on Companies Registration Activities 2011–12* (2012).
Company Law Review: Final Report (2001) (URN 01/942).
Cork Report Insolvency Law and Practice: Report of the Review Committee (Cmnd 8558, 1982) (HMSO).
Davies Report, *Women on Boards* (2011) (Department for Business, Innovation and Skills).
Department of Trade and Industry, *Modernising Company Law* (Cm 5553-I) (TSO).
European Commission, *Should Aid be Granted to Firms in Difficulty?* (2009) (Competition Directorate).
Financial Law Panel, *Shadow Directorships* (1994).

Garwood Report (Insolvency Regulation Working Party), *A Review of Insolvency Practitioner Regulation* (1999).

Greene Committee, *Company Law Amendment Committee Report* (1926) (Cmd 2657).

Hampel Report, Committee on Corporate Governance: Final Report (1998).

Harmer Report, *General Insolvency Inquiry* (1988) (Australian Law Reform Commission Report No. 45).

Higgs Committee, *A Review of the Role and Effectiveness of Non-Executive Directors* (2003).

INSOL, *Directors in the Twilight Zone III* (2011).

Insolvency Service, *Enterprise Act 2002 Corporate Insolvency Provisions: An Evaluation Report* (2008).

The Insolvency Service Executive Agency: Company Director Disqualification (1993) (National Audit Office).

The Insolvency Service Consultation on Reforms to the Regulation of Insolvency Practitioners (2011).

The Insolvency Service, *2011 Annual Review of Insolvency Practitioners Regulation* (2012).

The Insolvency Service, *Review of Disqualification Proceedings Taken in the Case of European Home Retail plc and Farepak Food and Gifts Ltd* (2012).

Institute of Directors, *Corporate Governance Guidance and Principles for Unlisted Companies in the UK* (2010).

Jackson Report, *Review of Civil Litigation Costs: Final Report* (2010) (HMSO).

Jenkins Committee, *Report of the Company Law Committee* (1962) (Cmnd 1749).

Law Commission, *Regulating Conflicts of Interest of Directors and Formulating a Statement of Duties* (Report No. 261) (1999).

National Audit Office, *Company Director Disqualification* (1993) (HMSO).

National Audit Office, *The Insolvency Service Executive Agency: Company Directors Disqualification – A Follow-up Report* (1999) (HMSO).

Office of Fair Trading, *The Market for Corporate Insolvency Practitioners* (June 2010) (OFT 1245).

R3, *The Value of the Insolvency Industry* (2008) (Centre for Economic and Business Research).

Sharman Inquiry, *Going Concern and Liquidity Risks: Lessons for Companies and Auditors* (June 2012).

Turnbull Report, *Internal Control: Guidance for Directors on the Combined Code* (1999, revised 2005) (Financial Reporting Council).

Turner Report, *The Failure of the RBS: Financial Services Authority Board* (12 December 2011) (FSA).

UK Corporate Governance Code (2010) (FRC).

UK Stewardship Code (2010) Financial Reporting Council.
World Bank, *Doing Business* (2012) www.doingbusiness.org

WEBSITES

Association of Business Recovery Practitioners – www.r3.org.uk
British and Irish Legal Information Institute – www.bailii.org
Confederation of British Industry – www.cbi.org.uk
Financial Reporting Council – www.frc.org.uk
HM Courts Service – www.hmcourts-service.com
INSOL – www.insol-europe.org
Insolvency Lawyers' Association – www.ilauk.org
Insolvency Practitioners Association – www.insolvency-practitioners.org.uk
Insolvency Service – www.insolvency.gov.uk
Institute of Directors – www.iod.com
OECD – www.oecd.org
UNCITRAL – www.uncitral.org

Appendix I Applicability of selected statutory stewardship obligations and enforcement thereof

COMPANIES ACT 2006

s. 170 (scope of general duties) – directors and shadow directors
s. 171 (duty to act within powers) – directors and shadow directors
s. 172 (duty to promote success of the company) – directors and shadow directors
s. 173 (duty to exercise independent judgement) – directors and shadow directors
s. 174 (duty of reasonable care) – directors and shadow directors
s. 175 (duty to avoid conflicts of interest) – directors and shadow directors
s. 176 (duty not to accept benefits from third parties) – directors and shadow directors
s. 177 (duty to declare interest in proposed transaction) – directors and shadow directors
s. 182 (declaration of interest in existing transaction) – directors and shadow directors (s. 187)
s. 190 (substantial property transactions) – directors and connected persons
s. 387 (management accounts) – officers
ss. 441/451 (filing accounts) – directors
ss. 854/858 (annual return) – directors (including shadow directors), secretary and officers
s. 1157 (judicial pardons) – officers and auditors

INSOLVENCY ACT 1986

s. 133 (public examinations) – officers and persons concerned in the management
s. 206 (fraud in anticipation of winding-up) – officers, past and present, including shadow directors
s. 207 (transactions in fraud of creditors) – officers

s. 208 (misconduct in the course of winding-up) – officers, past and present, including shadow directors
s. 209 (falsification of books) – officers and contributories
s. 210 (material omissions from statement of affairs) – officers, past and present, including shadow directors
s. 211 (false representations to creditors) – officers, past and present, including shadow directors
s. 212 (misfeasance) – past/present officers or persons concerned in management
s. 213 (fraudulent trading) – any person knowingly a party to the carrying on of the business in such way
s. 214 (wrongful trading) – directors, including former directors and shadow directors
s. 216 (phoenix bar) – directors, including former directors and shadow directors
s. 218 (prosecutions) – past and present officers and members
s. 235 (duty of cooperation) – past and present officers, employees, independent contractors, administrators, administrative receivers and liquidators
s. 236 (provision of information about company's dealings) – any officer or person capable of providing information

COMPANY DIRECTORS DISQUALIFICATION ACT 1986

s. 6 (unfitness) – directors, including shadow directors

Appendix II List of selected statements of insolvency practice

Statements of Insolvency Practice (SIPs) are issued by the Joint Insolvency Committee, which consists of representatives of the recognized professional bodies and the competent authorities.

SIP 1 – **Introduction to SIPs**
Note: This explains the purpose and status of SIPs. It stresses that SIPs are to be interpreted as being subject to the Fundamental Principles in the Insolvency Code of Ethics. These principles emphasise the need for integrity, objectivity, professional competence, the need to preserve confidential information, professional behaviour and transparency.

SIP 2 – **Investigations by Office Holders in Administrations and Insolvent Liquidations**
Note: One of the key points here is that any investigations should be proportionate. The relationship between the IP and the creditors in the context of investigations is highlighted.

SIP 3 – **Voluntary Arrangements**
Note: this covers both company voluntary arrangements and individual voluntary arrangements. IPs are advised to keep distinct work done as a nominee from their input as a supervisor. The viability testing of voluntary arrangements is to the fore. In a CVA, if the proposal originally put forward by the company is modified before creditor acceptance, it is advised that the IP obtains the consent of the directors beforehand, even though there is no formal requirement in this respect.

SIP 4 – **Disqualification of Directors**
Note: This concentrates upon the reporting obligations of directors with regard to those directors who appear to be unfit. IPs are advised to adopt a de minimis filtering process. IPs are also reminded of the law of defamation, though their reports are assumed to be protected by qualified privilege. Reports on suspected unfit directors should be kept confidential. There is no separate fee for this reporting activity; it is deemed to be part of the office.

SIP 7 – **Presentation of Financial Information in Insolvency Proceedings**
Note: This outlines formats for the preparation and presentation of an office-holder's accounts. Information given to creditors (especially on remuneration/expenses) should be clear and transparent. Receipts in respect of a hive down must be separately noted.

SIP 8 – **Summoning and Holding Meetings of Creditors Convened Pursuant to s. 98 of the Insolvency Act 1986**
Note: There is detailed guidance here on a range of practical issues concerned with notification of, and attendance at, the s. 98 meeting. If the company has recently changed its name before the decision to go for a CVL was taken, any notice should include reference to the former name. Procedures for the appointment of liquidator and the establishment of a liquidation committee are outlined. IPs are reminded that they should not solicit appointment as liquidator.

SIP 9 – **Payments to Insolvency Office Holders and their Associates**
Note: Apart from emphasising the need for transparency, SIP 9 (which was reformulated in 2011) indicates that remuneration should be appropriate, reasonable and commensurate with work necessarily undertaken. For judicial comment see *Re Buildlead Ltd* [2004] EWHC 2443 (Ch), [2005] BCC 138, *Cooper v Houston and Finnegan* [2005] NICh 1, [2007] BPIR 1206.

SIP 10 – **Proxy Forms**
Note: This highlights good practice.

SIP 11 – **The Handling of Funds in Formal Insolvency Appointments**
Note: The importance of proper financial records is emphasized as is the fundamental rule that funds relating to a particular insolvency should be kept separate from those of the firm of insolvency practitioners.

SIP 12 – **Records of Meetings in Formal Insolvency Proceedings**
Note: This simply highlights best practice.

SIP 13 – **Acquisition of Assets of Insolvent Companies by Directors**
Note: The purpose of this SIP is to raise awareness of improper/undervalue self-dealing transactions involving directors and their associates. It is made specifically applicable to shadow directors. Where an insolvency practitioner sells company assets, there is a duty to obtain the best price.

SIP 14 – **A Receiver's Responsibility to Preferential Creditors**
Note: This seeks to allay concerns that receivers are re-characterizing security as being fixed in nature when in truth it should be seen as floating and therefore

should be subject to the obligation to meet preferential claims. This SIP was particularly important in the days before the ruling in *Nat West Bank v Spectrum Plus* [2005] UKHL 41, [2005] BCC 694, which clarified the distinctions between fixed and floating charges and found against artificial fixed charges. SIP 14 also stresses that it is important that realization costs are properly apportioned between fixed and floating charge elements of a security so as not to jeopardize the claims of preferential creditors. This SIP will remain of importance with the advent of the reserve fund for unsecured creditors because improper re-characterization of security could be a threat to unsecured creditors.

SIP 15 – **Reporting and Providing Information on IPs' Functions to Committees in Formal Insolvencies**
Note: This aims to harmonize reporting standards and practices.

SIP 16 – **Pre Packaged Sales in Administrations**
Note: This is now the most high profile of the SIPs. Introduced in January 2009 to allay public concern about the prepack phenomenon, it is now seen as the minimum standard required to ensure that a prepack secures any judicial approval. See for early analysis *Re Kayley Vending Ltd* [2009] BCC 578 per HHJ Cooke. Note also *Re Halliwells LLP* [2010] EWHC 2036 (Ch), [2011] BCC 57. But it should be stressed that compliance with SIP 16 is not a guarantee of judicial support – see the comments of the court in *Re UK Steelfixers Ltd* [2012] EWHC 2409 (Ch), [2012] BCC 751. As the title suggests, it applies only to prepacks entered into in the context of administration. The SIP reminds IPs of their duties to creditors in general and requires them at the earliest opportunity to explain the rationale for the prepack and to give full details of the transaction. Some 17 important information points are specified in para 9 of this SIP. The Insolvency Service monitors compliance rates on an ongoing basis. With the withdrawal of the threat of legislation, this SIP will retain its importance.

SIP 17 – **An Administrative Receiver's Responsibility for the Company's Records**
Note: Formerly SIP 1, this was renumbered in May 2011. It seeks to address the questions of custody of company records during the period of administrative receivership and their treatment after the administrative receivership has been concluded. This might depend on whether the company has then entered liquidation. Under Reg 20 of the Insolvency Practitioner Regulations 1990, administrative receivers were obliged to keep company records for 10 years from the date when the administrative receivership was concluded. This particular regulation was repealed in 2005: for the current position see Insolvency Practitioner Regulations 2005 (SI 2005/524).

Index